Although the history of centrally planned economies has been widely studied, the development of socialist thinking on the subject has remained largely uncharted. In this pathbreaking work, Pekka Sutela presents a detailed analysis of recent and contemporary Soviet economic thought and theory.

Dr Sutela traces the competing currents in the Marxist tradition of socialist economies from the Revolution to the present day. In particular he shows how the Gorbachev economic reform programme of 1987 rose from the work of Nobel Prize economist L. V. Kantorovich and his followers. However, this programme failed and the author explains in some detail why this happened. Since then, Soviet economists have tried to abandon their traditional theory of central planning and move along the path towards a market economy. Through extensive research as well as his close and long established contacts with leading Soviet economists, Pekka Sutela is able to show how Soviet economic thinking has moved from dogmatism through reformism to pragmatism.

Economic thought and economic reform in the Soviet Union is a most timely study. Current developments in the economy of the USSR are attracting a great deal of attention. This book will therefore be of interest to policy makers, the business and financial worlds as well as to students and academic specialists of Soviet studies and comparative economics.

ECONOMIC THOUGHT AND ECONOMIC REFORM IN THE SOVIET UNION

Cambridge Soviet Paperbacks: 5

Cambridge Soviet Paperbacks is a completely new initiative in publishing on the Soviet Union. The series will focus on the economics, international relations, politics, sociology and history of the Soviet and Revolutionary periods.

The idea behind the series is the identification of gaps for upper-level surveys or studies falling between the traditional university press monograph and most student textbooks. The main readership will be students and specialists, but some 'overview' studies in the series will have broader appeal.

Publication will in every case be simultaneously in hardcover and paperback.

Cambridge Soviet Paperbacks

Economic Thought and Economic Reform in the Soviet Union

PEKKA SUTELA

Special Adviser on Soviet and East European economic affairs at the Bank of Finland and Docent in Economics at the University of Helsinki

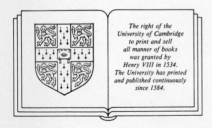

The right of the
University of Cambridge
to print and sell
all manner of books
was granted by
Henry VIII in 1534.
The University has printed
and published continuously
since 1584.

CAMBRIDGE UNIVERSITY PRESS

Cambridge
New York   Port Chester
Melbourne   Sydney

Published by the Press Syndicate of the University of Cambridge
The Pitt Building, Trumpington Street, Cambridge CB2 1RP
40 West 20th Street, New York, NY 10011–4211, USA
10 Stamford Road, Oakleigh, Melbourne 3166, Australia

© Cambridge University Press 1991

First published 1991

Printed in Great Britain at the University Press, Cambridge

British Library cataloguing in publication data

Sutela, Pekka
    Economic thought and economic reform in the Soviet Union.
    1. Soviet Union. Economic policies
    I. Title
    338.947

Library of Congress cataloguing in publication data

Sutela, Pekka.
    Economic thought and economic reform in the Soviet Union/Pekka
Sutela.
        p.   cm. – (Cambridge Soviet paperbacks: 5)
    Includes bibliographical references and index.
    ISBN 0 521 38020 0. – ISBN 0 521 38902 X (pbk.)
    1. Economics – Soviet Union.   2. Marxian economics.   3. Soviet
    Union – Economic policy – 1986.   I. Title.   II. Series.
    HB113.A2S87   1991
    338.947 – dc20   90 20148 CIP
ISBN 0 521 38020 0 hardback
ISBN 0 521 38902 X hardback

To Iiris and Eevi

Contents

Acknowledgements

This book was written while the author was a Senior Research Fellow of the Academy of Finland. Additional funding has been provided by the Yrjo Jahnsson Foundation and the Volkswagenwerk Foundation. The book was written in three countries. It was started at the Department of Economics, University of Helsinki, continued at the Centre for Russian and East European Studies, University of Birmingham, where the author was a Visiting Research Fellow from January to September 1989, and finalised at the Bundesinstitut für ostwissenschaftliche und internationale Studien, Cologne, where the author was a Fellow of the International Fellowship Programme for Advanced Soviet and East European Studies from September 1989 until Spring 1990.

I am grateful for the facilities, support and possibilities for discussion offered. Some of the ideas of the book were also presented at a seminar at St Antony's College, Oxford in Spring 1989 as well as at two conferences organised by the Institut für die Wissenschaften vom Menschen, Vienna, in Autumn 1988 and Summer 1989. The comments of three anonymous publisher's readers were extremely helpful. I remain responsible for the contents of the book.

1 The Soviet political economy of socialism

Introduction

The position of economic science under Soviet socialism is an apparent paradox. On the basis of official doctrine one would expect social sciences in general and economics in particular to have a central policy-forming influence. After all, while Marx may have seen his work primarily as a criticism of the classical political economy of Adam Smith and David Ricardo, most Marxists after him and especially the Marxist–Leninists among them have had a different claim to make. Their doctrine, the Marxist–Leninists have always argued, is the only proper scientific theory of any society and of socialism in particular. Even more important is their claim on the specificity of socialism: in contradistinction to capitalism it does not come about and function spontaneously. It must be brought about by conscious action, planned and managed following the objective laws of society as discovered by Marxism–Leninism. Given the determining role the economy is postulated to have in the society, the fundamental importance of economic science would seem to follow. Managing society must be based on social science, Marxism–Leninism argues.

On a second look, nothing seems to be further from the truth. Not only have outsiders often censured Marxism–Leninism as an empirically empty ideology, as apologetics, and Soviet planning as 'planning without theory', but official Soviet spokesmen have also admitted that both the scholarly level of social sciences and their use as a policy tool leave much to be desired. Such criticism has been especially conspicuous during the last few years. It was voiced by the then Secretary General Yuri Andropov and his immediate successor Konstantin Chernenko at the June 1983 Soviet Communist Party Central Committee Plenum, but it has deeper roots. In fact, such criticisms have been recurrent, and the leadership of the Soviet academic establishment and of the party-state have hardly ever

1

expressed satisfaction with the state of economic science and its applications in the planning and management of the economy.

The criticisms of social science in general and economics in particular have gained more weight with the policy of *perestroika* – restructuring. First, at the XXVII Communist Party Congress in 1986, Secretary General Mikhail Gorbachev demanded a 'major re-alignment of social sciences towards the concrete needs of practice', and then, at the January 1987 Central Committee Plenum, he noted that in many respects the available social theory was still 'at the level of the thirties and forties'. Throughout the current *perestroika* period, the proposals and advice of economists and other social scientists have been called on in an unprecedented way. In fact both the friends and the foes of reform have argued that the undeveloped state of economics is a major hindrance to meaningful change.

A typical example of the conservative criticisms of economics can be found in a letter to the journal *Oktyabr* by V. I. Konotop, who was until 1985 the first secretary of the CPSU Moscow region committee:

Now certain solid journals like to print pieces by theoretical economists [who are] in fact proposing a substitution of the fundamentals of planned economy by the anarchy of entrepreneurship . . . But why did these theoreticians for decades sit, as it is now often said, in dugouts, without giving an exact [and] understandable theory of the political economy of socialism?[1]

Practical workers like himself, Konotop claims, had led the country forward, while all the theoreticians do is 'without a deep theoretical foundation to copy a system of social and productive relations which is alien to the spirit of socialism'. Instead of doing that now, they should have come forward earlier with practicable proposals for developing the planning and management of the economy. In a true conservative spirit, Konotop sees the roots of present mistakes in the unfortunate neglect of earlier and better times.

While a demoted party apparatchik like Konotop accuses the economists for having neglected their work, the economists' point of view is understandably quite different. In early 1987 *Kommunist*, the theoretical and political journal of the Soviet Communist Party Central Committee, presented four leading academic economists, all prominent spokesmen of *perestroika*, with questions about the state of their discipline.[2] When asked whether Soviet economic scholarship is capable of responding to the challenge posed by the restructuring programme, one of the economists (A. G. Granberg of the famous Novosibirsk Institute of Industrial Economics) chose not to answer and two (L. I. Abalkin of the Academy Institute of Economics and P. G. Bunich of the Moscow Institute of Management) gave a mainly positive answer. The fourth, A. I. Anchishkin, an academician and the then head of the Academy of Sciences Institute for the Economics and Forecasting of Scientific-Technical Progress,[3] gave a clear negative answer: 'One must confess with all clarity that economic science as well as, in fact, social sciences as a whole, proved not to be ready to answer the questions that were posed by the XXVII Congress, the January 1987 Plenum [and indeed] by the whole of our development.'

The fault, Anchishkin argued, was not that of the economists. He gave five reasons for the deplorable state of affairs. *First*, a demand for scientific truth had not 'always' existed. In fact, Anchishkin claimed, an administrative economic system had no interest in discovering economic laws. The mastering of simple material balance type planning techniques is sufficient for it. *Second*, economics has often been conditioned by ideological dogmas which stand in contradiction to real economic processes. *Third*, economic science, like everything else in the society, was fragmented by administrative barriers. *Fourth*, the technical and information basis of economics has been retarded and, finally, *fifth*, the standards of economic education have been low.

The views of Konotop, a conservative party man, and Anchishkin, a leading academic economist, are thus far apart. A third perspective is added by academician Fedorenko, who not only was the long-time administrative head of Soviet academic economics as the academician secretary of the Department of Economics of the Academy of Sciences from 1971 to 1985 but was also the director of the main reformist economic research institute, The Central Economic-Mathematical Institute of the Academy of Sciences (TsEMI), from 1963 to 1985. The house theory of this institute, The System of Optimally Functioning Socialist Economy (SOFE), was often outlined in articles and books published under the name of Fedorenko. SOFE was, especially in the late 1960s, the main overt challenge to the overwhelmingly conservative political economy of socialism.[4] It will occupy many of the pages to follow.

In a speech commemorating his own seventieth birthday, Fedorenko does not hesitate to stress the achievements of his institute.[5] It is true, he says, that the situation in economic research and education is troublesome. This is especially true of political economy, but still 'economic science has not been fruitless. Proposals of primary importance have been put forward concerning the most important questions relating to economic policy and practice. It is a different thing that many useful proposals were not adopted or were postponed. This led to a loss of precious time.'

To substantiate his argument, Fedorenko goes on to enumerate such neglected proposals. The record is impressive: early experiments in full cost-accounting and self-financing later central to the economic strategy of *perestroika*, strategies of intensive growth, proposals for financial reforms as well as for a reform of the whole economy, are included in Fedorenko's list. In fact the mere length as well as the contents of the inventory make one suspect that Fedorenko's follower as the director of TsEMI, V. L. Makarov, may in fact be correct in claiming that the present restructuring of the economic mechanism is based 'on a number of proposals' that were earlier formulated within this particular school of Soviet economics.[6] A TsEMI spokesman in economic reform matters has gone even further. According to Yevgeni Yasin the *perestroika* strategy should be seen as a test of the proposals put forward by Soviet mathematical economists over an extended period of time.[7] This is an important perspective for the discussion to follow.

One could easily add other and more widely differing Soviet appraisals of the role of economic science and professional economists under Soviet socialism, both during the current period of change and before it. The spectrum of appraisals quoted above is, however, sufficient to delineate in a preliminary way the group of questions to be discussed in this book. We start with a background discussion of the development of Soviet economics in general, to be provided in this chapter. Chapter 2 gives an account of the early development of Soviet mathematical economics and especially of SOFE, the reformist challenger to orthodox economics referred to above. Much attention is given to the discussions of the sixties, as this was the main period of reformist proposals prior to the late eighties. Chapter 3 gives a discussion of the reformism of SOFE, while chapter 4 provides an overview of the Soviet reform debates from the early 1960s to the mid-eighties. Chapter 5 outlines developments within other currents of Soviet economic thought and chapter 6, finally, brings us to the Gorbachev period. Here we may try and answer the main question addressed in this book: is Soviet economic thought – assessed on the basis of published writings – capable of providing the ideas and guidelines necessary for an economic reform which would be both radical, implementable and productive? What kind of an economic reform have the Soviet economists been proposing in their writings? The reader interested in Soviet economic policies should be warned that the discussion to follow does not try to document the possible influence of Soviet professional economists on practical policies. That is a separate question, and one that would be difficult to answer, given the continuing secretiveness of Soviet policy-making.

The discussion to follow does not try to force Soviet economic debates into a pre-conceived framework. We have, instead, chosen to let the Soviet economists speak for themselves so that it is the reader who is given the privilege of interpreting the flow of discussion as it unfolds. Only at the beginning of chapter 6 is an interpretative framework for analysing the development of socialist reform economics offered. The argument to be presented there is – to provide a short outline – that succeeding generations of reform economics can be loosely interpreted along a single dimension.

Reform economics starts from an orthodox conception, dating back to the theoreticians of German and Russian socialist movements, which roughly compared the methods of functioning of the future socialist economy to those of a giant nineteenth-century capitalist factory. Seeing the inefficiency and indeed impossibility of such an economic model, early reformers relaxed some of the orthodox assumptions and tended to see capitalist corporation as their model. Further along the road, more and more characteristics of capitalism were added to the normative image of efficient socialism until – by the late eighties – a transition to genuine capitalism was advocated and also practised in such countries as Hungary and Poland. How the Soviet case fits into this interpretative framework, will be seen in chapter 6.

One should perhaps add that this book does not attempt a comparative appraisal of Soviet and East European reform economics. That task would be much beyond the scope of this particular project, and much tedious work remains to be done before such a comparative analysis can be performed.[8]

To a Western reader, much of Soviet social thought seems incomprehensible at first sight, and can remain puzzling even after long hours of study. In fact, few economists have ever judged it worth while to give much thought to it. The argument in this book, however, is that to understand the condition of contemporary Soviet economics, we have to start with its history. Indeed, it is actually useful to start with the Marxian economics of the previous century.

The Marxist heritage

The birth and development of the Soviet economics of socialism can only be understood as resulting from the interplay between Russia's history, post-revolutionary necessities as perceived by the country's new, self-styled Marxist–Leninist leading elite and the ideological framework of that elite. In a short discussion, an overemphasis on the last factor is perhaps permissible.

Marx left his followers with an awkward heritage. On the one hand, he, together with Engels who was possibly even more explicit, emphasised the scientific character of his socialism. In particular, he claimed to have found the objective economic and social laws that proved beyond any doubt the inevitability of the socialist revolution. On the other hand, the Marxist tradition that soon emerged stretched Marx's theory of capitalism – together with his scattered notes and remarks on other societies – into a general theory of history, supposedly valid for all times and places. This move was partly dictated by the propaganda needs of the socialist mass party that was slowly emerging. The social democrats, organised in the parties of the Second International, shared the science-obsessed and evolutionary attitude of late nineteenth-century culture, in spite of that being in disagreement with much of Marx's methodology. Opposition to evolutionism was one of the finer points of Marx's Hegelianism to which, as Aleksandr Bogdanov, the maverick Russian socialist politician and theorist noted in 1906, only a few Marxists adhered.[9]

In fact, Russia's first social democrats had a crucial role in the development of Marx's theory into a scheme of history. Grigori Plekhanov and other Russians were prominent gatekeepers of the Second International orthodoxy. Theirs was an ideological war on several fronts. The most vehement arguments were used within the broad socialist movement of the time. Historical development followed the laws discovered by Marx and Engels, the Russian social democrats asserted both against Western European revisionists and Russian populists. The former claimed that capitalism had changed, the latter that Russia's peculiarity made any Western European teachings irrelevant there. Nonsense, argued Plekhanov, Lenin and others: the Marxian doctrine of historical laws remained true everywhere and anytime. The strong emphasis later given to objective economic laws in the Marxist–Leninist political economy of socialism is partly rooted in this tradition.

The issue of Russian peculiarity has refused to die. Stalinist orthodoxy gave it a new twist by claiming Soviet socialism to be the peak of historical progress. The years of *glasnost* have brought back the debates of the nineteenth century. As then, Moscow literary journals now print articles by slavophiles, those who believe strongly in the peculiarity of Russia and oppose attempts at 'returning the Soviet Union to the mainstream of world civilization', as the westernisers want. Westerners, among them the leading reform economists of the country, are accused by extreme slavophiles of nothing less than trying to sell the country to imperialist capitalists. The liberals, arguing for the rebirth of civil society, a law-based state and a market economy, are outspoken as well. But the socialists, too, with their pleas for instituting a newly-defined real socialism in place of the actually existing one, still exist. In fact their position seems strong about the leaders of *perestroika*. After the seventy years' experiment with centrally managed socialism Russia's historical fate is again seen as open, and the alternatives first raised in the last century have come back. We will later meet with their spokesmen among the economists.

The Russian social democrats shared the general Second International emphasis on socialism based on science, large-scale production, planning and law-bound social evolution. For them the words of August Bebel, the first great leader of German social democracy, rang true: 'Socialism is science applied in all fields of human activity.'[10] Decades later, in his famous revolutionary pamphlet *State and Revolution*, Lenin would paraphrase Karl Kautsky's words on the future society. Kautsky, the leading theoretician of the socialist movement, wrote in the late nineteenth century: 'In the socialist society, which is after all just a single giant industrial enterprise, production and planning must be exactly and in a planned way organized, as they are organized in a modern large industrial enterprise.'[11]

This is the single factory image of socialism. Such characterisations were first repudiated by Soviet reformers in the late sixties. Only now, however, is it admitted that they are a central part of the theoretical heritage common to Kautsky and Lenin.

The social democratic orthodoxy, eagerly subscribed to by the competing factions of the Russian movement, claimed that socialism would first come about in the most developed West European countries. They speculated that a successful toppling of Russian autocracy could well signal the beginning of the era of European revolutions, but no Marxist could foresee that in the end Russia would be the only country with an endogenous socialist revolution. That was, after all, all too plainly against the objective laws of history as found in any textbook of Marxism. When the Russian revolution became a fact, the problem of reconciling it with the Marxian laws of social development remained.

The day after the revolution

The post-revolutionary Russian debates on the transition to socialism are well known, but there is little evidence of change in the image of socialism itself. For the Lenin of 1919 – as well as for the Lenin of 1899, who had wanted the Russians to imitate the German party programme as closely as possible[12] – 'building socialism means building a centralized economy, an economy managed from one centre'.[13] Even if money and markets should be necessary during the transition period, the socialist economy would be marketless and moneyless, somehow both centrally managed and democratically decentralised, without any contradictions between the common good and individual interests. This utopia, the classical social democratic approach to the economics of socialism, was forcefully restated in such important party documents as the 1919 party programme and *ABC of Communism*, the communist catechism by Bukharin and Preobrazhenskii popularising it.[14]

It was only in one of his last writings that Lenin noted the need for 'a change in our whole view on socialism'.[15] This is the remark that present-day reformers, often still anxious to show the impeccable Leninist roots of their readiness for doctrinal innovation, have to rely upon.[16] It is almost the only sentence of Lenin really in tune with *perestroika*. For decades Stalinist ideology could rely upon the traditional view of socialism. The 1919 party programme was not rewritten until 1961.

To understand the development of Marxist ideas of socialism a parallel with nineteenth-century mainstream economics may be appropriate. According to one interpretation at least, the classical early economists like Adam Smith and David Ricardo were primarily interested in the growth properties of the market system as a wealth-creating machine. Socialists like Kautsky and Lenin tended to see the future economy in a similar perspective. This can be called the Classical Approach to the economics of socialism. Later its followers would be primarily interested in questions of industrialisation, accumulation and growth.

During the latter half of the nineteenth century a neoclassical tradition emerged in mainstream economics. Its emphasis, as elaborated by Stanley Jevons and Leon Walras, was on the allocative and efficiency properties of the market system. Consequently, glimpses of a neoclassical approach to the economics of socialism also appeared in socialist literature. It laid stress on the high degree of organisation and efficiency in socialism. Its elements can already be seen in the famous planning principle of Marx, the comparison of 'useful effects' of products with the inputs necessary for their production.[17] Such outstanding Bolshevik theoreticians as Aleksandr Bogdanov and Nikolai Bukharin combined elements of the neoclassical approach with a basically classical framework, but it was left to Stanislav Strumilin to be the first Russian Marxist to propose a fully neoclassical approach to the economics of socialism. This happened during a debate on future planning principles immediately after the revolution.

During the so-called War Communism period of 1918–21 economists started, with official backing, to work out a system of non-monetary accounting. The issue was topical as the transition to socialism was thought to be imminent. Consequently, money and markets were supposed to disappear almost overnight. The proper socialist methods of planning had therefore to be worked out. Various accounting systems, based in most cases either on energy or labour inputs, were proposed, before the project was abandoned with the coming of the New Economic Policy in 1921.[18] The socialist future was postponed as markets and money were accepted as a temporary compromise between doctrine and reality.

Two contributions to the non-monetary accounting debate stand out. The first was that of Aleksandr Chayanov, the leading Soviet agrarian theoretician of the twenties who was purged in the early thirties and finally rehabilitated in 1987. Reasonably enough, he argued that the Marxian theory of capitalism was inappropriate for analysing socialist Russia. To Chayanov, socialism was reminiscent of a patriarchal peasant economy. In both cases, he argued, 'the principle of efficiency' was implemented directly, by conscious decisions based on physical units. Chayanov's implicit message comes through loud and clear: he had much more to offer to Soviet Russia than Marx ever had.

In short, Chayanov challenged the ideological hegemony of Marxism, denied its applicability in Soviet Russia and proposed its substitution by his own theory of the peasant economy. Not surprisingly, the Marxists did not agree. They were not going to abandon their doctrinal beliefs after the revolution just because Marx's theory did not seem to have anything to say about the post-revolutionary society. Chayanov was criticised by Strumilin and other Marxists.[19] They argued that even if Marx was the theoretician of capitalism many of his insights remained valid. This was not only true concerning the elements of traditional socialist utopianism he had shared. To the Marxists, his theory of history, his labour-centred approach to production and other such teachings were still valid.

Actually, Strumilin's approach was in many respects not all that far from Chayanov's. Following the neoclassical tradition of the economics of socialism he argued: 'On the most general level the problem of planning is the problem of the most beneficial use of the social means of production. Concretely, this leads to solving a mathematical problem on how to allocate the productive resources of the country so as to bring about the maximum satisfaction of social needs at a minimum of labour costs.'

Strumilin claimed more novelty for his somewhat rudimentary mathematical formulation of this approach than it really had. The neoclassical economic problem of the centralised economy had already been thoroughly discussed by the Italian economist Barone in 1908. In particular, he had shown how prices, rents and wages not only belonged to a market economy, but were a necessary element of any rational resource allocation. This is a point which Strumilin implicitly accepted, when he used an optimising framework to describe the economic problems of socialism. He was willing to interpret traditional Marxist concepts like 'the magnitude of value' or 'distribution according to work' in such a framework.

The reason for returning to this ancient debate is the fact that basically the same reformulation of Marxist economics was proposed by the optimal planning school in the post-Stalinist Soviet Union. Both the Strumilin of 1920 and the optimal planners of the early sixties approached the socialist economy as if it were a single huge factory to be rationally organised or, indeed, an optimising peasant household. Strumilin and the optimal planners offered fundamentally similar reinterpretations of Marxism. At the same time they also argued for the importance of using prices in any rational economy, including a socialist one interpreted as a single factory. In this view rational prices are necessary for an efficient economy, whether it has markets or not.

Strumilin lived to become the conservative *doyen* of Soviet economics. He died only in 1974, at the age of ninety-four. He is not a forgotten ancestor of the optimal theory; he is a pioneer who forgot himself. Strumilin was heavily criticised for an allegedly formalist and technocratic approach to planning in the early 1930s. Later he himself became the foremost critic of the optimising social engineering approach to planning, an approach which he had been the first in Soviet Russia to propose. After 1925, the relevant 1920–1 articles were never reprinted in the voluminous collections of Strumilin's writings. The later attempts of the optimal planners to remind the aged economist of his early opinions were of no use.[20] To Strumilin, the optimising approach had become a particularly dangerous piece of revisionism. Its conclusions were now 'without any rational content'.[21]

Economics and the Stalinist revolution

In his polemics against Chayanov, Strumilin defended the use and reinterpretation of Marxist concepts for socialist planning. Chayanov, however, was in a sense more Marxist than the Marxists. Marx had himself stressed the object specificity of his theories, and the leading Marxists of the early twentieth century were unanimous in excluding the possibility of a specifically Marxist political economy of socialism.[22] This apparently strange idea is rooted in a marriage of the peculiar Marxian concept of science with socialist utopianism. For Marx the defining feature of any science is its ability to pierce through the directly perceptible appearances into the essence of an object. When these coincide, no need for a theoretical science arises. The Marxist utopians said that in socialist society all social relations would be transparent. Therefore, descriptive studies of geography and organisation would be all that was left of political economy.

The idea of a society with transparent social relations is both noble and utopian.[23] It left the post-revolutionary followers of Marx in an awkward corner. Politically, psychologically and ideologically they wanted to profess Marxism. Theoretically, that had been denied them. There seemed to be only two ways out. The first was to postpone the death of Marxism by arguing that as long as Soviet Russia was predominantly a peasant society, the laws peculiar to pre-socialist societies maintained their relevance. This was Evgenii Preobrazhenskii's argument in his theory of the two regulators, markets and planning, of the Soviet economy.[24]

Another possibility was seized on in their somewhat different ways by Aleksandr Bogdanov and Nikolai Bukharin.[25] In a nutshell, their interpretation was that Marx's theory was basically about the form which the 'general sociological laws', valid for all times and societies, have under capitalism. In concentrating upon capitalism Marx had, they argued, understandably neglected the study of the general laws in their pure form, liberated from the appearance they have under capitalism. This pure essence is the form which social laws will have under socialism. This is the sense in which socialist productive relations are evident for all to understand, Bogdanov and Bukharin argued. They set upon studying the general laws of efficient organisation.

It is often argued that the Soviet reformers of the sixties and the eighties were Bukharinist in the sense of proposing an economic model which would combine markets and planning. And indeed, the New Economic Policy of the twenties – strongly defended at the time by Bukharin – has been a source of inspiration for generations of socialist reformers. What is less frequently noted is the methodological similarity between the Bogdanov–Bukharin approach to efficient organisation and the social engineering ambitions of the optimal planners. Among the three founders of the optimal planning school, two (V. S. Nemchinov and V. V. Novozhilov) had already attained some professional prominence in the twenties while the third (L. V. Kantorovich) attended lectures in political economy during the very years when Bukharin's doctrines were being publicly condemned. The decision to adopt the Bogdanov–Bukharin methodology must have been to some degree a conscious one.

The coming of the Stalinist revolution in 1928–31 spelled the end of the golden period of Soviet economics. Even if the debates of the twenties had been politically constrained, they had brought about pioneering contributions in many fields of economics. Now followed the Stalinist barrenness of the thirties and the forties, when a magnifying glass is needed to see anything of interest happening in economics. The roots of the revival in Soviet economics were largely in the twenties, but the forms which this revival took can only be understood against the background of the Stalinist decades.

The full drama of the Stalinist revolution in economics is still to be told. In brief, it meant the total suppression of all previous scholarship, the killing of some of the best brains in the field and the occupation of research institutes, journals and universities by young Stalinists. They were to spend the decades to come in commenting upon the decisions of the party-state and arguing for the existence of real socialism in the USSR. This was their only professional competence. Only a few of the scholars of the twenties – Albert Vainshtein, the student of national income, being the foremost among them – survived the camps to reappear in science in the fifties. Others, like the brilliant statistician and mathematical economist Yevgenii Slutskii escaped into other fields such as mathematics. Just a few of those who had started their professional career in the twenties, V. S. Nemchinov and V. V. Novozhilov being the prominent examples in economics, led a somewhat normal if precarious academic life during the Stalinist decades.

The case of Strumilin illustrates well the change that took place in Soviet planning ideology with the Stalinist revolution. During the late twenties he had been the major proponent of ambitious 'teleological' planning against the more cautious 'genetic' current of thinking. As was typical of the case of economics, the Stalinist revolution both killed the geneticists, who had included the leading planning theorists of the country, and demoted the teleologists. As already mentioned, Strumilin was also publicly criticised. The 1920–1 articles referred to above figured prominently among his alleged sins.[26] There Strumilin had explicitly proposed a social engineering approach. Even later he had argued that planning is an endeavour necessarily based on exact technical calculations. He had also worried about market equilibrium. That amounted to a programme of capitalist restoration, it was claimed. Strumilin's 'universal-mathematical' approach had totally forgotten what is really crucial in the economy: class struggle, the primacy of politics, mass enthusiasm and the leading role of the party, enthused his critic in 1933.

In the end Strumilin fared much better than many others, but the criticisms hurled at him were typical of the times. All talk of equilibrium and efficiency as desirable goals was condemned. The real Bolshevik planning was to be about mobilising resources and enlarging bottlenecks, the new planning chiefs like Valerian Kuibyshev and Nikolai Voznesenskii explained. While the importance of engineering and natural sciences was extolled, Kuibyshev's collected speeches and articles from the years 1930–5, when he was chief of the planning commission, do not contain a single reference to the possible services of economics or economists.[27] It was later claimed that in 1938 Molotov banned any discussion by the economists on prices: that was not their concern.[28]

Despite this perhaps surprisingly there was some relevant economic discussion in the thirties. In fact, one can well argue that most if not all of the measures for rationalising the centrally managed economy, which have been experimented with in the USSR since the mid-fifties, had already been proposed in the thirties.[29] The intensity of discussion varied (with an up-turn just before the war), but it is important to note that some of the prominent political economists of the sixties – men like Aleksandr Birman, Yakov Kronrod, Aleksandr Notkin and Shamai Turetskii – had already in the thirties proposed different ways of rationalising the centralised economic mechanism. There was also, amidst the overwhelming arbitrariness, prohibitions and taboos, a willingness to offer specialist advice. This could hardly have existed without some willingness to listen, too.

It is easy to see why this should be so: total arbitrariness of decision-making is too wasteful to last for long. Nor were all Stalin's men alike. The elevation of Nikolai Voznesenskii, the former student and teacher at the Economic Institute of Red Professorship, to the chairmanship of Gosplan, the planning commission, in 1938, when he was just thirty-four, made a difference. He was soon showing technocratic tendencies, even if a present-day evaluation must be excessive: 'Nikolai Alekseyevich [Voznesenskii] invariably studied each large-scale economic decision from the position of economic theory, and every political economic conclusion was verified with the practice of planning and managing the national economy. The greatest scholars of the country – representatives of different branches of knowledge – took an active and most immediate part in the activities of the USSR Gosplan.'[30]

Voznesenskii was the leading planner of the country for more than ten years. He was also made a member of the Party Politbureau, but then suddenly demoted in 1949 and later executed. The reasons for Voznesenskii's demise are still somewhat unclear, but his technocratic approach to planning must have been significant. To see Voznesenskii's technocracy in a clearer perspective his approach should be contrasted with how a Soviet economist and advisor saw the men for whom he worked over several decades:

When I started working in the Kremlin in 1932, I idolised our leaders. Meeting them face to face, I understood to my terror that we are frequently led by illiterate people. Three or four years of education. None of them even had a command of the methodology of analysis. . . . And even we, people who were involved in preparing important decisions, only had very limited information, often of a perfunctory kind. We were badly informed about the tendencies of our life, the world as a whole. . . . Qualitatively the apparatus deteriorated from one year to the next . . . The most interesting thing is that such were the rules of the system. For any position, any person.[31]

From all that we know of Stalinism it is obvious that this description is more typical. But the complaints of the economists on the incompetence of the politicians have not died with Stalinism. The issue is as alive in 1990 as it was decades before.

A political economy of socialism?

For the Stalinist regime, the Marxist heritage was an awkward one. It stressed the law-bound character of social development but at the same time denied even the possibility of a Marxist political economy of socialism. The Stalinist regime certainly wanted to argue that Soviet socialism was not a result of arbitrary policies or historical accidents but the natural result of the iron laws of history. The idea that the only true and real Marxist regime in the world lacked the possibility of a theory of itself must have sounded strange indeed in the ears of the people who ran it. Stalin and company had no interest in theoretical niceties. They wanted a doctrine showing that Soviet socialism was in the *avant garde* of world development. So it was argued simply that Soviet developments are naturally law-bound and that therefore a political economy of socialism exists.

As late as 1931 this potential solution was strongly criticised as being nothing less than a prostitution of Marxism.[32] A few years later it was official orthodoxy. But then, many other parts of traditional Marxist thought shared a similar fate. The new doctrines on Soviet socialism were codified in an ideological drive started in 1936. The history of Bolshevism was rewritten, the general theory of Marxism–Leninism was set down, and the Party Central Committee decided in 1936 to have an official textbook of political economy written. The work progressed with difficulty, and only in early 1941 was a draft ready. It had to be abandoned, as the hapless authors were told that their premises were wrong. Not only did economic laws exist in socialism, but they are also 'objective', independent of human consciousness.[33] Such a characterisation of the laws was news to the profession. Stalinist economists had earlier argued that any existing economic laws had been created by economic policies.

The pre-1941 truth about economic laws had been easy to comprehend. In essence it boiled down to saying that what the party–state did was an economic law. Taken literally, the post-1941 truth seemed to abolish this identity. Policies did not create laws, they might merely correspond to them more or less closely. Laws existed and thus presumably also functioned independently of conscious action. Did that mean that policies, if mistaken, might fail due to faulty foundations? Had that happened in Soviet socialism? Perhaps objective laws, when found by scholars, could and even should be used as a criterion for the correctness of policies? Had an advisory or even critical role been opened for Soviet economists? Might not a period of realism and modesty, possibly even of open debate, follow in Soviet policies? Such were the optimistic expectations to which the new doctrine gave rise after it had been first publicly announced in an unsigned editorial of the prestigious journal *Pod Znamenem Marksizma* in 1943.

If, as has been speculated, Voznesenskii was the force behind the new doctrine, such may have been his intentions.[34] Under his leadership Gosplan, the planning commission, had indeed hired the assistance of numerous economists. Voznesenskii's 1948 book on the Soviet war economy was sanctioned by Stalin and enthusiastically received in the press.[35] It was hailed as a major breakthrough in Soviet economics.

In retrospect Voznesenskii's 1948 book is an attempt at rationalising central management. It was based on a particular reading of the post-1941 truth about economic laws. The political economy of socialism, Voznesenskii asserted, was to be a study of 'the laws of planning and organising production'. Far from being a domain of political decision-making only, planning, therefore, is part of the subject-matter of economics. This is the core of Voznesenskii's argument. He needed the economists' assistance not for decentralising the economy, but for making centralism work better.

Such a technocratic interpretation of the post-1941 truth on economic laws was not the only possible one. Another reading had been offered in 1944 by K. V. Ostrovitianov, who had been made the unofficial curator of academic political economy.[36] If Voznesenskii's political economy was technocratic, Ostrovitianov's approach can only be characterised as axiomatic-apologetic. The economic laws of socialism were in this approach to be derived from what were now regarded as the defining features of socialism. This is for Ostrovitianov the peculiar sense in which they were 'objective'. It is a case of objectivity by definition. With the definitional laws thus defined, the economists were to show how such alleged laws as 'socialist industrialisation', 'collectivisation' or 'planning' had been in fact followed in Soviet practice. According to this view of the economists' role in socialism their task was crude apologetics, not policy advising, as seems to have been the case in Voznesenskii's interpretation.

One can thus see the neoclassical efficiency oriented approach to the economics of socialism clashing with crude apologetics in the late forties. This clash was manifest in the justly famous debate at that time on investment criteria.[37] Economists like Novozhilov and Strumilin had proposed the use of formal efficiency criteria, while such orthodox proponents of arbitrariness as Mstislavskii declined to admit the existence of any problems of scarcity. Novozhilov, in particular, was criticised for submitting to 'the thinking – long ago unmasked in Marxist literature – of "maximum results with minimum costs"' and for not understanding that investment decisions are and should be fundamentally political.[38]

The writing of the political economy textbook, started in 1936 but interrupted by doctrinal developments and the war, was now finally drawing to a conclusion. As the last preliminary step Stalin wrote his main economic work, a brochure of assorted comments on various economists' opinions.[39] This pamphlet is usually remembered for its reassertion of three things: the existence of objective economic laws, the existence of money and markets in socialism and the admitted possibility of a contradiction between productive forces and relations in socialism. In fact, however, its crucial contents are in an answer to one L. D. Yaroshenko.[40] Yaroshenko, an obscure Gosplan economist, had argued that productive forces and productive relations had been fused in socialism. State administration had a crucial economic role. Consequently, the political economy of socialism had to be a study of planning and rational organisation of production. Stalin saw this proposal as blasphemy, pure Bukharinism and Bogdanovism. Economic policy, he asserted, was a matter for the political decision-makers, not for economists. That was his testament to Soviet economics.

Stalin's booklet seemingly reasserted a total rupture between all investigations of efficiency and the political economy of socialism. This impression was strengthened by the violent campaign against Voznesenskii's ideas that ensued. But the fact that such a campaign was deemed necessary shows that the neoclassical efficiency approach to the economics of socialism had survived the Stalinist decades. For a few years in the late forties, encouraged by the technocracy of Voznesenskii, it openly fought for acceptance. After the dictator's death in 1953 its voice would become insistent.

Criticisms of political economy

In general terms Stalinist political economy – indeed like all Soviet science – extolled itself as being the only truly scientific political economy in the world. At the same time, however, the work of Soviet economists was strongly censured:

The insufficient knowledge of Marxism–Leninism is revealed in the substitution of factual description of economic policy for political economy, in inability and failure to collect historical experience and to proceed comprehensively to the essence of economic appearances, in theoretical helplessness and scholasticism, in isolation from practice, in a dogmatic approach to solving practical problems, in simply repeating ready formulas and standpoints instead of scientific work, in basing work on citations, in failing to eliminate simplifications and vulgarisations of Marxism and in the practice of cramming and talmudism.[41]

Such criticisms were voiced repeatedly. Much of this criticism was ritual, but some may have reflected real concern. Little, though, could be done without fundamental political change. Only after Stalin's death did such criticisms begin to carry some weight. Already in early 1954 the Party Central Committee adopted a resolution demanding more relevance in economics. Another notable intervention was made by Deputy Prime Minister Anatolii Mikoyan, who at the XXth Party Congress in 1956 urged the economists to start a critical reappraisal of 'certain' theoretical dogmas of Stalin.[42] In particular, he encouraged creativity and stressed how 'any scientific economic work' is impossible without statistical analysis. Meanwhile even the simplest statistics only became available slowly.

The basic task of the Stalinist political economy of socialism had been to argue for the reality and law-determined character of Soviet socialism. As such it was too important a part of Soviet ideology to be totally abandoned. Instead, the admitted defects of political economy were explained by the personality of Stalin, especially by his insistence on the separation of the doctrines of political economy and economic policies.

A basic consensus reigned among the post-Stalinist leadership about the need to enhance productivity and the standard of living. Economists were expected to contribute towards this goal. The essence of Khrushchev's science policy was succinctly put by L. F. Ilichev, a Central Committee Secretary: 'practical results are the decisive criterion for the value of science'.[43] The normal criteria of scientific truth were not mentioned and Lysenko's phoney agronomy

was one project to capitalise on this approach. In economics the ideal
of social engineering, violently condemned at the time of the Stalinist
revolution, was now resurrected. Its prominent proponent was academician Vasili Nemchinov, a statistician and the driving organisational force behind the rise of Soviet mathematical economics since
the late fifties. In numerous programmatic statements he explained
how:

It is especially important, at the present time, that economists should become
social engineers and economics an exact science. Economic research should
not be based on reworking literary sources but on the concrete facts and
figures of living reality. An economist must be able to fine-tune the management mechanism of social production and to regulate the functioning of this
mechanism. Only then will he be able to satisfy the requirements set upon
him.[44]

Nemchinov warned again and again about the dangers of arbitrary
planning and management. In socialism, he pointed out, such 'voluntarism' can lead to losses no smaller than those caused by the
'anarchy' of capitalist competition.[45] Nemchinov's criticisms were
originally directed against Stalinist planning, but they were also
applicable to more recent times. Such voluntarism and various 'hair-
brained schemes' were, after all, what Khrushchev's regime was
accused of after he was forced into retirement in 1964. The new
Brezhnev leadership promised, among other things, modernisation
of the society and a scientific approach to managing the economy.
This seemed a final rehabilitation of the neoclassical approach to the
economics of socialism. For a short period of time even a radical
reform of the economy seemed possible.

Meanwhile, the need for such a reform was being acknowledged,
as the economists' first attempts at social engineering had met with
problems. It was noted that any partial attempts at rationalisation
were either condemned to inefficiency or impossible to implement.
The economy rejected the measures the economists tried to
implement. Because of irrational planning practices enterprises were
not interested in efficiency-enhancing methods. Working better only
led to tighter plans and lost income. Therefore the efficiency
approach could not limit itself to such partial measures as introducing
computers, mechanising planning calculations, using information
systems and optimality algorithms. Neither was it sufficient to
change the criteria according to which enterprise activity was evalu-
ated and managers rewarded. Understanding this was crucial for the

advocacy of a radical economic reform that started in the sixties and has retained its timeliness ever since. These discussions are surveyed in later chapters of this book.

go to Pg 49

Old or new political economy?

The problem that the political economy of socialism now faced was as simple as it was crucial. It was totally unable to enlighten policy-making. This fact was laid bare for all to see during the grand late-fifties discussion on the law of value and price policy.[46] Everybody agreed that existing prices were fundamentally arbitrary and irrational. They often encouraged wastefulness and punished thriftiness, efficiency and good quality. What should be done? was the natural question to put to the economists.

In 1941, when he asserted that economic laws did exist in Soviet socialism, Stalin had used one particular law, the law of value, as an example. It existed in the Soviet Union, he announced. The choice was a most unfortunate one. The law of value was understood by Marx primarily as a shorthand expression for the way in which markets function in the capitalist society. As a price theory it is clumsy and flawed, especially if understood to deny the influence of needs and demand on value and prices. More reasonable interpretations are also possible and were later put forward in Soviet as well as in Western economics. Soviet political economists, unfortunately, had no method of distinguishing between true and false theories. They could argue that the law of value existed, but did not know what that might mean. In particular, they derived several different price formulas from the alleged law. They had no way of agreeing which formula should be the preferred one.

Quite obviously, then, the political economy of socialism, the only kind of economics of socialism that had been taught and studied in the USSR, was impotent in practice. The situation called for a different approach. But there were also misgivings of a different nature. Political economy had been used as an apology for Stalinism, and this was now openly admitted. As the Central Committee Secretary Ilichev once said to an Academy of Sciences audience: 'The first priority was not to promote economic practice according to the demands of economic laws, but to "adapt" the categories of political economy to the huge failures that took place in practice *so as to justify those imperfections*' (emphasis mine).[47] As Ilichev went on to point out that the situation had favoured economists who were incapable of empirical analysis but fluent in citations, the open encouragement given to new approaches in economics is evident.

To propose, even indirectly, that Stalinist political economy should be abandoned was, however, too much. This is what L. A. Leontev did in a 1961 article.[48] Leontev was – until his death in 1971 – one of the best-known political economists, a corresponding member of the Academy and a long-standing journal editor. During the forties he had been a prominent populariser of the doctrine of objective economic laws. Now he contrasted Stalinist political economy in a most unfavourable way with the work of economists of the twenties. The latter, he argued, provided a good example of the kind of work that economists should be doing. Some of the alleged laws of political economy were devoid of all rational content, he concluded.

Ilichev, the Central Committee Secretary for ideological matters, was not willing to go nearly as far as that. At an ideological conference he picked out Leontev's article for criticism: 'The path which he has taken and incites others to take also is erroneous and can only lead to serious mistakes, negate all that is positive in the development of economic thought in our country, and make the whole political economy of socialism open to doubt.'[49]

Exposing the whole of the political economy of socialism to doubt would almost amount to putting a question mark over the whole of Soviet socialism. The official de-Stalinisation of the early sixties was not willing to go that far. The political economy of socialism was there to stay. Though one more frontal attack against political economy was coming (chapter 3), the reformists generally preferred either to reinterpret the by now traditional laws of political economy in a novel way or simply to ignore its scholastic controversies. The former strategy, 'scholarly revisionism', had ideological advantages, made the arguments of the reformers easier to comprehend by political economists and also came naturally to many of those who had themselves been educated in political economy. But it also tied its practitioners to a framework which remained deeply unsatisfactory. The latter strategy, 'apparent pragmatism', was free of this drawback but made its exponent the underdog in a field where political economy claimed to define the main theoretical contours.

The organisation of economic science

The relationship between theoretical political economy and applied branches of economic study only became an issue after the volume of such studies started to multiply in the late fifties. The topic was first explicitly raised, it seems, by the veteran academician Ostrovitianov in 1964, and he also edited a monograph that outlined the conservative orthodox understanding of the 'system of economic sciences' in 1968.[50]

The monograph divided the economic disciplines studying socialism into three groups in a declining order of abstractness. The most abstract were the general economic disciplines. They included the political economy of socialism as the centrepiece, but also economic history and the history of economic thought. In the second rank were various special or interbranch disciplines, e.g. the science of economic planning, economic statistics, labour economics, the study of finance as well as the study of the socialist world economy. The third and final group included the various branch economic disciplines such as the economics of industry or agriculture. The alleged hierarchical structure of the economic sciences meant that the disciplines of a lower rank were always supposed to be based on the theoretical findings of the discipline of a higher order. They were all supposed to be applications of political economy. On the other hand, political economy would remain an abstract study with little if any connection with empirical matters. Furthermore, the monograph specifically pointed out that the use of mathematical methods did not give rise to any new economic discipline.

Ostrovitianov emphasised that neither political economy nor other economic disciplines studied economic policies as such. Their task was 'to provide the scientific foundations of economic policy'. In the case of the science of planning (or management) it was possible to argue that 'the adoption of any decision of principal importance must be preceded by a wide-ranging consultation with specialists'. Concerning political economy proper Ostrovitianov complained of a tendency to define it too widely, so as to include various empirical topics. He wanted to keep his theories free from empirical details. This, as will be seen in chapter 5, was something his younger colleagues were not ready to accept.

This differentiation between theoretical study and empirical research is further strengthened by existing institutional barriers. In the USSR, fundamental research is concentrated in the Academy of Sciences research institutes. Universities are mostly for teaching. Scholarship pursued there has generally been and still remains much more conservative than that of the Academy institutes. Among the Academy institutes, the Institute of Economics in Moscow has the main responsibility for developing the political economy of socialism. Not surprisingly, its profile has in general been quite conservative. During the sixties new Academy institutes, The Central Mathematical-Economic Institute (TsEMI) in Moscow and the Institute of Industrial Economics (IEiOPP) in Novosibirsk became not only the main centres of reformist economic thought but also the most important centres for developing methods of planning and management. They both had strong and ambitious directors. TsEMI was led from its foundation in 1963 until 1985 by academician Nikolai Fedorenko and IEiOPP from 1967 to 1986 by academician Abel Aganbegyan.

The Academy is organised in departments, which are supposed to coordinate the work of all the institutes within them. Though institutes are basically led by the director, the position of the academician secretary of a department does give its holder some influence over other institutes as well. Fedorenko was the academician secretary of the department of economics from 1972 until 1985. He was succeeded by Aganbegyan.

Other academy research institutes with relevance to economic reform include The Institute for the Economics of the Socialist World Economy (IEMSS), The Institute for the Study of USA and Canada and the Institute for World Economy and International Relations (IMEMO). The first has long been directed by academician Oleg Bogomolov and the second by academician Georgi Arbatov, while the directorship of IMEMO has changed hands more often. These institutes are not supposed to study the Soviet economy directly, but some of their researchers do. Their main importance is in transmitting information from their own fields both to general discussion and especially to policy-makers, to whom they have direct access.

The network of party institutes of higher education is also important in the social sciences. The Academy of Social Sciences in Moscow, which is directly under the Central Committee, has had an important role and was especially prominent in the seventies. Important economic bureaucracies like Gosplan and Gosbank, the state bank, also have their specialised research institutes. They have better access to empirical information than the Academy institutes. Because of the degree of academic freedom that the Academy has been able to secure, the best scholars usually, however, prefer to work there. The prestige of the Academy is high. The research institutes with the least prestige and scholarly achievement are those of the branch ministries.

The Academy is only relatively independent, especially in the politically delicate field of social science.[51] Its scholars often have the greatest difficulties in gaining access to useful information, and they are naturally subject both to party control within the academy and to censorship. Neither are the institutes immune from high-level political pressure. An example of this was seen in the early seventies. The Academy Institute of Economics had tried, with the support of the Academy leadership, to reorient its work away from scholastic political economy towards questions more relevant to policy issues.[52] The Academy line was arguably in tune with the early Brezhnev period emphasis on scientific decision-making, but it had not foreseen the change towards conservative orthodoxy that was under way. In December 1971 the Communist Party Central Committee adopted a resolution which roundly condemned the work of the Institute.[53] It had neglected the study of fundamental political economy.

The importance of ideological orthodoxy was in many ways emphasised in the early seventies. This was due to the Czechoslovak crisis, the worsening of relations with China, the rise of domestic dissidence as well as the increasing general conservatism of the Brezhnev leadership. The ideological climate had turned decisively from the reformism of the late sixties towards conservatism, and this affected the Academy as well. The Department of Economics published a self-criticism which admitted serious theoretical mistakes. The 'autonomous functioning' (citation marks are used in the original) of markets had been overemphasised, the role of centralism had been understated and, worst of all, even the possibility of competition in socialism had been mentioned.

The Institute of Economics was not the only one disciplined in the early seventies. There was a general conservative crack-down in Soviet social science. Institutes were reoriented, their directors and researchers sacked and censorship tightened. The leadership of the Institute of Economics was also duly changed and research in the fundamentals of political economy re-emphasised. The problem, however, was that fewer and fewer people were interested in it. Ever since the early seventies the institute has had problems in attracting postgraduate students and talented scholars, especially in the field of political economy. This has been the subject of repeated complaints. The marginalisation of political economy has continued, apparent pragmatism has prevailed.

As well as being neglected by most economists, political economy has been unable to find internal cohesion in the cross-currents between scholarly revisionism and orthodoxy. The 1954 textbook of political economy was the last one which was official in the sense of codifying a monolithic doctrine binding for all. That was only possible by papering over the differences in opinion that already existed in the early fifties. By the late sixties there were three main textbooks on the market. In addition, many economists published monographs on 'the laws and categories of the political economy of socialism'. The various compendia had much in common. They all tried to imitate the way in which Marx presented his theory in *Capital* as a dialectical interplay of categories. All the textbooks were also almost hermetically sealed against factual analysis or statistics. And naturally they all presented mere variants of Soviet ideology. But the differences between the compendia are also real, and any notion of an official political economy of socialism is correct only in a relative sense.

As the idea of a single truth is deeply ingrained in Marxism–Leninism, such a situation was considered abnormal and the Academy of Sciences set the goal of producing a book giving *the* political economy of socialism as early as 1968.[54] After much effort, a three-volume work called *The Socialist Economy* was finally published in 1984.[55] The authors admitted that 'far from all debatable problems have been solved completely'.[56] By the time the volumes had reached their readers this was an obvious understatement. Instead of a refined analysis of the 'categories and laws of political economy', a totally new approach was being demanded from the economists (chapter 6).

2 The mathematical challenge to orthodoxy

In chapter 1, we saw how the Soviet political economy of socialism was born as a form of Marxist–Leninist ideology, how it proved totally barren of relevant policy advice and how – even in the seventies – continued party insistence upon its primarily ideological role condemned it to marginalisation among professional economists. It was discussed in official declarations and forewords to scholarly books, but actually neglected by most economists in their professional work. It still had some importance as the general frame of reference into which all economics, especially that of not a purely technical nature, had to fit somehow. For most economists, because of their education, it was also the natural discourse within which to pursue their theoretical and policy generalisations. Furthermore, as we shall see in chapter 5, the importance of policy issues within political economy grew. None the less, since the fifties, most reform economics was to be found outside political economy. In particular, there was an open challenge to the leading role of political economy in the late sixties. Economic reformism and reformism in economics coincided in the new Soviet mathematical economics of optimal planning.

Contemporary observers were struck by the rapidity with which Soviet economics seemed to change during the late fifties and early sixties. Just before that, all Soviet social science had seemed one Stalinist wasteland of intellectual barrenness, and suddenly, as if from nowhere, groups of economists, administrators and mathematicians had sprung up, advocating administrative rationalisation, economic reform and a re-examination if not abandonment of long-held Marxist doctrines. Not for the first nor the last time, the 'end of ideology' in the Soviet Union was prophesied, theories of convergence of social systems gained in popularity and a 'mathematical revolution' was diagnosed in Soviet economics.[1] None of these expectations materialised, and with hindsight we can see the causes, effects and limitations of the undeniable and real changes that have taken place in Soviet economic thought with greater clarity. What happened in the sixties is the topic of this chapter and chapter 3, but a consideration of the background to the 'new Soviet economics' is needed first. As already pointed out, not all Russian and Soviet economics belonged to the Marxist mainstream made orthodoxy by the revolution. The thin Russian tradition of mathematical economics is of particular interest, because it was as a mathematical theory of optimal planning that Soviet reformism was to have its only grand theory so far.

The background

A history of Russian and early Soviet economic thought remains to be written, but the main outlines of the development are well known. As in other respects in Russia, the development of economics had been conditioned by the combination of European influence and semi-Asiatic problems so peculiar to the country. Recurring waves of Western intellectual fashions from positivism to Marxism have swept the country and each has recruited its ardent followers. Such scholars were Westernisers in the style of Viktor Volkonskii, the prominent reformist economist who broke new ground in 1967 by associating himself with a unified 'world economic science' in distinction to the Stalinist division of all social thought into Marxist–Leninist science (The Truth) and bourgeois ideology (The Untruth).[2] No less influential, however, were Slavophile opinions emphasising the peculiar characteristics of the country. Partly reflecting German historicism, such judgements denied the suitability of any Western social science for Russian soil and soul. These too have their latter-day followers, often in open resistance to the modernising tendencies of the Westerners.[3]

Overall, what Russian economic thought, mostly derivative as it was, may have missed in originality, it has gained in diversity. Only a few of the pre-revolutionary Russian economists have deserved even a footnote in standard Western textbooks of the history of economics, but the variety of their interests is notable: Tugan-Baranovskii on economic history and business cycles, Dmitriev on the mathematical labour theory of value and Slutskii on consumer theory are those most frequently remembered. The latter two are also the first prominent Russian mathematical economists.

The 1920s witnessed a well documented if brief flowering of Soviet economic scholarship. The Soviet economists of the twenties mixed into a fruitful combination pre-revolutionary Russian economics and statistics, European Marxism and closely observed American empirical research. The intellectually exciting post-revolutionary agenda of fundamental social change and a still relatively permissive political climate contributed to innovation. This happened in agrarian theory,[4] the beginnings of development economics,[5] and growth theory[6] as well as planning methodology[7] and mathematical economics in general.[8] The economics of the twenties has not lost its attraction for scholars, and the parallels between some of the debates of the twenties and those of the sixties are conspicuous.[9] In the *perestroika* period, this parallel, which could only be hinted at earlier, is now openly discussed. Many reformers point to the New Economic Policy of the twenties with its variety of forms of ownership and widely functioning markets as the suitable model of socialism for the late twentieth century, too. Reversing the earlier officially sanctioned interpretation, they see the twenties as socialism proper and the Stalinist decades as a tragic lapse from the normal, indeed even from the 'true' Leninist definition of socialism.

Most Russian economics of the pre-revolutionary period and of the twenties was naturally not of a mathematical character. The mathematical method, however, was sometimes practised. As late as 1931, I. G. Bliumin, a leading analyst of Western economic thought, could have a solid monograph on mathematical economic theory published by the Communist Academy.[10] Bliumin not only provided a detailed and matter-of-fact if critical discussion of several leading mathematical economists from Cournot to Cassel, but also defended the use of mathematics in Marxism. The existing symbiosis between the mathematical method and subjectivism is paradoxical, he argued, as an 'objective' understanding of economic phenomena actually gives more opportunity for the use of advanced methods. The more advanced the theoretical analysis, the better the prospects for the use of mathematics, Bliumin argued. He was echoing Marx's own words on the use of mathematics as a criterion for the progress of any science. Bliumin duly wound up his discussion with a vision of a future Marxist mathematical school of economics.

This was an attitude rapidly vanishing from the scene. The same year, 1931, in which Bliumin's book was published, saw an attack by Valerian Kuibyshev, Gosplan's chief, on an alleged 'arithmetical-statistical deviation' in planning.[11] In the view of the Stalinist planning bureaucracy earlier plan proposals, usually submitted by non-Bolshevik specialists, had – in addition to their other faults – been too abstract and general and lacking in detailed factual foundation. In a word, they had not been meticulously directive enough; they had not incorporated the ethos of the Stalinist command economy. Planning, as far as it was to have any rationality, was to be seen as a matter of mobilising resources. It was a task for engineers, not for economists. This attitude was to persist and triumph. For decades economists were excluded from planning. The Planning Commission was – like the whole country – led by engineers.

The exclusion of economists from top planning positions still continues. In summer 1990 academician Oleg Bogomolov, one of the radical Soviet proponents of a market economy, argued that a basic reason for the half-heartedness and confused thinking of government reform policies was the predominance of non-economists in the economic bureaucracies preparing and implementing crucial decisions.[12] A common language between reform economists and bureaucrats does not exist.

Many of the economists of the twenties were sent to prisons or labour camps. Some were executed. In this heady and repressive atmosphere of the thirties Leonid Kantorovich, a young Leningrad professor of mathematics, was asked by the local plywood trust to think about a method of rationally organising its production.[13] He gladly accepted the task of assisting Soviet industrialisation. But instead of simply outlining some practical proposals for the trust the young mathematician ended up with both a generalisation and a solution of the task he was set. This was the origin of a new branch of mathematics, linear optimisation.

The first published version of Kantorovich's method in 1939 had a printing of 1,000 copies. While it was enthusiastically received by a narrow circle of Soviet specialists it was hardly noted by plannersin general. By the late thirties Kantorovich had already applied his brain to a more grandiose task, something that seemed to fulfil his early conviction that mathematics should not only be profound but also of practical use. Going beyond the realm of the organis ationof factory production, he asked, could not and should not the planning of the whole national economy be seen as a task of optimisation under constraints, the attainment (as Kantorovich wasto formulate it) of maximum production subject to various resource availabilities, technologies and a pre-determined product mix?This formulation of the optimal planning framework was to become the centrepiece of the new Soviet economics of the late fifties.

The planning task as formulated by Kantorovich was actually not a new one: it was a way of presenting the neoclassical approach to planning. What was new was Kantorovich's ability to formulate and solve the problem under linear conditions with a large number of constraints. While the mathematics of linear optimisation are not of immediate concern here, the somewhat peculiar economic character of Kantorovich's approach should be pointed out. The assumption of a given goal function to be maximised (or minimised, depending on the formulation) is the fundamental limitation of the analysis. Kantorovich assumed the maximand to be a pre-determined product mix. In so doing he kept well in line both with the axioms of Soviet forced growth policy and with the priority of political decision-making, which was assumed to fix the product proportions in question. But saying that political decision-makers impose the structure of production, leaving the planners to maximise the given output, seems to concede no role whatsoever to consumers. Later on, this neglect of the demand side was acknowledged and the search for the proper objectives of the socialist economy started in earnest. Socially and politically, this gave a totally new twist to the optimal planning approach.

Of most interest, perhaps, is the fundamental underlying assumption of optimal planning theory. Planning the national economy is quite simply seen as an extension of planning enterprise production. Decades later academician V. L. Makarov, a pupil and collaborator of Kantorovich, characterised the mathematician's methodological approach as being based on 'the possibility, immanent to socialism, of *constructing* the economic system. Because socialism, in distinction from earlier formations, has an author – Marxist–Leninist doctrine – the economic system too must be constructed consciously, proceeding from the theoretical conception of this doctrine' (emphasis added).[14]

To put this into other words, in the same way as a plywood trust was, in the Soviet planned economy, given the task of maximising the production of veneer from given resources, the economy as a whole also has a given task, and the economic problem boils down to organising production in an optimal way relative to that task. This, naturally, is an extremely narrow technocratic sub-optimisation approach which by consciously neglecting all social and political issues makes the economist a humble servant of the state – in this case a servant of the Stalinist state.

Not surprisingly, Makarov is willing to see Kantorovich's 'production–technological' approach as just the first approximation necessary
for the mathematician's model building. The economist in Kantorovich, he argues, was never happy with stopping at that. The next
question about which Kantorovich, so Makarov argues, 'thought
much and intensively', concerned the economic and social conditions
which would bring about the movement towards efficiency. Posing
this question implied crossing the border from being a servant of
Stalinism to being an economic reformer.

Makarov's interpretation is a friendly one. Less sympathetic commentators have often accused Kantorovich of an overly technological
understanding of optimality. The social questions of choice, freedom
and power do not figure prominently in his published writings.
Though Kantorovich later fought hard for issues like price reform, he
does not seem to have outlined any alternative to the traditional
centrally managed economy. His proposals were about rationalising
it, not about finding an alternative to it. There is, however, no doubt
about the correctness of another part of Makarov's interpretation.
Kantorovich, and the optimal planning theory in general, did share
the assumption (or even axiom) of the constructability of the socialist
economy. For the optimal planners, the building of a model of an
efficient economy also meant drawing up a blueprint for an optimal
socialist economy. Furthermore, they believed that such a blueprint
could be implemented within the main political and institutional
arrangements of existing Soviet socialism. One-party rule and the
predominance of state ownership were accepted parts of those
arrangements. The optimal planners were rationalisers, not revolu-
tionaries, Soviet optimal planning theory is social engineering writ
large.

There is also a more radical way of looking at Kantorovich's formulation. Optimisation by definition means the choice of the best alternative available. The optimality approach always assumes the
existence of alternatives, choice and, consequently, of responsibility
for the option selected as well as for the alternatives forgone. Relative
to the Stalinist orthodoxy which argued that all policies were
determined by economic laws, this was revolutionary. Choice, furthermore, can only be optimal relative to definite criteria. Whose
goals have – or, indeed, should have – the decisive say? Kantorovich
accepted the priority of the planners' goals as reflected in the product
mix. Later, in the sixties, new interpretations arose. It was argued
that in an optimal socialist society citizens' preferences must be the

decisive criterion of optimality. Society, therefore, needed a democratic mechanism for the articulation of such preferences. The planners should implement citizens' goals, not those of a political dictatorship. It was furthermore argued that the citizens' preferences are best revealed in their market choice as consumers. Market equilibrium, therefore, should be the feedback judging the correctness of planners' decisions.

In the early forties such possible implications of optimal planning still lay in the distant future. In spite of the pressing military tasks imposed upon a mathematician in beleaguered Leningrad, Kantorovich finished a book manuscript in November 1942. The manuscript was duly submitted to Gosplan, the planning commission, for approval, and an expert committee was nominated to assess the applicability of Kantorovich's work in practical planning. Kantorovich had shown how the properties of the optimal planning task, especially the crucial duality between physical and value dimensions of the economy, could be interpreted as offering a way of using the price mechanism to rationalise central planning and management of the economy.

In fact, the easiest way of appreciating the importance of Kantorovich's work is to relate it to the earlier socialist calculation debate among Western economists.[15] As mentioned in chapter 1, Enrico Barone had shown in 1908 how prices are implicit in any rational calculation of costs and needs. They are the rational method of comparing costs and results. Therefore, any society either has to use markets to arrive at prices or must find another way for simulating this function of the markets.

Ludwig von Mises and Friedrich Hayek, the leading figures of the Austrian school of economists, argued during the interwar period that only the market mechanism can discover rational prices. No planning agency could possibly calculate rational prices as the amount of information needed would be prohibitive. Neither could all relevant information be formalised for calculations. On the other hand, socialism could not use markets, as the whole idea of planning was to substitute markets by something better, centralised decision-making. Furthermore, markets, even if their necessity had been admitted, could not function in a society based on state property. Rivalry, risk-taking and entrepreneurship would all be impossible, given the state monopoly of ownership. The economic impossibility of the socialist dream seemed to have been proved. Without markets and rational prices the planned economy was doomed to inefficiency, 'groping in the dark', possibly even to imminent crash.

The best-known socialist answer had been given in the thirties by the Polish socialist economist Oskar Lange. He proposed that the central planners should in fact use prices, arrived at not in markets but in a simulation of the competitive game. In the sixties Lange himself was to recommend the centralised use of powerful computers to process the information for rational planning. These, Lange seemed to be saying, were the proper substitutes, for markets.[16] Computers would finally legitimise centralism. Kantorovich's theory provides the argument behind such centralist answers to the socialist calculation debate. Linear optimisation showed theoretically how the planning agency could solve the 'thousands of equations' necessary for arriving at an efficient use of resources. Furthermore, Kantorovich was able to show how so-called shadow prices showing the marginal contribution of each scarce resource and good towards the objective function could be used to guide enterprises towards the optimal utilisation of resources. No markets, rivalry, private ownership or entrepreneurship would be needed – or so it seemed.

In 1942 Soviet economic experts' opinion concerning Kantorovich's proposals was, however, 'in the main'[17] negative. One professor of statistics accused him of 'speaking about the optimum, while Pareto [the great Italian economist of the turn of the century] also spoke of the optimum and Pareto was a fascist'.[18] Kantorovich had to withdraw his manuscript. The USSR was not yet ready for this method. Not only were the computers needed for making Kantorovich's method practicable unobtainable, but the rationalising approach itself was bound to be controversial even among those economists and planners who understood its core. As we saw in chapter 1, the socialist economy was supposed to be about increasing constraints, not about an optimal adaptation to them. Such counter-arguments to rationalisation were to be heard right up until the sixties.

The first Soviet economist apparently to understand the potential of Kantorovich's method was V. V. Novozhilov, a professor of engineering economics at Leningrad's prestigious Polytechnical University. His primary interest was in efficiency calculations,[19] and his work was criticised in the debate on formal investigation criteria in the late forties (chapter 1). In the early fifties Novozhilov was fired from his university. During the debates he declined Kantorovich's offer of assistance. In the circumstances, a mathematician's support would have been a handicap.

Kantorovich and Novozhilov were not the only mathematically oriented economists who fell victim during those years to Stalinist xenophobia. A. L. Lurie, later the author of the first Soviet textbook on the use of mathematical methods in economics, was criticised for his studies in transport economics. Pavel Maslov, an economist-sociologist-statistician from the Moscow Financial Institute was condemned for writing a book which attempted to acquaint Soviet scholars with Western advances in econometrics and statistics. The book was printed but withdrawn from circulation after it was found to have characterised Marx's method as deductive, neglected the achievements of Soviet statistics and even – the greatest sin of all – praised Western cost of living indices, totally failing to mention that their sole real task was to help cover up the inevitable impoverishment of workers under capitalism.[20] It was to take Soviet statisticians several years after the declaration of *glasnost* before they were able to publish their first cost of living indices.

The third future great name of optimal planning, in addition to Kantorovich and Novozhilov, was academician Vasili Nemchinov, who committed in the late forties most of the sins an academic party member with a conscience could possibly commit. Not only did he defend Maslov (and academician Evgeni Varga, the object of another witch hunt) but he had also written about the need to introduce econometrics into the USSR. But econometrics, exclaimed K. V. Ostrovitianov, the Stalinist curator of economics, is after all just 'the archebourgeois mathematical school of statistics' and as such clearly inadmissible in the USSR.[21] Worst of all, Nemchinov, a professor of the Timiriazev Agricultural Academy, had bravely resisted the infiltration of Lysenko's phoney agronomy. This finally led to his dismissal from the Agricultural Academy in 1948.[22]

Winds of change

The dictator finally died in 1953. The post-Stalin leadership was concerned about low economic productivity and wanted to raise the general standard of living. They demanded, in a way unknown during the Stalinist decades, a contribution from the economists to increasing the efficiency of the economy. This rapidly opened up new possibilities for mathematical economics. The use of even simple mathematical methods seemed to promise fast results with minimal investment – and without questioning the existing institutional setting. In 1954 the Leningrad State University decided to publish Kantorovich's 1942 manuscript. The decision was withdrawn, however, after the economist Strumilin, as a publisher's referee, declined to recommend the book for publication. The reason he gave was somewhat ridiculous: the book 'did not correspond to generally accepted views'.[23] It was to take five more years and – according to Aron Katsenelinboigen[24] – a lot of ideological polishing before the book that was to win both the Lenin prize and the Nobel prize for Kantorovich was finally published.[25] Seventeen years had passed since the writing of the book.

'The book literally struck one by its originality', recalled Nikolai Petrakov almost thirty years later. By then Petrakov was a corresponding member of the Academy, deputy director of TsEMI and a leading proponent of economic reform. He would soon become a personal adviser to Secretary General Gorbachev. But in the late fifties Petrakov was still a mere recent economics graduate of the Moscow State University. 'The book contained no definitions or general ruminations on the "requirements" of various economic laws or about how "they regulate" social development. The book was about THE THING, about how diligently, with maximal effectiveness to use the limited production possibilities, how rationally to manage the economy.'[26]

As a manual of social 'housekeeping', as Petrakov puts it, Kantorovich's theory was immediately raised as the banner of the new economics, social engineering writ large. For the next few years it was to be the centrepiece of Soviet economic debates. Crucial as it was, the publication of Kantorovich's book was not the only sign of the changing times. Possibilities for empirical research were symbolically opened by the publishing of a statistical yearbook, the first in decades. Scholarly autarky started to crumble, as foreign visitors, international symposia and book translations became somewhat less of a rarity. Connections with East European countries were of special importance, as prominent socialist scholars there were at that time defending the use of mathematical methods in planning and social sciences as being Marxist orthodoxy. Discussions on economic reform, as well, were much further advanced in countries like Poland, Czechoslovakia and Hungary.

Perhaps of equal importance were Western scholars like Norbert Wiener, the founder of cybernetics, who emphasised the enormous potential of modern methods in national economic planning. In the West, this was the time of a widely shared belief in rational economic policy and planning, of the new utopianism of economic system design and the convergence theory. In the USSR, such ideas were often seen as a confirmation of the 'objective requirements' of the scientific and technical revolution. Its benefits could only be fully reaped under socialism, it was argued. Furthermore, it was often asked, was it not something of an insult to Russia that methods first pioneered there were being used primarily in the capitalist countries? Surely there should be a way of differentiating between the scientific method itself and the bourgeois use to which it had been turned? Both the input–output method – whose roots go back to the Russia of the twenties – and linear optimisation – which had been independently developed in the USA a few years after Kantorovich – were the subject of such musings.

The traditional informal and largely arbitrary planning approach still had its public defenders. As late as 1956 Gennadi Sorokin, a leading Gosplan economist, repeated Kuibyshev's warning about a 'statistical-arithmetic deviation' in planning.[27] This, however, was a losing position. By 1958 I. G. Bliumin – the same Bliumin who had in 1931 prophesied a future Marxist mathematical economics – argued that Western economic scholarship could be divided into two parts, a bourgeois political economy on one hand and various practical methods on the other. While the former was a part of hostile ideology, the latter could and should be used in the Soviet Union as well, if augmented by the proper theoretical framework.[28]

The political economists soon sketched a division of labour between political and mathematical economics that was to their liking. They tried to preserve a monopoly of theoretical research for themselves. Any general problems could only be studied by political economy, while various practical problems could and should be studied by mathematical methods. In this way the political economy establishment, while carving a small niche for mathematical methods, hoped to reserve the leading theoretical and ideological role for itself. This boundary survey was doomed to fail, however. Mathematics is by no means limited to a study of measurable entities, and Marx for one wanted to use mathematics in theoretical research. Furthermore, and of greater importance, many mathematical economists were not satisfied with the humble role given to them by the political economists. While the latter were unable to provide an economic theory of socialism, some of the former were soon to launch a frontal attack on the monopoly of political economy – and on the economic system it had for decades tried to legitimise.

The attack

Once started, the apparent mathematical breakthrough in Soviet economics was fast. By the early sixties nobody openly denied the applicability of mathematical methods in economics, and in 1963 the government both decided upon measures for speeding up the introduction of computers in the economy and sanctioned the founding of TsEMI, The Central Economic-Mathematical Institute of the Soviet Academy of Sciences. Two years later TsEMI started publishing its house journal, *Ekonomika i matematicheskie metody* (The Economy and Mathematical Methods). Concurrently the teaching of mathematics to economists widened from the small study groups organised by Kantorovich, Nemchinov and Novozhilov into an integral part of the general economist's curriculum. It was soon possible to graduate as a mathematical economics specialist, though such specialists have remained a small minority among Soviet economics graduates. Within this minority, most have been specialists in management information systems and planning techniques. Mathematical economic theory and econometrics have been almost non-existent. In general, standards of training have left much to be desired.

In the late 1950s academician Nemchinov, who had become the leading public proponent of the use of mathematical methods, was still giving a very narrow characterisation of the role of mathematical economics. According to him 'the object of Soviet econometrics, which is a supportive branch of science, is the theory of economic and planning calculations and the means of their mechanisation'.[29] By the early sixties the field had been widened. Nemchinov's list of central research topics for mathematical economists now included price formation, input–output and other macro-economic models, the use of optimisation models in solving various specific problems (especially in transport) as well as the development of mathematical statistics.[30] But for Nemchinov 'economic-mathematical methods' still remained the term to be used of the new discipline, and he always emphasised its applied role: 'Experience shows that under socialism econometrical research has boundless possibilities if it is based on Marxist–Leninist economic science and puts itself into the service of national economic and enterprise planning.'[31]

Nemchinov died in 1964 having just installed Nikolai Prokofevich Fedorenko as the head of the new institute of mathematical economics, TsEMI. Fedorenko was not a practising mathematical economist himself, but an organisation man and a specialist in the economics of the chemical industry. He was to head TsEMI for more than two decades. His position as the academician secretary of the Department of Economics of the Academy from 1972 to 1985 made him the leader and organiser of all economic research within the

Soviet Academy of Sciences. Fedorenko was an ambitious man. Using the institute and the academy position as a power base, he soon launched a variant of optimal planning theory which was not only a competitor to political economy as the general theory of socialist economics but also a blueprint of economic reform. This approach was to be called SOFE, The System of Optimally Functioning Socialist Economy, and since the mid-sixties it has been the major reformist doctrine in Soviet economics. It will be discussed in some detail below (p. 41). The approach, systematised and refined over years, was finally at the root of the economic reform programme announced in 1987 by Secretary General Gorbachev. That particular reform programme only survived (as will be seen in Chapter 6) perhaps for a year. Some of its weaknesses had their origins in SOFE.

SOFE is more a general approach than a consistent body of theory. It has been open to interpretations in terms of different degrees of reformism. Furthermore, not all Soviet economic reformers have derived their proposals from the optimising logic of SOFE. Still, SOFE has been the only, at least moderately consistent, reform economics the USSR has produced, at least before 1989. Its failures, gaps and mistakes have reflected wider tendencies in Soviet reform thinking. In the same way its varying destinies have mirrored change in Soviet political attitudes towards reform.

SOFE is not the product of Nikolai Fedorenko. To understand that one has to appreciate the way in which the Soviet academic establishment functions. The Soviet Academy of Sciences, the main network of centres for basic research in the country, has long had a reputation for independence and even democracy. This has been based on the exceptional independence the academy enjoys within the Soviet state. Academicians are elected for life by their peers, and there have been celebrated cases when party pressure has failed to sway the academicians. But actually such scope for independent decisions only exists for the academicians themselves. Within an institute a strong leader has wide scope to harness the bulk of research to serve his own ambitions. This is just what Fedorenko did. After he had learned the basics of the optimal planning paradigm – and had seen that they made sense in terms of his earlier practical experience – he made SOFE his own. Books and articles actually written by researchers of his institute were published under Fedorenko's name. This was the custom of the country. The recollections of Aron Katsenelinboigen, one of the most important early Sofeists, published after his emigration to the USA, give a vivid picture of this mechanism.[32]

The optimal planners were never modest in their promises concerning the future effect of implementing their methods. Both Kantorovich and Novozhilov promised an upward shift of 30 to 50 per cent in total production while Fedorenko and two other academicians, writing in the government newspaper, *Izvestiya*, prophesied a doubling of growth rates as the result of applying cybernetics in the economy.[33] The same promise was repeated when TsEMI was launched. Such promises must have been effective in securing resources in the short run, and the researchers may have believed in them. But even the first practical applications ran into problems. Not only were the models to be used extremely crude, but they also rested on the fundamental assumption that efficiency was in the interests of enterprises. This, however, was not the case. To protect themselves from the often arbitrary plan figures imposed by the ministries and planners, enterprises had to have reserves of unused capacity. They also had to exaggerate their input requirements. Consequently, enterprises were not willing to submit the information needed for optimal plans. Those who were foolish enough to do so, saw their plan targets raised, supplies of resources cut and, consequently, income diminished. Striving for efficiency thus all too often brought huge economic losses to enterprises.

In this way opposition to efficiency enhancing measures seemed to be coming from the lower echelons of the economy. But such opposition, it was quickly emphasised, was caused by the way in which the enterprises were subordinated to ministries, planners and regional economic authorities. The hierarchical structure of the economy was not itself seen as a problem; it was taken as a self-evident feature of socialism. The basic problem was perceived in the fact that higher administrators engaged in a detailed and often unpredictable 'petty tutelage' over the enterprises. The latter were thus deprived of any degree of freedom in their activities and their institutional environment became unpredictable. This was widely diagnosed as the main problem in the existing economic model. Practical managers naturally agreed.

There seemed to be two possible ways out. The first one was to argue for a comprehensive economy-wide reform instead of piecemeal change by rationalisation. Such a reform would seek to make efficiency the most advantageous policy for enterprises. The second way out – proposed when the chances of reform seemed slim – was to argue for compulsory implementation of the new progressive methods. The first alternative will be discussed in chapter 3. The second, an attempt to beat some of the irrationalities of the command economy by means of commands, was first proposed by Leonid Kantorovich in 1967,[34] repeated by Abel Aganbegyan, the head of Novosibirsk's prestigious and generally reform-minded Institute of Industrial Economics in early 1968[35] and finally reproposed by Fedorenko ten years later.[36]

It took longer to understand that the high-level decision-makers of the economy, the planning bureaucracy, were often even less interested in reform than the enterprises. They were for many years implicitly or explicitly regarded as unselfish servants of the system with no power aspirations or interests of their own. All the 'petty tutelage' was simply seen as a consequence of a badly designed hierarchical division of labour, not as a natural way of exercising ownership rights in a situation where the planners and ministries were responsible for the performance of 'their' empires. Since the late sixties, however, the bureaucrats have often been accused of sabotaging the reform of 1965. During the seventies planners generally supported the mechanisation of plan calculations but fiercely opposed any reform that would lessen their concrete power over resource allocation. This was to lead to important conclusions when the reform strategy of perestroika came to be outlined.

The optimal planners wanted both a new model of the socialist economy and a new theory of it. Though the basic optimisation paradigm of Kantorovich was still seen as the necessary foundation for this approach, it was no longer sufficient. It was felt that it needed amendment in at least three directions.[37]

First, Kantorovich proceeded as if the Soviet Union had been a massive plywood trust, thus actually repeating the Kautsky–Lenin single factory image of the socialist economy. An attempt to describe the Soviet economy in a single model was, however, all too unwieldy for practical purposes. No computers could process the necessary amount of information in a reasonable time. TsEMI scholars like V. F. Pugachev and V. A. Volkonskii were soon following contemporary foreign research in showing how the single planning task could either be decomposed into manageable parts or be itself composed of smaller blocks. This work, together with similar research in Novosibirsk, outlined an important agenda for the coming years. On the one hand, it seemed to promise a practicable way of implementing formal, mathematical models into planning work. On the other hand, such models were used normatively, as an image of a rational organisa

tional structure. In the decomposition case the structure of the socialist economy would remind one of the divisional pattern of the
modern corporation, while the compositional structure came close to
a cluster of several enterprises, bound together by contracts or
markets. The compositional approach recalls the traditional top-down
structure of the Soviet economy while the decompositional approach
was open to a market oriented and decentralising interpretation.

Another drawback of Kantorovich's original model lay in its hand-
ling of final demand. The structure of production had been taken as
given, determined somehow by the planners. Was there a way of
rationalising the goal setting process itself? Soviet researchers came
forward with two solutions, neither of them original but differing in
their approaches to the philosophy of planning.

One group of scholars, Nemchinov among them, proposed a normative approach to consumption planning. In their view specialists are
able to determine a scientifically based structure and level of consumption. The 'true' needs of people, thus calculated, should be the basis of
consumption planning. This approach reflected a willingness to submit
consumer choice to centralised decision-making. The other approach,
first formulated in Soviet literature by Volkonskii, took consumer
preference as reflected in market choice as the point of departure for
planning. These scholars argued for a more individualistic approach
to planning. For them the information generated on the market
would be both the starting-point of plan formulation and the primary
criterion for judging the correctness of the planners' decisions.

The third direction in which Kantorovich's original model was
developed proved crucial for the uniqueness of SOFE as social
engineering. Following the spirit of the welfare economics of Jan
Tinbergen, the Dutch Nobel prize laureate in economic science, a
research team led by Aron Katsenelinboigen produced the first version of SOFE in the mid-sixties.

SOFE: The first stage

Tinbergen's basic idea is powerful in all its simplicity. He argues that
economics is able to outline the optimal organisation of the economy
in a way which transcends existing institutional patterns and inefficiencies.[38] Furthermore, as Tinbergen argued in his famous theory of
convergence, the various economic systems of the world are in fact on
the way towards such an optimum regime.

Katsenelinboigen's group professed no belief in convergence, but argued – as a spokesman of TsEMI put it – that 'from the point of view of mathematicians and all reasonable people, the most important qualitative characteristic of the socialist economy, differentiating it from the capitalist society, is the possibility of building in principle an optimal national economy'.[39]

What Tinbergen had seen as common to capitalism and socialism, the Sofeists wanted to see as a property of socialism only. Optimality, they argued, is something inherent in socialism. Such pronouncements should not merely be dismissed as make-believe confessions of faith forced upon scholars by the Soviet ideological constraints. The idea of socialism as a goal-directed society *is* fundamental to Marxism, and there is little reason to doubt that the early Sofeists were sincere in their professed Marxism. That was a handicap brought about by their education.

Katsenelinboigen's group adhered strictly to the idea of goal-directed socialism in their work of the late sixties.[40] They defended the idea of a single objective function of the socialist economy in terms of systems thinking. Socialism, they argued, happens to belong to the class of consciously guided systems, and in their view that necessarily implied the existence of an objective function. Furthermore, they added, only this idea would provide the necessary degree of consistency for SOFE.

In the first phase of SOFE the strategy of research was interpreted in a very straightforward way. The design of an optimally functioning socialist economy was to be derived from a minimal set of axioms, non-provable basic properties of the system. These axioms varied somewhat from one exposition of SOFE to another, but the fundamental treatise published in 1968 under Fedorenko's name lists four of them:

1 The economy is a complex system. It has a large number of elements with many linkages.
2 The economy has an inherent goal function and faces scarcity of resources.
3 The economy is a hierarchical system.
4 The economy functions in conditions of incomplete information.[41]

The first and the fourth axioms are common to different economic systems, while the other two are supposed to make up the difference between capitalism and socialism. The capitalist society is torn by class antagonism; it can have no common goal function. Socialism, on the other hand, is based on common ownership and therefore on a fundamental community of interests. The common goal necessarily exists.

Katsenelinboigen's group joined contemporary Western systems theoreticians in arguing that reality, 'the world', consists of a hierarchy of systems, each with its sub-systems and super-systems. Each super-system dictates the goal of its sub-system. Thus, the goal of the economy was given by the society as a whole, while the economy, for its part, dictated the goals of sub-systems like enterprises. This was clearly a conception strongly slanted towards totalitarianism. The early Sofeists approached society as if it only consisted of the hierarchy of state industry. Other, possibly independent ownership forms, or civil society as a whole, were forgotten. Over twenty years later Mikhail Gorbachev would emphasise that the idea of hierarchical socialist society is 'a copy of the authoritarian-bureaucratic system which we abandon, [it] is an expression of the antidemocratic ideology of Stalinism'.[42] But for the theorists of the sixties the existence of hierarchy was axiomatic.

Furthermore, the idea of hierarchy was interpreted to mean that the highest echelon of the economy, the planners and the leaders of the party/state, were the sole articulators of the needs of 'the society as a whole'. The lower echelons were supposed to have only their own, partial interests, while the highest echelon had no particular interests, only general ones. The local interests of the lower level had a short time-horizon, while the highest echelon also saw further into the future. The politicians and bureaucrats were thus identified as the noble guardians of the common good. Furthermore, with very few exceptions,[43] the Sofeists habitually tended to relegate the territorial division of the country to secondary status, if it was mentioned at all. This Moscow-centrism – not shared by Novosibirsk economists – is a serious weakness in a multi-national half-continent like the USSR.

Sociologically such views of the socialist hierarchical society were obviously extremely naive. Politically they were dangerously close to the totalitarian image of society. Janos Kornai, the Hungarian economist, concentrated his 1967 criticism of the work of Katsenelinboigen's group exactly on this point.[44] Not surprisingly, even in the USSR the Sofeists were sometimes accused of being super-centralisers who wanted all social decision-making to be of the top-down kind.

The Katsenelinboigen group was not the only theory forming

influence in early SOFE. Viktor Volkonskii's interpretation of the optimising approach was derived from general equilibrium theory. It emphasised horizontal linkages and consumer choice, not vertical subordination. Citing the optimality properties of competitive markets Volkonskii argued in a 1967 book that 'the greatest achievement of world economic science is the strict proof of the . . . possibility of setting up a system of optimal decentralised management founded upon commodity-money or *khozraschet*-relations'.[45]

Katsenelinboigen wanted the optimal plan to simulate the price generation process on markets, Volkonskii called for a market-like mechanism to generate prices. Volkonskii was not explicit as to whether this mechanism would simply be the market or something else – perhaps a bargaining process – but his concentration on motivation and coordination had a different flavour from that of Katsenelinboigen's group.

Volkonskii was not the only opponent of overly centralised interpretations of optimal planning. In 1965 A. M. Matlin had already renounced any interpretation of optimal planning as an attempt at creating a 'centralised machine' for planning and management.[46] Katsenelinboigen and Faerman emphasised in 1967 that for them SOFE is 'no Leviathan', not an all-powerful state machinery.[47] In more detail Katsenelinboigen's group answered the charge of supercentralism in a 1969 book.[48] The problem, they argued, was to strike the right balance between the existence of a global objective function on the one hand and the need for the articulation of specific interests in the economy on the other. People do have genuinely different preferences, and, furthermore, there is uncertainty about the environment of the economy. Take the example of horizontal and vertical linkages. The alleged fact that pure quantity guidance – planning, as Katsenelinboigen put it in 1969, or the command economy, as it would be called now – is theoretically feasible shows that a pure hierarchical economy without prices is feasible. In actual fact, however, prices and horizontal linkages are indispensable. Enterprises always have their specific local resources which they have to be able to utilise. The possibility of departing from the plan must also exist. The time, computing facilities and other resources available to planners are always limited and plans are only approximate. Even the best plans cannot foresee random change in the economy. Therefore, Katsenelinboigen and others concluded, the plan should be given only in aggregate and any detailed decision-making should be based upon horizontal contracts between enterprises and other economic units.

On a closer look this argument is actually less radical than it may first seem. Even in this formulation the hierarchical relations of planning are primary and everything else is secondary, in part only a practical complication. In reality a purely vertical quantity guidance had never existed and plans have always been to some degree aggregative. Katsenelinboigen's argument could well be interpreted as providing no more than the reasons why unofficial middlemen, *tolkachi*, and official horizontal contracts existed even in the heyday of Stalinism. As a foundation for reformism the arguments presented by Katsenelinboigen are therefore extremely weak. They amounted to no more than saying that the single factory image can never be implemented in a pure form. This is, of course, not a fundamental criticism of the image itself.

It seems therefore appropriate to conclude that the underlying single hierarchy approach, the single factory image of Kautsky and Lenin, was the basic defect of Stage 1 of SOFE, as developed by Katsenelinboigen's group. Another problem was no less prominent. As a Soviet economist was to put it later, the Sofeists approached economic reform as if it were a question of designing a new piece of machinery.[49] Reform was seen as a question of social engineering, of setting the goals and noting the constraints and of optimising the economy accordingly. Existing reality was indeed sometimes criticised for not adhering to rational mathematical models.

There was, however, no analysis of why reality existed as it did. In fact, there was no explicit analysis of reality at all. Nor was there any analysis as to why a desirable change might actually be possible. The reformability of Soviet socialism was taken for granted. Furthermore, there was no theoretical analysis of the process of transition from one model of the economy to another. There was no theory of economic policy and no discussion of the proper sequencing of reform measures. Nor could there have been. Most of the problems of economic and social policy that have been seen as crucial in East European reform experience do not, after all, even arise in the optimal planning framework. That framework really has no place for money as a liquid asset, credit, foreign trade or the conversion of military production. Questions of competition, ownership, the legal framework and entrepreneurship are all absent. This was the technocratic and romantic phase of Soviet economic reformism. The bitter disappointments of the late sixties and the seventies were still ahead, and the capacity to devise mathematical algorithms for optimal planning seemed to be the crucial constraint in reforming the economy.

The total disappearance of history, social and political relations in SOFE, Stage 1, is astonishing, especially as it comes from self-professed Marxists. No wonder that not all economists with reformist inclinations shared the narrow abstractness of early SOFE. As early as the early sixties Abel Aganbegyan concluded that Kantorovich's model was too narrowly techno-economic, neglected all dynamic and investment problems, and was therefore not an appropriate tool for analysing socialist reproduction.[50] By the late sixties V. V. Novozhilov, one of the cofounders of the optimal planning paradigm, who died in 1970, was emphasising the need for a historical approach and arguing for a transition from what he called 'techno-economic quantitative optimising' to a 'qualitative' reform of production relations.[51] Still, SOFE, Stage 1, was the only more or less consistent Soviet reform theory of the sixties.

There is probably no single explanation of why Katsenelinboigen's abstract approach came to dominate in early SOFE. Partly it must have been because it was there: an immensely ambitious framework, but sufficiently simple in its basic ideas to be able to offer concrete reform proposals. In addition, many of the proposals were closely in tune with what practical Soviet managers were arguing for on the basis of their everyday experience. The sheer scale of Katsenelinboigen's construct must have impressed those who wanted something totally different but still clearly socialist to take the place of the political economy of socialism. And, finally, both the foes and proponents of SOFE were conscious of its close similarities with the methodology and ethos of the Bogdanov–Bukharin theories of rational organisation. SOFE was embedded in a historical alternative to Stalinism.

The party-state encouraged studies in optimal planning because of the practical results they promised. Such encouragement is visible in the state prizes given to Kantorovich, Nemchinov (posthumously) and Novozhilov in 1965 as well as in a Central Committee decree of 1967 which named optimal planning methods as an important field of study. But the Sofeists wanted to go further, they wanted to topple the political economy of socialism, an established branch of Marxism–Leninism. In a justly famous 1966 discussion on optimal planning Nikolai Fedorenko distinguished between two kinds of political economy.[52] The existing one is 'descriptive', a commentary on goals, institutions and policies, while the future one should be 'constructive', a guide to forming goals, institutions and policies. In discussion, some Sofeists went even further. Albert Vainshtein, one of the few economists of the twenties who had survived through long years in camps, commented by saying that description is, after all, a useful activity, but part of political economy had been plainly destructive.

The main fault of political economy was seen in the fact that it had no way of distinguishing between false and true 'economic laws'.[53] The claimed superiority of the SOFE methodology was in its ability to derive laws from as general a description of the economy as possible. At the same time some laws of political economy could be shown to be illusory. The one arguing that the production of means of production should always grow faster than consumption goods was often presented as an example of that.

Even here, however, the Sofeists' opinions varied. Fedorenko's characterisation of SOFE as the new socio-economic theory of socialism varied in content. Sometimes SOFE was supposed to be the new political economy of socialism, sometimes just its core. Attitudes towards traditional doctrines like the labour theory of value as a price theory also varied. From an opportunistic point of view, that had its political advantages. The uncertainties of SOFE allowed the derivation of different sets of reform proposals, varying in their degree of radicalism, and thus suitable in the context of changing political environments. What SOFE lost in consistency, it seemed to gain in longevity.

Compared with abstract theorising on allocation mechanisms, empirical research continued to be relatively neglected. Several factors contributed to this. The meagre availability of information, the sad state of the Soviet computer industry and the character of university education in economics were among them. There were only two main exceptions to this picture. The first is input–output studies into the structure of the economy, pursued among others by Stanislav Shatalin, a fierce critic of political economy and a radical reformer who in 1990 became a member of Gorbachev's Presidential Council.[54] Second are closely related studies into growth, efficiency and technical progress.[55] Both fields had reformist implications. Input–output studies not only helped in drafting more consistent plans, but also by their very approach shifted attention from the goal of maximal forced growth to that of balanced development.

The growth studies both helped to explain the causes of past economic slowdown and forecast further slipping of growth rates. In the early seventies such forecasts were angrily rejected by the planners. This naturally did not prevent the slowdown from continuing. Another point is also worth noting. Already in 1967 A. I. Anchishkin and Yu. V. Yaremenko argued that the success of economic reform should not be judged by growth rates.[56] Any successful reform will bring about structural change which leads both to a better satisfaction of needs and a temporary slowing down of measured economic growth. The success of reform should therefore be judged upon the possibilities of economic choice it helps to bring about, Anchishkin and Yaremenko concluded. Obviously, if Soviet leaders had listened to such opinions in 1985, they would not have embarked upon both *perestroika* (restructuring) and *uskorenie* (growth acceleration). The path of *perestroika* would have been much easier.

The picture painted in this chapter of the Soviet reform economics of the sixties is a bleak one. Of the necessary ingredients for a potentially successful reform programme – a description of the present, a sketch of the desired future and a strategy of transition – they only seem to have had the second. Even this was seriously flawed. Chapter 3 describes in more detail the reform programme that was derived from the theoretical framework just explained and puts it in the context of Soviet reform discussions in the sixties as a whole.

3   The reformist programme

What is an economic reform?

The post-Stalin Soviet leadership was never totally satisfied with the performance of the economic system. Declining growth rates, pervasive imbalances and inefficiencies, an inability to innovate and to serve consumer needs – all these systemic defects have served as a continuous pressure for change. During the last thirty-five years political response to such pressure has varied. There have been times when the leadership has believed in the sufficiency of fine-tuning by economic policy measures: resources have been reallocated from one branch or region to another, prices have been adjusted and wage scales redrafted. The results of such policy measures have been modest, and the policy leadership has therefore repeatedly groped for more far-reaching change in the economic system.

Changes in the economic system proper, as distinct from policy measures, can be called economic reforms.[1] The reforms that the Soviet Union has gone through so far have been partial. They have affected only some or perhaps just one of the fundamental institutions of the economic system. In the seventies such reform activity came to be seen as a continuous process of 'perfecting' (*sovershenstvovanie*) the economic system. Such reforms have not reached the goals set for them, either because they have been badly designed and executed or because an economic system – somewhat like a living organism – has a tendency to reject alien parts and thus render all partial reforms necessarily inefficient. If the latter is the case only a comprehensive economic reform – one encompassing the whole economic system – has any chance of succeeding. This is, of course, the conclusion behind Gorbachev's *perestroika* reforms. Those reforms go even further by emphasising that the interconnections between economy, culture and polity make decisive progress in any one of them highly improbable without supportive change in the others. This, present-day Soviet analysts maintain, is the fundamental lesson to be learned from the abortive reforms in the Soviet Union and other centrally planned economies.

The conclusion is in many respects plausible, and it might be used as a measuring-rod for assessing earlier reform aspirations. Here, however, we adopt a different approach. To avoid forcing the search by Soviet economists for an appropriate reform strategy into a pre-determined scheme, we first let the Soviet economists talk for them-selves. Only in chapter 6 is a stylised framework offered into which we can locate the phases of Soviet reform debates. By doing this we finally arrive at a position where we can assess the dynamics of Soviet economic reform.

It took Soviet economists decades to understand the limited poten-tial of any partial reform. In the immediate post-Stalin years dis-satisfaction with the economic system focussed upon the inefficiencies and irrationalities of the way in which enterprises operated. Five aspects of the problem, in particular, were singled out for critical scrutiny.[2] The first one concerned so-called *success indi-cators*, the criteria upon which enterprise performance was assessed.

The traditional success indicator was gross output or *val* (*valovaya produktsiya*). While enterprises were also often given other perform-ance indicators like production costs or labour productivity, it was *val* that made or destroyed managers' careers. Any neglect of quality, costs or schedules could be expected to be forgiven, if the overall target of gross production was reached or better still surpassed. Gross output has the advantage of being easy to measure and monitor. Within the traditional Soviet national income accounting system, it is also consistent with growth maximisation. But, on the other hand, the defects of *val* are enormous. By including labour, materials and intermediate inputs its use as a performance indicator encourages waste and inefficiency. By emphasising current production, maximis-ing gross output discriminates against technological progress with its inherent uncertainties and discontinuities. The quality of goods pro-duced, or consumer satisfaction in general, is totally neglected or even consciously sacrificed.[3] To counter such tendencies the planners often took the seemingly easiest route of adding new success indi-cators. A peculiar success indicator cycle arose. In a reform their number would be cut to increase enterprise autonomy. Soon, however, their number would start to increase, until the time of the next reform arrived. As the indicators used were all too often con-tradictory, the reign of *val* continued – as indeed it has in many ways continued until now. The economists' search for a 'philosopher's stone', a single success indicator with all the possible advantages and no drawbacks, continued until well into the late eighties, until it was generally realised that the primary problem lies not in the indicator to be used, but in the basic idea of having such hierarchical superiors as branch ministries to assess enterprise performance.

The second problem, related to the first, is the low and declining *efficiency of investment*. The Soviet growth spurt in the thirties was spurred on by a doubling of the share of investment in national income. The lion's share of investment went into raw materials extraction and heavy industry. By the late fifties this motor of Soviet growth was producing diminishing returns. This worrisome trend had many causes. Increasing extraction costs and low technical progress were among them, but so were also a general tendency to over-invest and the lack of any rational investment criteria. Such problems were much discussed by the economists.

The third problem, also closely connected with the first, was that of *incentives*. Even if a proper way of measuring enterprise performance had been found, the crucial question of motivation would have remained. How does one ensure that enterprises operate so as really to maximise the success indicator? It had been realised in the early thirties that mere commands, exhortation or the career prospects of enterprise managers were not enough, and the answer had been proposed in the form of material incentives.[4] In its crudest form the use of material incentives just implied piece-work for workers and premia for overfulfilment for managers. With a growing understanding of the defects of *val* this no longer seemed the universal solution. Whatever the performance indicators selected, however, the principle of material incentives dictated that the incomes and general material well-being of the enterprise and its employees had to be connected in a transparent and effective way with the success indicator(s). There was a lively discussion on these issues in the late fifties.

Fourthly, there was the problem of *prices*. Though the importance of rational prices for monitoring, measuring and motivation of enterprise operation had been well understood by economists as early as the thirties, price policy had been (as seen in chapter 1) an area explicitly closed to scholarly discussion. Such a situation could not last, given that Soviet prices were in many cases completely irrational, failing to reflect either production costs or utilities. In principle, they had been formed on the basis of branch-average production costs, adding a profit mark-up. In practice, production costs were only very incompletely taken into account, profit mark-ups varied wildly, and the habit of freezing prices for long periods – while in some ways convenient for planning – meant that any relationship that prices might have had with supply and demand conditions was more or less accidental.

Finally, there was the position of the *ministries*. Enterprises had, due to their large numbers, never been directly subordinated to the planning agencies. Industrial branch ministries were used as an intermediary echelon of the economic hierarchy, and in fact they had become the most powerful economic institutions. They – sometimes with further intermediaries – managed the enterprises and defended their own interests against the planners. In attempting to guard themselves against supply interruptions and other uncertainties created by the economic system the ministries had attempted to achieve autarky by themselves producing as many production inputs as possible. This neglect of specialisation through faulty coordination had led to unduly high production costs, irrational haulage of goods and regional imbalances.

Such criticisms of the economy were widely shared. Reform proposals have always been much more varied. There are many reasons for this. First of all, as seen above, economists simply have not had a well-developed theory of the economy. Political economy could only offer slogans of extremely dubious value. Mathematical economists have had the optimising logic as a unifying framework, but they have been a small minority whose theories have often met with incomprehension or outright hostility. Furthermore, optimal planning theory was founded on extreme simplifications. There was good reason to doubt the applicability of its conclusions.

In addition, most Soviet economists have not been accustomed to thinking in terms of well-defined models. Their education has emphasised verbal reasoning with little stress on consistency and even less explicit linkage with reality. Most relevant economic information either did not exist or was of extremely poor quality. There has been no tradition of statistical or econometric inference. On the contrary, such exercises were strongly discouraged during the Stalinist decades.

Finally, ideological taboos and doctrinal constraints were numerous. Nobody could, until the late eighties, openly argue for the creation of markets for factors of production, allowing private entrepreneurship or – to present the other side of the coin – argue for abolishing the supreme economic power of the ruling party. Any proposals for reform had to be capable of presenting as further developments of socialism. This tradition still leads to the somewhat ridiculous situation whereby prominent Soviet scholars present Sweden, Austria or even Switzerland as the most socialist countries in the world.

Perhaps the best way of characterising Soviet economics as a whole is to call it 'abstract quasi-empiricism'. Abstract, because the discussion of alleged socialist economic laws has always been an important part of it. Quasi-empiricist, because such laws have been characterised with the help of scattered examples and statistical figures generally without any discussion of their representativeness. Different parts of the economic discourse have emphasised one or another facet of the discussion. Political economy has been scholastic while applied economic disciplines have been quasi-empirical or apparently pragmatist, as the term was used in chapter 1.

Khrushchev's reform

Political considerations had a key influence on the kind of economic reform that Khrushchev embarked upon in 1957. He decided to tackle the 'departmentalism' of the ministries and other central economic organs, where much of the political opposition to his policies resided. Khrushchev's reform consolidated the position of his own power base, regional party and government organisations, by subordinating most economic activity to newly created regional economic councils, *sovnarkhozy*.

Though the problem of departmentalism was real, Khrushchev's reform was economically ill-advised. Creating *sovnarkhozy* left most of the Soviet Union's economic problems unaddressed, and where it tried to act it probably created more confusion than it solved problems. To put it simply, in addition to creating administrative uncertainty, *sovnarkhozy* substituted localism for departmentalism. Branch autarky gave way to attempts at regional self-sufficiency. Coordination within branches suffered.

It was not surprising, then, that the reform failed to prevent growth rates for national income and labour productivity from dropping quite dramatically by the mid-sixties. Furthermore, it antagonised the powerful central economic bureaucracies. Not unexpectedly, one of the first measures of Khrushchev's successors after 1964 was to recentralise economic management by reinstituting the subordination of enterprises to Moscow-based branch ministries. This was probably economically reasonable, but it also contained an important political message to the central economic institutions. The Brezhnev

leadership gave them back the concrete power over resource allocation that Khrushchev had tried to take away. At the same time the
new regime promised the administrators the degree of job security
that later contributed to making the Brezhnev period the only
genuinely conservative one in Soviet history.

The failure of the *sovnarkhozy* contributed to a serious weakness in
Soviet economic research, especially in Moscow-based research.
Though the necessity of complementing management by branches or
economic complexes with regional management was admitted,
sometimes even emphasised, the possibility of primarily regional
administration seemed for a long time to be a lost cause. Only the
pressure of regional political movements in the late eighties changed
the situation, and economists accustomed to thinking in terms of
Moscow-centred hierarchies were badly prepared for the new
situation.

The Liberman controversy

The later conservatism of the Brezhnev period was not yet evident
during the first years of the new leadership. In fact the regime
seemed to court reform. It declared that the time of Khrushchevian
'voluntarism' was over and promised a new scientific approach to
planning and managing society. Policy inputs by scholars were
encouraged. And, of course, the fact that Khrushchev's *sovnarkhoz*-
reform had failed to address most of the problems identified earlier
had not gone unnoticed by economists. Khrushchev had indirectly
contributed to the increasing dissatisfaction with the existing economic model by having the party adopt a new programme. It set
extremely ambitious economic goals, crowned by the call for the
attainment of material abundance – 'communism' – by the eighties.
Even the economist who wrote this part of the programme understood a few years later that the goal was utopian.[5] Not only had the
goal been founded on misleading statistics, but the existing economic
system was unable to reach the implied levels of productivity. In fact,
as early as 1962 the economic situation had deteriorated sufficiently
for a public discussion of economic reform to be allowed again.[6] This
controversy was heralded by the publication in *Pravda* on 9 September 1962, of a call for a new enterprise incentive system by Evsei
Liberman, an economics professor from Kharkov.[7]

Liberman's article was at the time widely celebrated. In retrospect
its limitations are plain. Liberman did not aim at changing the econ-

omic system fundamentally; he was primarily concerned with the need to rationalise the plan implementation process so that enterprises would seek to use their full productive capacities, improve the quality of goods produced and restrain their demand for additional inputs. Enterprises would under Liberman's scheme still receive mandatory plans from above as before, they would just have more autonomy in implementing them. At the same time central management, now freed from 'petty tutelage' over enterprises, would have more time for its main task, strategic planning. Liberman, like many reformers after him, seemed to be under the illusion that planners really would like to exchange their concrete power over resource allocation for the job of outlining long-term development plans. Publicly at least, the Soviet economists of the sixties never addressed the possibility that the planners might like the old system just because of the power it gave them. Perhaps the economists really believed in the assumed selflessness of the planners.

Liberman's main originality lay in proposing that in place of a multiplicity of performance criteria there would be only a single one, profitability defined as the ratio of profits to working capital. Its planned and actual level would determine the enterprise incentive fund and thus directly influence managerial and worker incomes. There would, however, be a side condition. No bonuses were to be paid if the plan regarding output levels, product mix and delivery schedules went unfulfilled.[8] These would be the plan targets received by the enterprise from above. In other respects it was to work out its plan by itself.

The idea of profitability as a socialist decision-making criterion attracted at the time much Western curiosity. In numerous comments it was seen as an example of convergence of economic systems. One should, however, note the limited nature of the role of profits in Liberman's scheme. In particular, profitability was not proposed as the criterion for resource allocation. Profits were to act as an incentive for implementing a plan determined by planners using unspecified criteria of their own. It is furthermore extremely doubtful whether profitability might have had even the limited role Liberman was advocating. Existing prices would have given enterprises totally misleading signals, guiding them in directions often in conflict with the motto Liberman gave to his proposals: 'What is advantageous for society must be profitable for each enterprise.' Liberman admitted the need for a price reform, but was extremely vague about it. Price fixing, however, would remain the prerogative of the central planners. Liberman's proposals were definitely not about market socialism.

The vagueness of Liberman's programme has often been pointed out. In some cases the contradictions in his proposals reflect deep problems of Soviet reality rather than just muddled thinking. The issue of price reform is a case in point. On the one hand, Liberman believed in this effectiveness of prices as a demand constraining device. To take an important example, fixed capital had in the Soviet Union been allocated to the enterprises free of any charge. This was widely believed to have encouraged its inefficient use. Liberman strongly advocated the establishment of rental charges for fixed capital as an incentive to economising. But, on the other hand, Liberman doubted the centrality of the whole pricing issue, arguing that the buyer 'has no difficulty including any price in his investment estimate or in his planned costs, no matter how high it may be raised by the supplier'.[9]

This was an important argument. It amounted to pointing out what the Hungarian economist Janos Kornai was much later to call the soft budget constraint.[10] According to this approach the chronic deficits of materials, intermediate goods and investments in the centrally planned economy are not due to their low prices. Such deficits rather have their roots in the fact that the state has a paternalistic attitude towards 'its' enterprises. On the one hand, it subordinates them to the planners' discretion, on the other, it covers almost any expenditure and losses incurred by the enterprises. Finance, under such conditions, is not a binding constraint for enterprises, whereas the physical availability of resources is. And, indeed, as Liberman said, if enterprise budget constraints are soft, enterprises really can include any prices in their costs, the resultant losses are covered by banks or the state budget, and, as Liberman argued, 'prices are not very important to the economy'. Liberman's argument was wholly in the spirit of Kornai's theory.

In Liberman's case, however, this was an incidental insight which did not inform the rest of his reform proposals. He did not argue for a hardening of the budget constraints by introducing real capital markets, competition, the possibility of bankruptcy or the dismantling of the hierarchy of state ownership. Instead, he inconsistently noted one important implication of soft budget constraints while continuing to advocate reform measures which actually assume the sensitivity of enterprises to prices, that is, which assume the existence of hard budget constraints. Such inconsistency is naturally just what one would expect from the abstract quasi-empiricism characterised above. But there was also a political constraint involved. In the sixties proposals for allowing bankruptcies or emphasising the necessity of competition were extremely rare. By the early seventies they would be condemned as serious political mistakes.

The limitations of Liberman's proposals were not peculiar to him but were widely shared at the time. Nobody advocated a change in the fundamental status of state ownership or central planning. Enterprises were still to remain a subordinate link in the hierarchy of economic management, subject to commands from above. Political, not economic criteria, would still prevail in plan formulation. Prices were still to be centrally set, and state ownership would remain overwhelmingly predominant.

The publication of Liberman's article opened a wide-ranging and relatively well-known debate on economic reform both in the USSR and in the centrally managed states of Eastern Europe. Here we concentrate on the Soviet discussion. Most of its participants had no doubt about the necessity of change in at least some of the characteristics of the economic system. Mere policy changes would not suffice. Some debaters, it is true, warned against any change, arguing that even a partially decentralising reform of the kind advocated by Liberman would in fact weaken centralised control over the economy, bring about worsening disequilibria, undesirable structural change and the danger of inflation and unemployment. The status quo, even if not perfect, they were saying, was decidedly better than a future with such dangers.

Such conservative feelings represented, however, a minority of published opinion. But while the diagnosis on the defects of the traditional economic system was widely shared, reform proposals varied. There was a minority opinion which saw the application of modern computing technologies and related mathematical methods as an opportunity for increasing the degree of centralised decision-making in the economy. Most participants in the public debate, however, shared the goals of increasing enterprise autonomy in plan execution and of rationalising the management of the state hierarchy of industry in general. Within this general framework opinions differed concerning technical questions such as the performance indicators and formulas of centralised price setting to be adopted. The proposals were often partial, contradictory and vague.[11]

The Kantorovich–Novozhilov framework

The early Soviet reform proposals best founded on an explicit economic framework were those of the optimal planners. Though the approaches of Kantorovich, Novozhilov and Nemchinov had much in common, it is useful to distinguish between the Kantorovich–Novozhilov approach on one hand and the proposals of Nemchinov on the other.

The backgrounds of Kantorovich and Novozhilov had little in common. The former was a mathematics professor who came to economics via practical engineering economics. While Kantorovich was probably ignorant of Western economics, Novozhilov had a solid pre-revolutionary economic education. This did not prevent him from professing orthodox Marxism in his writings. Still, both the mathematician and the economist shared the common efficiency approach to planning. As early as the forties Novozhilov was the first economist to use Kantorovich's method of linear programming for outlining methods of rationalising planning. In particular, he emphasised the centrality of the interest rate on capital and scarcity rents of physical resources in optimal allocation. This amounted to restating what Barone had written about the need for prices almost four decades earlier. Novozhilov also 'reinvented' opportunity cost, the central concept in any choice under scarcity which had been totally neglected in Soviet Marxism. Together with a strong emphasis on the necessity of market feedback for rational planning, that was perhaps the most lasting message of Novozhilov to his Soviet colleagues.

Kantorovich always remained fascinated with the more technical issues of optimal planning. His mode of thinking was more that of a planning technocrat than a reformist. Novozhilov's approach, on the other hand, was more an economic interpretation of optimal programming than a coherent theory in a strict sense. In particular, he went to great lengths to show that shadow prices could well be interpreted in a way that was consistent with the Marxian theory of value. But these were theoretical controversies with only indirect implications for economic reform. Of more immediate interest is the fact that the optimal planning paradigm could be and was interpreted in diametrically opposite ways. The first interpretation was to understand mathematical planning techniques and shadow prices as modern means of achieving centralism. Originally, both Novozhilov and Kantorovich seemed to incline towards this position.

Novozhilov, in particular, distinguished between two kinds of centralism. The first one is direct centralism, where an attempt is made to implement the goals set by the centre using administrative commands. This is the traditional method of central planning. The other one, much preferred by Novozhilov, is indirect centralism, where the optimal plan is implemented by using shadow prices derived from the plan. Kantorovich had shown how in an optimal plan any scarce resource or good receives a valuation or shadow price which shows its marginal contribution to attaining the given objective function. Furthermore, profit-maximising enterprises, when faced with these prices, will automatically, without any commands from the centre, select such production plans as together maximise the objective function. Shadow prices thus induce them to fulfil a plan which is optimal relative to the centre's preferences.

In fact, Novozhilov argued, such use of commodity–money relations – to use the standard Soviet expression – will lead to increased centralism in the sense that enterprises will reach the centre's goals better this way than under traditional command.[12] Price guidance, Novozhilov argued (but did not prove), is in this sense a more effective form of centralism than guidance by obligatory plan targets.

Until the early sixties Novozhilov seems to have believed that with modern computers and advanced mathematical methods the centre would be able to derive optimal prices for all resources and thus guide all economic activities in an indirect way.[13] It soon came to be realised, however, that no optimal plan could possibly determine the production, distribution and use of all the millions of goods in the economy. Even the biggest computers were unable to handle the necessary amounts of information, which in any case were not available. Therefore, only the main outlines of production and the most important, possibly aggregated, prices could be derived from a centralised plan. This fact would contribute to decentralisation. The range of options open to the enterprises was to increase in two respects. First of all, enterprises were to be left free to adjust their behaviour to prices given to them by the planners. They were not to be told exactly what to do; they were to find out for themselves what the planners wanted them to do. This would, Novozhilov and others argued, create new possibilities for creativity and initiative and thus necessarily enhance efficiency. On the other hand, enterprise independence was to increase because managers were only to receive plans from above in an aggregated form. All the details were to be worked out by the enterprises themselves.

On one hand, therefore, the goals set by the centre would in the reformed economy be reached better than was ever possible by traditional command methods. The planners, as we have emphasised above, liked the traditional system because it seemed to give them total control over economic processes. In reality this was an illusion. Economic processes deviated greatly from any plan: in attempting to plan everything, traditional centralism loses control of the economy. Rationalising planning in the direction of indirect centralisation would diminish the deviations between plans and reality, Novozhilov and others argued. In this sense reforms were to further centralism. On the other hand, enterprises were to have increased independence in fulfilling and carrying out the goals set in plans. In this sense the reform was to enhance decentralisation. Altogether, it was claimed, the economic reform would be at the same time both centralising and decentralising.

Kantorovich emphasised that though his method was formally reminiscent of capitalist market competition, in reality 'one differs radically from the other'. There would be no markets in his scheme, just the use of shadow prices derived by computers to simulate markets.[14] Computers were even claimed to have advantages over markets. They would process information faster and avoid the fluctuations typical of markets searching for equilibrium.

Such claims are bold but unfounded. At least four counter-arguments seem warranted. First of all, there is the problem of initial information for calculations. As already mentioned, enterprises have good reasons for exaggerating their resource needs and understating output capacities. Furthermore, not all relevant information can be formalised into data for transmission. Second, especially given the state of Soviet computers and communications as well as the inevitable abstractions made in plan models, there are limits to the amount of information that can be processed. Third, the models used in calculations do not only make unavoidable abstractions. They also reflect the modellers' knowledge and blind spots. Not all the ensuing limitations are technical. In the Soviet case, in particular, the models proposed only tried to depict the officially sanctioned routines of planning and management, not the multitude of unofficial and outright illegal actions that enterprises daily engage in. Fourth and most importantly, the computer solution only discusses the use of existing information. There is no reason why the system proposed would create optimal conditions for the creation of new information.

All in all, the computer solution was misleading because it was limited to simulating the calculating properties of markets. In fact markets are not only a way of simulating a huge computer, they are primarily an institutional framework for human action. Computers do not provide such a framework. It can also be argued – though the issue is controversial – that neither do they usually bring a new institutional setup with them, though this is what many computer enthusiasts and reformers wanted. They have, in the Soviet Union and elsewhere, usually been grafted onto existing institutions and routines. Change in institutions and behaviour may follow as people perceive their new possibilities, but that does not necessarily happen. The opposite was the case with the hugely ambitious computerisation programme for the Soviet economy in the seventies.[15] In the end computers were being used as big, expensive and not always very convenient calculating machines. Not only did the existing economic model make rational use of computers impossible; the machines themselves were used to lengthen the life of that model. In this sense the computerisation programme finally proved not so much futile as detrimental.[16]

Some of the objections to Kantorovich's evident inclination for all-encompassing optimal planning were already voiced by Novozhilov. He argued against an excessive concentration upon the formal aspects of optimal planning. The main lesson of the planning models, Novozhilov claimed, is the insight they give to the development of the institutions and routines of the planned economy. His own emphasis was on the need for market feedback.[17] For more detailed reform proposals Novozhilov usually referred to the last writings of academician Vasili Nemchinov.

Novozhilov died in 1970. His attitude to economic reform was probably best summarized by Nikolai Petrakov in a 1966 pamphlet. Petrakov's two points catch well the spirit of indirect centralisation (or economic management methods, the term which soon became popular). First of all, 'behind any methods of economic management stands the state, which by its administrative action articulates the economic demands of the society as a whole. Without this, economic management would dissolve into anarchy. The whole question lies in what is being "administered", in which form state (societal) tasks are given to enterprises.' Etatism is thus absolute; economic reform is a question of its forms. And second:

The essence of economic methods of guidance comes down to setting enterprises in such conditions that they, guided by concrete economic interests, [and] economic criteria, would at the same time act according to the interests of the whole national economy. . . . The basic task of the centralised planning apparatus will be in giving enterprises economic parameters such as capital charge, interest rate, contract violation fines, prices and so on. Guided by these parameters, enterprises will take independent economic decisions. This path means a higher level of efficiency of planned socialist production, because it brings about a maximal enlargening of the economic independence of enterprises as well as of the initiative of all toilers in uncovering the internal reserves for developing production.[18]

This was the indirect centralisation philosophy of reform. For radical proposals on a more practical level we have to look at the last writings of academician Vasili Nemchinov.

Nemchinov's Khozraschet economy

If Liberman's proposals were well within the framework of partial reform, academician Vasili Nemchinov came closest among Soviet economists of the sixties to outlining a programme of comprehensive radical reform. This was done in a series of articles from 1962 until his death in 1964. His last article, published in *Kommunist*, the Party journal, in 1964, is of special interest: almost twenty-five years later Secretary General Gorbachev in a crucial speech on economic reform singled it out as the theoretical inspiration for the economic reforms of *perestroika*.[19] And indeed, not only is Nemchinov's article the most notable Soviet reform contribution of the sixties, but it also outlines an approach which is easily recognisable in Gorbachev's reform efforts as outlined in 1987.

We should perhaps start by noting what Nemchinov did *not* propose. His reform blueprint should be seen in the context of the Khrushchevian ideological framework of the early sixties. The 1961 Party Programme decreed that transition from socialism to communism was imminent. Among other things that was interpreted to mean an ongoing homogenisation of ownership forms, a process whereby state ownership was to be made not only predominant but also universal. Publicly at least, Nemchinov subscribed to these political trends. Though his original expertise was in agricultural economics, even he, the most radical of Soviet reform economists, wrote as if the whole national economy consisted of and should consist of a single hierarchy of state ownership. In this respect the *perestroika* reforms, with their attempts at breaking the state monopoly of ownership, are on a different level of radicalism from anything Nemchinov or other Soviet economists of the sixties proposed.

Further, Nemchinov – like other reformers – regarded reforms as a way of strengthening, not diminishing the role of planning in the economy. On the road to communism, he argued, planning comes to encompass more and more aspects and parts of society. Old methods of planning are no longer able to cope with the increasingly demand- ing task.[20] Developing modern mathematical and computing methods of centralised planning, therefore, in no way contradicts the necessity of changing the interrelations between planners and the enterprises. They are two different but interrelated tasks. The econo- mists, Nemchinov argued, can offer their services as social engineers for both purposes. Both cases were instances of a more general task, that of putting planning and management on a modern scientific basis.

Nemchinov's attitude to markets was the other side of this coin. 'Free markets and market competition contradict', he wrote, 'the planned and balanced development of society.'[21] Real planning had to be mandatory for the producers. This did not imply that it had to suppress all monetary categories in the economy. On the contrary, parameters like planned prices or profit-sharing rules should be seen as another effective tool of central planning. Without such tools and scientific methods planning may well lead to losses as large as those occasioned by the 'anarchy' of markets, Nemchinov emphasised. An efficient economy had to find ways of avoiding both the anarchy of planning and that of markets: this was Nemchinov's central message.

And finally, Nemchinov, while concentrating upon the relation- ship between planners and enterprises, neither dwelt upon the inter- nal structure of enterprises nor the structure and status of hierarchically higher institutions. Questions of self-management or of the political structure of the society were thus outside his focus. It has often been emphasised that this was also a crucial weakness of the Kosygin reforms of 1965. They tried to change the functioning of enterprises while leaving the ministerial and planning bureaucracies with their previous tasks, responsibilities and, inevitably, also powers.

Novozhilov was one of the first economists to understand the prob- lem, to connect *perestroika* and *demokratizatsiya* – to use the later terminology. He emphasised, as seen above, that economic progress depended upon the 'creativity of the popular masses'. Its activisation, Novozhilov argued, presupposed the democratisation of manage- ment and the transformation of 'organs of planning and accounting into organs of self-rule'.[22] Exactly why this was so and how such a transformation might take place, even Novozhilov did not go into.

Neither could he have, given the limitations set by Soviet censorship. This probably also goes a long way towards explaining why the regional dimension of society was so little discussed in the sixties.

Thus Nemchinov did not propose a reform of the ownership structure, a transition to a market economy or a democratisation of society. What *did* he propose? He outlined quite thoroughgoing changes in the whole system of economic management of the economy. The basic proposals are parts of what he called a *khozraschetnaya sistema planirovaniya*, literally, a 'cost-accounting system of planning'. *Khozraschet* or cost-accounting, as it is usually translated, is one of the numerous Sovietese terms which are essentially untranslatable and have an extremely poorly defined content. At a minimum it means, quite literally, an accounting of costs and revenues. Often, when speaking of 'full *khozraschet*', the emphasis is on accounting of all relevant costs, sometimes including those like externalities not usually included in book-keeping. Furthermore, *khozraschet* usually also implies an attempt to cover costs with revenues, often even running a surplus or maximising profits. Finally, sometimes *khozraschet* implies that any units on it should have some real independence in pursuing their goals – whatever they may be. Such a term of many meanings is even more inscrutable when applied to regions instead of enterprises. No wonder, then, that arguments about proper *khozraschet* – not about that which exists but about that which should exist – are often among the murkiest in Soviet economics.

In Nemchinov's case the proper translation for *khozraschetnaya sistema planirovaniya* might be 'central planning with limited independence for enterprises', because that is what Nemchinov's system was all about. Such independence was to be of four kinds. First of all, Nemchinov, like Liberman, wanted the number of obligatory plan-indicators given to enterprises to be drastically diminished. Within the limits set by such indicators enterprises would be free to organise their activities as best they could. The enterprises' efficient operation was to be furthered by means of various normatives – another Soviet term for the parameters of indirect centralisation – fixed for a period of ten to fifteen years.

The stability of normatives is a crucial part of Nemchinov's proposals. Actually, for Nemchinov's goals to be realised, normatives have to be both fixed for a long period and uniform for the whole economy, a particular branch or at least a group of enterprises. Stable and uniform normatives would mean that regional authorities, ministries and planners had less scope for meddling in the enterprise's affairs. In particular, if the enterprise knew – to take a typical normative as an example – its rule for sharing profits with the state budget for a long period, the maximisation of its profits would not be inhibited by a fear of confiscatory taxation once any profits were shown. On the other hand, if normatives have been tailored separately for each enterprise and can be changed at will, management by normatives collapses totally into traditional commandeering. In the example just given, no enterprise would be interested in profit maximisation as any profits shown could be immediately confiscated. There would be neither economising nor increased autonomy.

The idea of stable normatives is an important example of Nemchinov's emphasis on the necessity of a legal regulation of hierarchical relations. Traditionally, any decisions by a hierarchical superior had been binding on the subordinate unit with the force of a law. Now enterprises were to be legally protected against any administrative arbitrariness. Nemchinov did not, however, explain how this was to be united with a continuing predominance of state ownership. A cynical view of the much lamented arbitrary decision-making by superiors would, after all, call it an exercise of property rights by the state.

The idea of stable normatives, crucial in Nemchinov's proposed *khozraschet* economy, has another weakness, too. They were to be fixed for a long period of time, in Nemchinov's proposal for even ten to fifteen years. But what kind of information is to be used in forecasting, when the central tools of state policy are fixed for such a long period? No government in the world has been willing to tie its hand on, for instance, taxation in this way. From the policy point of view, therefore, Nemchinov's *khozraschet* economy would be incredibly inflexible. There seems to be no natural way between the Scylla of petty tutelage and the Charybdis of no policy reaction, as long as the hierarchical subordination of state enterprises is preserved.

The idea of stable normatives also faces a third problem. The enterprises have in practice information which the planners do not have. This is one, though not the only, asset they use when bargaining over plan targets and resource supplies with their ministry and the planners. The substitution of most plan targets by normatives would not change the actual situation. A bargaining over normatives would ensue, and another reason why normatives would be neither stable nor uniform is added to the list.

And, finally, as long as enterprises are state property planners would be subject to political pressure to protect existing jobs and incomes. In an environment where economic results depend largely upon factors beyond enterprise competence, managers and workers will demand specially tailored changes in taxes, prices and other normatives whenever economic adversity threatens. Planners have only very limited possibilities for distinguishing to what degree adversity has been inflicted by the enterprise itself. Anyway, as long as the political goals of full employment, relative economic security and restricted open inequality reign in the society, the planners have to rely upon such tailoring of normatives. Stable and uniform normatives thus remain a chimera. This was confirmed by actual developments in Hungary in the seventies and in the USSR after 1987. Planning by normatives, the Nemchinovian basis of Gorbachev's economic reforms as announced in 1987, was generally judged a failure after just a year or two.

The second characteristic of the *khozraschet* economy was 'plan-orders'. Enterprises, having received the few remaining obligatory plan targets and normatives, would inform the planners about their projected production possibilities and resource needs for the next plan period. Using this information planners would draw up a plan of the economy. This plan would be disaggregated into so-called plan orders, which would be presented to the enterprises in a way similar to putting up any orders. The enterprises would then make competing proposals for these plan orders, thus taking up responsibility of fulfilling the plan. Such orders were to differ from traditional plan commands in that there was to be voluntary acceptance and they were to be advantageous for both sides. For the enterprise, they were to be profitable; for the planners, they were to give the most efficient way of implementing the central plan.

In Nemchinov's *khozraschet* economy, plan orders were to be the prime method of uniting the interests of enterprises with those of society as a whole. Once concluded, contracts for plan orders would be legally binding for both sides. Mistakes in plans, being the responsibility of planners, would not invalidate existing contracts. Thus enterprises were not to be punished for the mistakes made by planners.

Third, enterprises, having concluded their contracts on plan orders, were also to conclude contracts with one another concerning material deliveries, construction, transport and also all the details of product quality and schedules left unspecified in plan orders. This was to be the way of disaggregating the plan. Enterprises were to receive all their means of production through wholesale trade, paying a price, not by centralised distribution and free, as traditionally under Soviet socialism. The transition to wholesale trade in the means of production, Nemchinov argued, would eliminate prevailing shortages.

Fourth and lastly, enterprises were to be free to sell any production over and above plan orders. They were also to set the price for any non-serial products. Most prices, though, would be set by the authorities. Even the prices of non-serial production should be firmly based on official price formulae. There would thus be no real market prices. Still, this is probably the first proposal for a dual-track planning system. Part of production would be strictly centrally determined by plan orders, but there would also be another part, decided upon by the enterprise itself. A variant of the dual-track system has been in use in the USSR since 1987.

Contracts would not imply markets, Nemchinov emphasised. There should be no question of creating spontaneity within the planning system.[23] Spontaneity was an ugly word even for the foremost Soviet economic reformer. Nemchinov is not totally explicit about the differences between markets and the proposed system of contracts. One difference is clear: contracts should always be closely regulated and monitored. Prices, in particular, would be under strict control. On other relevant questions Nemchinov is less explicit. He does not say whether the enterprises would have the right to decline plan orders, or whether a given share of production should always be tied to them. Neither does he address the question of entry and exit to markets. Such issues, however, are crucial for the real degree of independence that the enterprises might have.

Finally we may note that Nemchinov shared the reformers' general *naïveté* towards the planners. Thus, the statistical authorities and planners – aided by up-to-date computers and mathematical methods – were to collect as much descriptive information on the economy as possible. Nemchinov clearly assumed that such information would not be used for the petty tutelage of the enterprises. In his view the planners should, could and would make the distinction between descriptive and planning information a water-tight one. They would be given more tools of power, but they were not supposed to use them.

SOFE on reform

Kantorovich, Nemchinov and Novozhilov were the founders of the optimal planning school. By the mid-sixties the main work of developing the theory and its reform implications was concentrated in the Central Economic–Mathematical Institute (TsEMI) of the Academy of Sciences in Moscow. Chapter 2 outlined the theoretical development of optimal planning theory into SOFE, the System of Optimally Functioning Socialist Economy, as the house theory of TsEMI came to be called. It is now time to look at the main reform recommendations it produced in the mid-sixties.[24]

The proposals of SOFE can be conveniently classified under seven headings. (1) The first is *rolling planning*. Plans with different time-horizons should be drawn up for the economy, and they should be tied together into rolling planning. Looking forward from the present, consecutive plans would become less and less detailed, more and more forecast-like. As time progressed, plans for the future would be both revised in the light of experience and made more detailed and binding, as their horizons drew closer.

This proposal, earlier advocated by Nemchinov, was supposed to break with the traditional discreteness of planning: a five-year plan is adopted every five years and detailed to the same degree for each of its years. Under rolling planning, a plan for the next five years would be redrafted every year, and only the next one or two years would be planned in any detail. The same, in principle, would be true for yearly plans. They would be revised on a rolling basis and only the most immediate months or quarter would be planned in every detail.

Under the old system enterprises had often received their plans well into the relevant planning period. This, together with the use of an inelastic planning horizon, condemned them to *shturmovshchina*, 'storming', attempts at fulfilling output plans by the deadline at any cost and neglecting all considerations of quality. Rolling planning would make the economy more cost-effective and quality-conscious, SOFE argued.

(2) *Scientific planning*. Plans should no longer be based upon arbitrary rules, intuition and rules of thumb but on scientific calculations. All calculation, whether concerning goals to be set, resources available or technologies used, should be based on objective information competently processed. The arbitrariness of traditional planning should give way to well-informed decision-making. This assumed that under suitable arrangements, honesty could be made the enterprises' best policy. It also presupposed a huge increase in applied research on all levels of the economy, notably better educational standards for the planners as well as a willingness on their part – and on that of the politicians – to listen to expert opinion. In fact, an

important implication was that economists and systems engineers with their computer programmes would undertake much of the control over the system from the incompetent bureaucrats.

(3) *Interactive planning*. The economy would remain a hierarchical system, but its functioning should be reorganised. Instead of the top-down commands typical in the old system, future planning must be an interactive process between lower and higher levels of the economic hierarchy. To ensure room for enterprise independence and initiative, the planning process would be started from the bottom up. Enterprises and ministries would send planners information about production possibilities and resource needs. After much objective deliberation and scholarly calculation, the planners would send the enterprises both an aggregative plan and normatives derived from the plan as shadow prices. The aggregative plan would be formally optimised relative to the global objective function adopted, while the enterprises would use the shadow prices in solving their own, local optimisation problems. Profit was usually thought to be the best local optimality criterion, though there was some disagreement on this.

(4) *Information systems*. A country-wide network of computers and communications facilities for processing and transmitting information is needed as the technical basis for planning. A clear distinction must be made between descriptive and planning information. The former must be rich, the latter as sparing as possible. Through the information system, planning and management could make use of immensely more and better information than earlier. Because only the minimal information absolutely necessary would be used for planning purposes (as distinct from description and statistics), the information system would not grow into a straitjacket suppressing all independence and initiative.

(5) *Economic contracts*. The centre only decides upon a plan in aggregate units. The necessary disaggregation takes place in horizontal and voluntary contracts between enterprises. They stipulate the product mix, quality parameters and prices within the overall frame of the aggregate plan. Signing and executing such contracts is an important part of enterprise independence.

(6) *Shadow prices*. Shadow prices, derived from the optimal plan will be central in enterprise guidance. All scarce resources must have a shadow price, reflecting their marginal contribution to the objective function. When enterprises organise their operations so as to maximise their profits relative to given shadow prices, those operations that give the biggest increase in the value of the planners' goal

function will also be most profitable for enterprises. What is advantageous for the society at large will also be profitable to enterprises.

(7) *Khozraschet*. Enterprises, as just noted, must aim at profitability. Furthermore, the principles of *khozraschet* are also to be adopted on the higher levels of administration such as ministries. The supply of material inputs should change from planned allocation to a wholesale trade system. Credit, instead of free budget outlays, should be given more prominence in financing production. The position of banking would thus be made more important.

The above is only an outline of the SOFE proposals as put forward around 1964–6. As they have been discussed in detail by Michael Ellman,[25] there is no need to go into details here. Some remarks seem appropriate, though. The SOFE proposals are clearly in line with those put forward by Nemchinov. The main difference lies in the more technical character of SOFE. While its proposals had been substantiated in the optimal planning framework as developed by Katsenelinboigen, Nemchinov regarded mathematical economics and reform economics as two separate discourses. In particular, SOFE gives much emphasis to the use of shadow prices formally derived from an optimal plan and to the somewhat technical issues of rolling plans and information systems. The Nemchinovian idea of plan orders is missing, and so is the competitiveness proposed by Nemchinov. Instead of that, SOFE proposed the use of *khozraschet* on the ministry level. This is an issue to be discussed later. In general, though, both sets of proposals are firmly in the indirect centralisation tradition of optimal planning. SOFE emphasised the need for formal optimal planning, while Nemchinov's normatives obviously did not need to be mathematically derived. As will be seen in chapter 4, within a few years there would be important evolution away from the ideas of indirect centralisation.

The Kosygin reform

The reform proposals of Nemchinov and SOFE were, on the one hand, part of the build-up of the discussion leading to the measures announced in September 1965. On the other hand, in the case of SOFE, they should be seen as an attempt at developing that reform further. It was hoped that the reforms announced by Prime Minister Alexei Kosygin would be only the first step towards a new economic mechanism. In actual fact the 1965 reform decree remained the peak of official Soviet reformism until the late eighties. It contained three main measures.[26] First, the reform recentralised economic administration by reinstituting the system of Moscow-based branch ministries. Second, it overhauled the enterprise incentive system and third, there was a reform of wholesale prices. Together these measures were meant to put an end to many of the irrationalities which had plagued the economy. There were also official promises of further reforms, but they never came.

The Kosygin reforms are an attempt at rationalising the economic system while preserving its fundamentals. The decisions sought to create a more rational form of managing the hierarchy of state ownership, one better adapted to the needs of a modern economy, not at changing such structures in any fundamental way. Nor was there to be any basic change in strategic economic goals. It was hoped that the new measures would help the party–state to reach its goals better than the old system had been able to do. What exactly these goals were, was not made clear. The reform was not accompanied by any open reconsideration of strategic goals.

The government did engage in some changes in policies. In particular, the new Soviet leadership promised more incomes, stability and security for the managers, workers and farmers whose interests had been threatened by the erratic Khrushchevian policies. The main beneficiaries were the farmers. Following policies initiated under Khrushchev, some of the benefits traditionally enjoyed by industrial labour, like fixed minimum incomes and pensions, were also given to farmers. At the same time investment in agriculture, long neglected, was sharply stepped up.

The set of policies proposed by the new Brezhnev leadership was an expensive one. It was not only costly in terms of capital investment and promises of rising incomes for all, but also had a high price in terms of alternative policies forgone. The government had promised job security for all. In practice that was interpreted to mean the security of existing jobs. That made any reorganisation or pruning of the management system impossible and rendered the government incapable of a major structural overhaul of the economy. Any market-oriented economic reform was blocked by the promise of stable prices. The new agricultural policies, finally, contained the seeds of a catastrophe. Capital inputs soared without any lasting increase in production to match the consumer demand created by rising incomes and stable prices.

These are some of the basic contradictions in the economics of the Brezhnev era. The leadership's economic policies would only have been viable if a reformed Soviet economy had been able to generate the well-being whose distribution had been promised. The 1965 reform measures, however, soon proved to be incapable of securing that. The original decisions were in many respects unclear and contradictory. Though there has never been a convincing Soviet analysis of the reasons for the failure of the 1965 reforms, TsEMI criticised their contradictions openly as early as 1966.[27] Some of the defects of the 1965 decisions are generally accepted. Thus, they increased enterprise decision-making powers while maintaining overall ministerial control and responsibility for branch performance. Because of that, the ministries were bound to continue to interfere in enterprise activity. The decisions also talked of creating wholesale markets for means of production, but left such work to the very administrators who were supposed to be replaced by the markets. Not surprisingly, the markets failed to materialise. The central planners continued to have preferences on the details of enterprise performance. When the enterprises showed some initiative, often in directions not sanctioned by official policies, the planners responded by increasing the number of obligatory plan targets.

In retrospect the Kosygin reforms suffered the typical fate of a partial reform. The original design was flawed, implementation at best half-hearted and political support lukewarm.[28] Finally, the Czechoslovak crisis of 1968–9 seemed to show that given suitable circumstances an economic reform could radicalise with a speed that in the space of just a few years threatened the power of the party itself. The cause of Soviet economic reform was lost by 1968. Not only were the contradictions of the 1965 reform blueprint always resolved in a centralising fashion, but all public discussion of the economic ills of the country was soon strictly constrained. Complacency and belief in central management, theories of developed socialism and scientific management of society, were to be the official Soviet tune of the seventies.

The basic institutional structure that emerged after the 1965 reform continues to guide the Soviet economy. This is not true of all the ingredients of the reform. Most of the fine-tuning included in the 1965 reform was soon lost. In particular, the incentives schemes in use were soon as impenetrable and arbitrary as they had ever been. The price reform was supposed to correct some irrationalities, but it did not remedy the fundamental faults of the price system. The administrative recentralisation remained.

Not surprisingly, the 1965 reform failed to arrest the long-term

Soviet economic slowdown. Though the increasingly ineffectual and conservative Brezhnev leadership did not try another economic reform on the 1965 scale, it continued to tinker with the economic mechanism. Attempts were made to enhance central planning by the increasing use of mathematical models and automated information systems. Enterprise incentive systems were repeatedly changed, the hierarchical structure of industrial management was marginally altered by a 1973 decision and many of the 1965 goals were reasserted in 1979. Such change meant little for the continuously deteriorating over-all performance of the economy, but as negative experiences such measures were an important phase in developing Soviet reform thinking. Belief in partial reforms and in strengthening centralism deteriorated.

4   The years of radicalism and reaction

The new economic journalism

The economic reform discussion of the sixties differed in several respects from that of the late eighties. While professional economists like Abalkin, Aganbegyan, Bogomolov, Bunich, Latsis, Petrakov, Popov, Shatalin and Zaslavskaya have been among the prominent spokesmen of *perestroika*, the reform discussion of the sixties was dominated by non-economists. 'In fact, who are now most actively discussing economic problems?', asked Nikolai Petrakov in 1970, 'Journalists, writers, mathematicians, airplane constructors, automation specialists. The voices of the economists are only heard quite distantly in this choir.'[1] The Sofeists were a small minority, who mostly wrote for the specialised press. The impotence of political economists continued to be in evidence. Leonid Abalkin, one of the few reformist young political economists, commented on this in 1971.[2] Political economy had unfortunately never become 'a theory of rational economising', Abalkin complained. It had not been able to answer the challenge of the reform. It had opinions about economic laws, but not about their practical importance. Many reform proposals, however well-meaning, only hung loosely together, Abalkin concluded.

This does not mean that the economists had been silent. There were veteran economists like Nemchinov, Novozhilov and Aleksandr Birman, a professor of finance, who advocated the cause of reform in numerous articles and booklets. In addition, for the first time since Stalin's assumption of power, economists and economic journalists took the reform discussion onto the pages of widely read literary journals like *Novyi Mir*, the most progressive journal of the time. It had published Solzhenitsyn, but it also opened its pages to economists and economic journalists like Grigori Khanin, Otto Latsis, Gennadi Lisichkin, Nikolai Petrakov, Vasili Selyunin and also Leonid Abalkin. These writers were so-called 'children of the XXth Party

Congress' of 1956, young men whom Khrushchev's criticism of Stalinism had convinced not only of the impermissability of mass terror but also of the need to reinvigorate socialism by returning to its true Leninist foundations. True Leninism was no longer looked for in the extremism of the Civil War years of 1918–21 but in the relatively peaceful, pluralist and market oriented years of the New Economic Policy (NEP) of 1921–8.[3] Gennadi Lisichkin in particular argued that the roots of the Stalinist system were to be found in War Communist practices.[4] The new reform proposed was thus compared with the 'true Leninist' transition to New Economic Policies in 1921.

In these respects the reformist discourses of the sixties and late eighties are parallel. In the *perestroika* period as well, some of the very same children of the XXth Party Congress have advocated the cause of reform in journals like *Novyi mir*, defending it as a return to the true Leninism of the twenties. People like Khanin, Latsis, Lisichkin and Petrakov have again appeared in mass-circulation journals, in many cases after a less than voluntary absence from them. But now – and this is an important difference between the sixties and the late eighties – a return to true Leninism is no longer the most radical path publicly discussed. The Soviet twenties were a time of one-party rule, centrally controlled state industry and escalating attempts at planning. These are as much features of the Leninist NEP in the same way as the limited use of markets and pluralism of ownership, so strongly emphasised by the reformers. Such defining features of the USSR were not openly questioned in the sixties, but in the late eighties they are no longer sacrosanct. In the sixties Gennadi Lisichkin, perhaps the most market oriented among the reformers defended true Leninism against Stalinism. In the *perestroika* period he has emerged as a defender of Leninism against those who see it as the foundation of Stalinism.[5]

The only discussion of the sixties which came close to taking up the issue of ownership concerned agricultural reform. Several reformists, both journalists and scholars, took up the cause of so-called autonomous links. The idea of links was simple. A group of farm workers was given autonomous rights and responsibilities for organising farming as best they could. A link did not own the land it tilled, but in practice it cultivated it quite independently. Such links had been experimented with during the later Khrushchev years, and the experiment was restarted in the late sixties. Links recorded increases of production and income of up to several times until all such experiments were stopped in the early seventies. Why?

There were several reasons for this.[6] By increasing productivity the links showed the real extent of rural overpopulation. If collective and state farms had to compete economically with links, they would not be able to continue employing people whose level of productivity was very low. There was thus a real possibility of open rural unemployment. Neither this nor the increase in earning differentials induced by a wide use of links was deemed ideologically acceptable. Furthermore, autonomous links were a form of self-management, and the Brezhnev leadership had no intention of introducing self-management either in agriculture or industry. Agriculture was supposed to follow the existing organisational patterns of industry, not to start an initiative that might revolutionise the social institutions of towns as well. Finally, the whole structure of Soviet society was tilted against links. Farms are the lowest level of a hierarchy, and as long as the local and regional party and state bureaucracies are there to command farms, no real independence is possible within farms. To put it the other way round: a link system would have made the rural party and state apparatus powerless and almost unnecessary: they would do all they could to prevent this, in any case the Brezhnev leadership had promised that no such upheavals would occur. For all these reasons, the experiments with autonomous links were duly abandoned only to be resurrected in the eighties, when an increase in food production was badly needed, rural overpopulation no longer existed to the same degree as in the sixties, an increase in earning differentials had not only come to be accepted but was actually set as a goal and the democratisation of society tended to distance party committees from economic management. In 1989 a closely related idea, the leasing of enterprises, was made the centrepiece of economic reform in industry, too. While the Brezhnev regime had promised to preserve existing social relations, Gorbachev set out to revolutionise them. Autonomous links were one of the precedents found for doing this.

Autonomous links were not the only radical economic issue discussed in the sixties. Aleksandr Birman took up the possibility of insolvency and thus, implicitly, unemployment.[7] Boris Rakitskii proposed creating worker participation in strategic enterprise decision-making. He also argued for regional *khozraschet*, later an important part of *perestroika*.[8] Grigori Khanin, a Novosibirsk economist, wrote in *Novyi Mir* a series of remarkable book reviews in which he defended the cause of competition both in banking and in general, emphasised the need for comprehensiveness in reforms, and called for a reappraisal of Soviet economic history, arguing that his calculations showed that the growth rates recorded in official Soviet statistics were false.[9] In the mid-eighties Khanin's calculations aroused much debate. The old question of whether Stalin was really necessary is inevitably seen in a different light once it is admitted that the huge industrial growth recorded in official statistics is possibly a chimera.

A third difference between these debates and those of the *perestroika* period lies in the fact that the economic discussions of the sixties were pursued separately from the political and cultural ones. Both the economists on one hand and the writers, historians and social thinkers on the other were trying to promote pluralism, democracy and responsibility in society. They also shared the pages of the same journals, e.g., *Literaturnaya Gazeta* and *Novyi Mir*. Still, somehow, the two discussions never really met.[10] The link between the possibility of economic choice and political liberties, so obvious to the Western liberal mind, was hardly ever explicitly pointed out in published Soviet discussion until the late eighties. Perhaps this was due to censorship, perhaps the conclusion seemed disturbing to those reformists who regarded themselves as socialist. Accepting the fundamental liberal criticism of socialism cannot have been easy, and the idea of the incompatibility between central planning and democracy as well as the market economy as a necessary condition for political democracy became widely accepted among Soviet reform economists only after 1987.[11] In 1989 it even became possible to publish extracts from such a classical liberal statement as Friedrich Hayek's *The Road to Serfdom*.[12]

Market socialism?

For a few years after 1965 it still seemed that the confusions and contradictions of the Kosygin reforms might be resolved by developing the reform in depth and breadth. The Soviet government supported optimal planning and other new directions in economics in various ways, and Leonid Brezhnev's speeches – in addition to extolling a new, 'scientific' attitude to managing the society – still sometimes commented positively on the Lenin of the New Economic Policy. Until the Czechoslovak crisis it seemed that the socialist countries of Eastern Europe were entering a common period of reforms. In the Soviet Union the years from 1966 to 1970 formed the peak of economic reform discussions. For the first time since the twenties, a few Soviet economists openly argued for the wide use of markets in socialism.

This discussion had its limitations. The issue of ownership was only raised in relation to autonomous agricultural links. It was assumed that state ownership would continue to have a monopoly position in the non-farm sector. The markets under discussion were those for goods, not for labour and capital. Furthermore, markets were generally understood as a mechanism for transmitting information. They were to be *used* technocratically as a channel of feedback. They were not seen as a natural institution for human action. And, finally, the prevailing political and ideological constraints prevented an open discussion on the social consequences of markets and planning. The conservatives were able to extol the 'scientific principles of planning' and condemn markets for causing inflation and unemployment, for increasing income differentials and thus undermining alleged Soviet achievements. The pro-marketeers were not able to analyse the Soviet experience of centralised planning realistically.

An example of how restricted the discussion of the social role of markets had to be is given in Viktor Volkonskii's remarks on Aleksandr Birman. Birman had, as mentioned above, stressed the need for closing down terminally loss-making enterprises. Volkonskii wrote in 1967:

Of even more importance [than material stimulation] is the question raised by Prof. A. M. Birman on the unavoidability of the consequences of bad economising under the market system. The practice of economic management both in this country and abroad gives much material for analysing this problem, which is one of the key issues in the political economy of socialism and is also connected with socio-economic questions. Discussing it, though, is not one of the tasks of this article.[13]

This is a vivid example of the limits imposed by censorship. Volkonskii could say that the market mechanism would not function properly without sanctions against inefficient producers, that is, without the risk of bankruptcy ('unavoidable consequences'). He could also say that this is a crucial issue. There could not be effective markets without bankruptcies, but could there be socialism with them and with unemployment ('socio-economic questions')? These are the problems that Volkonskii raised, as any experienced Soviet reader well understood, but an article discussing them could not be published. Only in the late eighties could the reformers enjoy the same kind of public discussion rights that the conservatives have always had.

It is intriguing to note that in spite of the constraints set by censorship there was never a professional Soviet underground economic literature. Few prominent economists emigrated. When open reform-ist discussion was made impossible, most professional economists preferred to withdraw into technical studies and wait for better times. In the mid-eighties they would come forward often equipped with the same theories as in the sixties.

The Kantorovich–Novozhilov framework was about indirect centralisation as a way of implementing plans, not about markets. The same is broadly true of SOFE as presented under the name of Academician Fedorenko in a justly famous 1968 book.[14] In theory, as we have seen, an optimal plan might have no relationship to markets at all.

Assuming that the size of the task could be handled and that random variations would cause no trouble, prices and other norma-tives would be derived from the plan as shadow prices and be given out to enterprises as administrative commands. No markets would be needed – or so it was argued. In later conservative times, this was the interpretation of optimal planning that Fedorenko preferred to put forward.[15] Even when Fedorenko chose to emphasise the importance of scale and randomness, prices would fundamentally be based on planners' decisions reflecting 'social utilities'.

The exact status of markets in optimal planning was always left unclear. Many Sofeists emphasised – as had Novozhilov already in the twenties – the negative consequences of having non-equilibrium prices for consumer goods. Queuing, rationing, black markets and quality deterioration were not in the sixties as serious problems as they would soon become, but it was well understood that equilibrium prices are necessary. Remembering the impossibly huge task of set-ting and changing centrally the millions of retail prices, the only possible way of having equilibrium prices was to leave them to be determined by supply and demand on the market. As Sofeists said while defending market pricing against accusations of fomenting inflation, it is crucial to have correct relative prices. *If* a macro-econ-omic equilibrium exists, there is no danger of inflation.[16]

But, on the other hand, the basic logic of optimal planning said that prices were to be based on the plan. If one believes in planning, one has to argue that it could do better than markets ever could. Current market information, Fedorenko, Volkonskii and others claimed, was insufficient for planning consumption. Especially as over a lengthy planning horizon, new products will appear and consumer incomes and preferences change. Information on 'scientific norms of con-sumption', externalities and various social considerations, which is not available on markets, was also needed. It has to be generated within the planning process. This is why the prices derived from the optimal plan could not coincide with current market equilibrium prices. Otherwise planning would be without an economic rationale.

The same problems appear in a new form in the case of investment goods. Technical progress, random variations in weather and other variables exogenous to the planners' competence – as well as changes in such determinants of the economy as state policies – drive a wedge between current equilibrium prices and optimal plan valuations. As we saw above, Nemchinov had argued that traditional voluntarist planning was no better than markets. Novozhilov, on the other hand, emphasised that market feedback would always be needed. In principle, the optimal planners always asserted, rational planning, if it both uses indirect centralisation and allows for some – possibly regulated – markets, can be made to perform better than markets alone would do. But the proposed precise mix between plan and markets was never very clear.

In 1970 Nikolai Petrakov published an article in which he strongly advocated equilibrium prices both for consumer goods and – in passing – investment goods.[17] This brought forth a rejoinder from Boris Smekhov, another economist, who pointed out many of the potential differences between current equilibrium prices and optimal plan valuations already mentioned.[18] In his reply Petrakov accepted that a normative approach to consumption planning was also necessary. There should be both the planners' right to recommend (but only to recommend!) and the consumers' right to choose.[19]

Another rejoinder to Petrakov's 1970 article represented possibly the first Sofeist condemnation of market socialism. While stating their like-mindedness with Petrakov, Gorbunov and Ovsienko wrote that 'Socialism and the plan are just as inseparable as socialism and the social ownership of the means of production. Therefore the concept of "market socialism", which denies society-wide planning as an imminent feature of socialist production, is fruitless both theoretically and practically.'[20]

Petrakov, who had been criticised by name in *Pravda* for theoretical and politico-economic mistakes,[21] was forced to publish a critique of market socialism in 1973.[22] He called market socialism 'a reaction of liberal professors to the power of monopolies'. Even if perfect competition no longer existed in capitalism, it should be reconstituted as socialism, market socialists argued, or so Petrakov claimed. In fact, perfect competition was a utopia, and in socialism priority is given to the plan. Prices arising from the plan should be called 'prices of planned equilibrium', Petrakov proposed. While market prices are myopic, the prices of planned equilibrium take into consideration any forthcoming changes in production structure, productivity, incomes and other such determinants. Planning, Petrakov concluded, is able to do better than markets.

Petrakov's article reflected deep-rooted attitudes among Soviet economists. Soviet Marxism has long argued that capitalism has developed from free competition to monopolies. Introducing free markets in socialism would therefore be both utopian and reactionary, an attempt to return to the nineteenth century. This argument is still put forward by opponents of a market oriented economic reform, who continue to argue that powerful computers make the derivation and implementation of optimal prices possible.[23] Only slowly have Soviet scholars started wondering whether Marxism has not underestimated the role of competition in the development of capitalism[24] and whether, indeed, monopolisation should be seen as a state-induced aberration in capitalism, not as a consequence of natural development.[25]

Such considerations, whether well founded or not, do not of course change the fact that the Soviet economy is extremely monopolistic. According to a recent study, most Soviet enterprises are local monopolies.[26] The impermissibility of free pricing in a monopoly situation was emphasised by Yuri Sukhotin as early as 1970.[27] As long as Soviet economists believed – as many still do – that monopolisation and therefore centralisation is a technologically induced inevitable process common to both capitalism and socialism, they were unable to draw the alternative conclusion. Perhaps monopolisation is a state-induced evil which should be fought by appropriate policies – even, perhaps especially, in the USSR. On this perspective, widely adopted only during the last few years, market socialism begins to look possible instead of being 'utopian and reactionary'.

Petrakov's idea of prices of planned equilibrium was developed and refined by him and other TsEMI economists during subsequent years.[28] In the early eighties this proposal was fiercely condemned by the leadership of the State Committee for Prices as 'market socialist'. After 1986 TsEMI campaigned for these prices as the basis of the centralised price reform then planned for 1988. The Price Committee disagreed and prepared a price reform blueprint which TsEMI and many other economists found totally inadequate. Such disagreements contributed to a repeated postponement of the price reform.

Preserving the existing irrational structure of prices while increasing enterprise autonomy was one of the factors lying behind the deterioration of the Soviet economy in 1988–9.

It is a good measure of the change in Soviet economic thinking that after 1989 several TsEMI spokesmen on price reform strongly opposed any plans for a centralised price revision. Only free market prices, they now insisted, could bring about the equilibrium badly needed. Markets without free prices are now condemned as bureaucratic illusions.[29]

It is difficult to find a consistent market socialist among the Soviet economists of the sixties. Even Viktor Volkonskii, the TsEMI economist who according to some has written 'the ideology of capitalism adapted to Soviet conditions',[30] was in fact perfectly conscious of the limitations of a competitive economy. He warned of the cyclical properties of free markets and explicitly did not want to leave 'large' investment decisions to the market.

Another economist who seemed to have taken the side of markets in the 'markets or plan' controversy was Gennadi Lisichkin, an economist and journalist, in a much-discussed 1966 booklet.[31] Lisichkin rightly insisted upon the difference between genuine markets and the use of commodity–money relations as an accounting and control device. They are alternatives and have each a logic of their own, he emphasised. Any attempt to graft elements of one onto the other is bound to fail, Lisichkin argued. In a fusion the dominant one is going to absorb and neutralise any 'alien' elements. In Soviet history, the New Economic Policy of the twenties is the model of the market alternative, traditional central planning the model of using commodity–money relations. For Lisichkin there was no doubt that the principles of the twenties are 'the uniquely correct system of economic relations, until such time as full communism is built'.

Indeed, one of the generally accepted lessons of the thirty-five years of East European economic reforms is that though different combinations of planning and markets are viable, any reform must be able to decide whether it aims to maintain the priority of planning or whether a primarily market economy is set as the goal. The first case is that of Lisichkin's 'commodity–money relations', the second that of markets. On this perspective Lisichkin's argument should be seen as a far-sighted criticism of the predominant Soviet reformist attempt to combine indirect centralisation with some market elements. There was, however, a crucial limitation to Lisichkin's analysis. He understood markets very narrowly, only as 'a complicated structure of conditions under which the disposal (*realizatsiya*) of social product takes place'.[32] He is thus in fact only writing about product markets and even about them only from a specific angle. Even his market socialism, then, is of a limited variety.

SOFE, stage 2

By the late sixties SOFE was trying to liberate itself from the technocratic social engineering which had been much emphasised in the early work of Katsenelinboigen's group. Volkonskii, in particular, understood well that a social science approach was needed as a basis for discussing social optimality. In a 1969 conference he presented an unpublished paper which among other things enumerated the concepts and categories which, in his opinion, are necessary for the discussion of optimality. Among these the speaker included the democratic mechanism for the self-regulation of social life, the 'value' orientation of society, the role of science (i.e. of the specialists) and so on.[33]

The barrier between economic and political discussion was starting to crumble. The social engineering approach to optimal planning was condemned as seeking to create 'superautomatons' which are based on 'a model of an all-directing, absolutely authoritarian planning centre' and thus embracing 'the idea of totally centralised command planning'.[34] By 1969 the approach of Katsenelinboigen's group, the target of such criticism, had also undergone some evolution. As pointed out in chapter 2, their 1969 book[35] elaborated upon the need for horizontal linkages in the economy. The group had also abandoned the somewhat totalitarian ideal of a single objective function for the economy and without mentioning democratisation by name now argued for regulated – possibly controlled – procedures for social goal setting and for a permitted pluralism of values. Though hierarchical relations were still seen to have priority over horizontal linkages in a socialist economy, it was now suggested that horizontal ties between enterprises would also be used to improve resource allocation relative to the plan received from above. Any attempt to attain a perfectly optimal plan requires too much time and other scarce resources. One had to take an approximate plan as the starting point and let enterprises depart from it, when the need arose.

The new approach to optimality was spelled out in more detail in a 1971 book by Nikolai Petrakov.[36] He criticised both the technocratic social engineering of SOFE, Stage 1, and the general equilibrium approach offered by Volkonskii. Petrakov's approach was based on systems thinking. Abandoning the simple idea of a social goal function Petrakov emphasised the need for 'the existence of a mechanism for defining, specifying and correcting' social goals. Passing beyond the image of markets as only a mechanism for transmitting existing information he stressed the ways in which new information is generated. Generation of new information and interest articulation alike imply the existence of social pluralism. Decisions should emerge not as a dictate of assumedly monolithic leadership, but as an informal compromise taking account of the diversity of existing interests. Instead of social engineering, Petrakov was calling for politics.

On the philosophical level, Petrakov had in his 1970 *Novyi Mir* article explicitly abandoned the metaphor that both Kautsky and Lenin had used. Socialism, he wrote, is not just a large machine.[37] It consists of people with different interests. Planners are no exception to the rule. They are not only burdened by a psychology developed during the years of direct centralism, but also have their own interests. Left uncontrolled, they may well draft plans which reflect only those. Plans were thus too important to be left to planners.

Petrakov proposed that the greater part of enterprise production plans should be based upon market demand in the form of their order books. Only 'the most important' production elements should be determined centrally. Most production would be based on market demand, but be centrally regulated through changes in resource payments, taxation and finance. Certain resources would remain under direct central allocation.

What, if any, would be the role of optimal planning and shadow prices under such a dual-track planning system? Petrakov's proposal is a variant of Nemchinov's *khozraschet*-economy, and the government's economic policies would regulate economic activity primarily through various economic normatives like resource payments, rents, interest and tax schedules. At least some prices would also be centrally fixed, though Petrakov is unclear on the relation between centrally set and market prices. Normatives, meant to be stable over a five-year period, would be derived from formal planning calculations, possibly even as shadow prices from an explicitly optimised plan.

Petrakov's 1971 proposal of a dual-track planning system is an important bridge between the sixties and the eighties. It is a development of Nemchinov's arguments. In 1986–7 the Gorbachev leadership chose the dual-track system, by then defended by a majority of reform economists, as the basis of its reform blueprint. In doing so, it was exploiting the mainstream of Soviet reform economics.

Petrakov's proposal shared many of the problems of Nemchinov's *khozraschet*-economy. How large a share of production is centrally planned and allocated? To what degree does the plan try to know more than markets? What exactly is the relation between planning calculations and market prices? How could normatives be stable? What is to be done with monopolies? How does one create markets? What is the role of finance? Such questions, and many more, were to be faced only in the late eighties. It was soon apparent that the stable normatives approach had to be abandoned. In the seventies even it had been condemned as market socialism.

Against market socialism

Even the cautious Liberman proposals were met with accusations of opening the door to 'market anarchy', bringing with it inflation, unemployment and diminishing control on the part of the planners over economic development. Not surprisingly, it was the political economist veterans of the Stalinist revolution who led the counter-attack against reformism from the late sixties onwards. People like Ostrovitianov, Pashkov and Strumilin thought they had seen it all before. Just as decades ago, a fight between bourgeois and Marxist thinking was being fought on Soviet soil.[38] Real and imagined similarities between the proposals of the reformists of the sixties and those of the economists of the twenties were used as political weapons. The atmosphere was further heated by the first dissident activities in 1967 which were met with much conservative fervour by the authorities.

The planners added their considerable weight to the conservative counter-attack soon after the Czechoslovak crisis of 1968–9.[39] A year later the head of Gosplan's Computing Centre put SOFE in the same company as 'the gibberish choir of revisionists, social modellers and overthrowers of Marxist–Leninist theory'.[40] These planners were not against introducing computers and mathematical models, if their use was based upon the Marxist–Leninist principles of planning – that is, if the new methods were used to preserve and strengthen the existing system of command economy. In their view the problem with economic reforms was that 'in practice the various forms of so-called self-regulation of the economy mean a weakening of the role of the socialist state and the party of the working class in the management of the economy'.[41] When the reformers argued that without decisive reform measures a further growth slowdown was to be expected in the Soviet economy, the conservatives answered by accusing them of borrowing various bourgeois tools for their calculations.[42] And finally, by the mid-seventies, when the slowdown could no longer be explained away, the Central Statistical Administration started cutting drastically the amount of published economic statistics. Such high-ranking economic institutions as the State Committee for Prices, the Ministry of Finance, the State Bank and Gosplan made independent academic research in their administrative fields nearly impossible by withholding information and severing formal contacts with the academic community.[43]

By the early seventies the planners had immediate reasons for concern. The reformers, though they saw that the cause of radical reform had been lost, continued making proposals for at least ration-alising the economic management systems. Thus, the Central Econ-omic–Mathematical Institute argued in 1972 that Gosplan, the planning committee, should be transformed into a 'scientific–econ-omic institution for long-range planning'.[44] This would have stripped Gosplan of most of its concrete power over resource allocation. At the same time it would have given the planners tasks for which they had at that time no competence whatsoever.

From the planner's point of view dangers also lurked in the topical proposals for creating automated information processing systems.[45] This was not only a question of technical rationalisation, as leading Moscow and Novosibirsk academic economics institutes – Fedorenko's TsEMI and Aganbegyan's Institute of Industrial Econ-omics – were campaigning for blueprints proposing fundamental reorganisation of planning work. Gosplan officials much preferred to use computers simply for mechanical calculation, involving no sub-stantial change in their work style. Using information systems in that way was, of course, calculated to enhance the planners' control over the economy.

Analysts have generally concluded that the academic economists' proposals were essentially impracticable. As no progress towards markets seemed possible, they had to propose huge mathematical model systems for which neither the computing capability nor the necessary information was available. An immense amount of work was devoted to such models in the seventies. Practical applications remained few. But the economists, as distinct from the planners, had something with real potential for rationalisation to propose. Still, the planners continued their attacks on SOFE in particular claiming that they supported the development of planning methods but opposed suspect theoretical constructs like SOFE.[46] SOFE, an article in the Gosplan journal asserted, must be condemned as:

an attempt to introduce a special concept of 'optimal planning', calculated to supplant the supposedly non-scientific system of empirical planning; striving to unite vulgar utility theory with the labour theory of value, to present price as a measure of utility; ignoring the principle of democratic centralism as the basis of the socialist economy, exchanging it for the so-called principle of hierarchical structure; borrowing notions from bourgeois theories (marginal utility theory, the notion of market socialism and the theory of factors of production, the ideal of automatic regulation of the socialist economy by 'optimal plan prices'); denying the laws of reproduction; and gradually exchanging the Marxist–Leninist theory of reproduction for the bourgeois theory of equilibrium.[47]

For a few years it seemed that there was an abyss between academic economics and economic planners. Prominent Gosplan Research Institute economists like A. I. Anchishkin had to change their affiliation from Gosplan to the academy. The Gosplan journal, *Planovoe Khozyaistvo*, routinely criticised anything the academic economists were doing. The latter, on the other hand, fought losing battles to maintain at least some momentum towards modernisation in planning and management. This does not mean that all academic economists were modernisers. While mathematical economists in general advocated modern planning methods as a way to better plans and therefore to less immediate interference by the planners in enterprise affairs, there were also a few conservatives who openly applauded mathematical planning methods as a way to more direct centralism.[48]

As will be seen in chapter 5, party economists were much more constrained in their criticism of the reformers than the planners. Still, two well-known economists from the Central Committee Academy of Social Sciences argued against the reformers that any influence of the market upon plans was inadmissible as it left production dependent upon the vagaries of demand.[49] In their view even the use of markets as a mechanism of feedback was thus not permitted.

What remained of reformism?

SOFE, Stage 3, of the late seventies and early eighties tried to prove its theoretical Marxist–Leninist orthodoxy and trod with great caution when proposing any change in the economic mechanism. While markets could no longer be proposed, quite far-reaching changes in the planning system were still being advocated. The main reformist proposals can be divided into three groups.[50]

(1) *Long-range planning*. Yearly and five-year plans should be supplemented with long-range (fifteen to twenty years) general plans of social and economic development. Such plans, combining forecasts and some directives for resource allocation, should concentrate on issues of technical development and social change.

The idea that the socialist system would best show its advantages in long-term planning is an old one. N. A. Voznesenskii, the head of Gosplan in the forties, had at an early stage set the creation of such a plan as his goal. Voznesenskii's attempts failed, and the next fairly serious attempt at long-term forecasting emerged with the preparations of the 1961 party programme. Its goal of overtaking the developed capitalist countries in economic terms and reaching full communism by the eighties was, however, totally utopian.

By the late sixties a new generation of Soviet economists, pupils of Kantorovich and Nemchinov, armed with input–output analyses and production functions, was forecasting a continuing slowdown in Soviet economic growth, if measures were not taken to speed up technical progress. One such measure might be the general plan. Economists like Aleksandr Anchishkin, Boris Mikhalevskii and Stanislav Shatalin became the champions of long-range planning. The issue of forecasting was a contested one itself. In the late sixties Soviet sociologists, encouraged by party decisions on developing forecasting, had proposed themselves as independent consultants on the long-term development prospects of Soviet society. Mikhail Suslov, the Party Secretary for ideology, led the suppression of such independent sociological futurology in 1971.[51] The reason offered was that such consultants might become a 'second party', a group of social critics. This was the field into which economists were now breaking with their proposals for a general plan. The party was suspicious, while Gosplan officials, as we have just seen, both objected to the pessimistic – actually highly realistic – results the economists' computers were giving and also often failed totally to see any general use for forecasts in a planned economy.[52] Many treated the whole idea of forecasting with suspicion. It was seen as something opposed to real command planning.

In 1972 the government accepted the idea of a fifteen-year Integrated Programme of Scientific–technical Progress and its Socio-economic Consequences. In practice the programme, coordinated by the Academy of Sciences, was not a plan but a scholarly forecasting exercise with little connection with the work of Gosplan. In 1979 the span of the forecast was lengthened by the Party Central Committee to twenty years, but at the same time its scope was narrowed by excluding socio-economic considerations from it. This probably happened because Gosplan did not want the exercise to grow into a potentially competing parallel to its own work.[53] In the same way as in 1971, the 'threat' of independent expertise was overwhelming in the minds of the decision-makers. This, together with the deteriorating quality of available statistics, further diminished the role of the forecast.

Still, the academic economists continued their work on forecasting. According to academician.Aganbegyan the official attitude to such research only changed in 1982 when Yuri Andropov became the CPSU Secretary General and Mikhail Gorbachev took responsibility for economic issues within the CPSU Central Committee Secretariat.[54] The economists' opinion took on a new importance after a decision in 1984 to have a special Central Comiittee Plenum on technical development. Aganbegyan and other economists were active in preparing the materials which finally became the basis for Secretary General Gorbachev's first programmatic statements on growth acceleration and *perestroika*.

(2) *Programme methods of planning*. The second area of proposals for reforming planning concerned the wide introduction of so-called goal-programme methods. In somewhat different forms, such proposals were put forward by several institutes and individual economists during the seventies.[55] Among them were TsEMI, The Novosibirsk Institute of Industrial Economics and Moscow State University, where the work was led by Professor Gavriil Popov, who was later to emerge as a leading radical politician. These were not proposals of purely theoretical interest. The use of goal-programme methods in actual planning was also increasing.

In spite of various differences, the proposals for programme planning had a common core. They aimed at transforming two features of traditional planning. The first concerned the way in which the economy is partitioned for descriptive and planning purposes. Traditional planning has for most of its history been based on the sector–ministry division of the economy. This has always led to problems in coordination across ministries. To fight this, Khrushchev opted for a regional scheme of economic planning and management. Not surprisingly, many of the problems of branch autarky reappeared in a regional form. Goal-programme planning is an attempt to avoid both the Scylla of branch ministries and the Charybdis of regional authorities. In short, it argues that many planning tasks – the building of a main railway with its infrastructure, the development of a region, the opening up of a major source of raw materials – are by nature inter-branch. Resources are needed from many branches, and social and infrastructure investments are as necessary as narrowly productive ones. No wonder that goal-programme planning became generally known as 'the inter-organisational approach'.[56] Such an approach needed inter-organisational decision-making. While some of its proponents argued that any new decision-making bodies needed should only be temporary,[57] others claimed that the increasing role of inter-branch programmes would make the establishment of large superministries (one for the energy sector, another for the agro-industrial complex, a third for transport as a whole and so on) necessary.[58]

The second specific feature of goal-programme planning is its goal-oriented nature. Traditional planning has always been based on existing resources. Planning has primarily been aimed at increasing and using them. The approach advocated in the seventies aimed to generalise the experience of the area where Soviet planning has arguably been most efficient, the organisation of military and space sectors. These are often presented as areas where goals have been relatively well defined and planning has been goal- not resource-determined. The second fundamental idea of goal-programme planning was consequently to shift the general planners' emphasis from resources to goals. In this sense goal-programme planning has been seen as a development of SOFE.[59]

Many of the questions raised by such proposals are technical. There are also at least three important implications for economic reform. First of all, goal-programme planning generally goes beyond the jurisdiction of a single branch ministry. Generalised, goal-programme planning would render existing ministries without many of their former functions, and leave them stripped of much of their traditional power. If new permanent administrative structures were created for managing the programmes, the old ones, the real mainstay of concrete economic power in socialism, had to be demolished.[60] Either this had to be done, or one would be simply creating a new, higher level of hierarchical management. The latter alternative would only complicate further the existing organisational maze. Unfortunately, the Gorbachev era has experimented with just such bureaucratic additions, in the form of various Council of Ministers bureaus for large economic complexes.

The second economic implication of goal-programme planning is potentially no less revolutionary. If goal oriented planning is to be efficient, the goal complexes to be created should not be too numerous. Goals, after all, are to be thought of as priorities, and one cannot have the whole economy as a priority. In this respect goal-programme planning differs radically from optimal planning, which tried to envisage and impose a global economic objective function, one covering the whole economy. It is impossible to lock all the economic activities of the country inside one programme or another, though even this has been proposed. Such a solution would con-tradict the allocational priority thinking crucial for any successful programme. Therefore one ends up with an economy which has numerous areas or pockets outside any explicit programmes. If goal-programme planning is just a complement to existing balancing methods, this is not of crucial importance. If, on the other hand, the new approach were to substitute for branch planning,[61] it would be natural to leave such non-programme pockets outside the scope of formal planning. One could even think that programmes would only cover the true priority sectors of the economy, and most production would be for markets. In this perspective the goal-programme plan-ning approach differs radically from the optimal planning tradition, which envisaged a single unified plan for the economy.

Though it could not be openly proposed in the seventies, goal-programme thinking could easily point to a New Economic Policy form of organisation of the economy. In the twenties, only basic industry was centrally managed, while the rest of the economy was either subject to indirect economic regulation or completely outside planning. GOELRO, the 1921 plan for organising Soviet Russia, is not, surprisingly, often mentioned in this context as the predecessor of goal-programme planning. A TsEMI scholar argued in 1989 in favour of substituting five-year plans by a number of programmes of different time-spans. This would both release the economy from the straitjacket of an artificial five-year rhythm and leave large parts, perhaps even most of the economy, unplanned but subject to various economic policies.[62] It seems certain that this is the direction in which planning will be developed under the Gorbachev reforms.

And finally, what is the proposed role of Gosplan under goal-programme planning? At least some of its proponents have argued

for limiting the role of Gosplan just to being the organiser of programmes.[63] This would imply a huge shift of economic power.

Certainly, the idea of goal-programme planning is not without its
problems. In practical terms the obvious unwillingness of branch
ministries to be dismantled is the crucial handicap. And while the
existing branch structure has at least the benefit of already existing,
there is no obvious and natural way of partitioning the economy into
new goal complexes. In fact Soviet scholars presented several different proposals for such a partition. If, on the other hand, goal-
programmes were simply to be grafted on the existing organisational
structure, many of its putative gains would be lost. It is thus perhaps
not too surprising that two of the best-known goal-programmes of
the seventies, the programme for the Russian non-black-earth agriculture and that for the Baikal–Amur railway, are seen with hindsight
to be among the major planning failures of the period.[64]

The third problem with goal-oriented planning concerns the very
idea of goal orientation. In space technology and military applications
goals may be relatively easy to determine, but that is hardly the case
with most planning. This is, after all, one reason why the planning
for resources is traditionally predominant wherever any planning is
done. The versatility of many resources and intermediate goods is
from this perspective a crucial advantage. They can be redirected
when new needs are recognised. The somehow 'objective' determination of social goals, on the other hand, is notoriously impossible.

(3) *The economic mechanism.* No explicit proposals for a market-oriented reform were possible after the early seventies, though positive
references to the Hungarian reform experience could be published.
Raimundas Karagedov of the Novosibirsk Institute of Industrial Economics concluded in 1974 that the Hungarian system had 'proved its
viability and can be regarded as a model of planned management of
socialist production with a future'. Furthermore its importance
'stretched beyond the borders of the country in question'.[65] In a later
article he emphasised that one cannot really speak of increasing
centralisation and decentralisation at the same time (as the theories of
indirect centralisation had done), as decision-making powers could
only lie in one pair of hands. He again cited the Hungarian example
as a consistent reform.[66] Viktor Volkonskii was another economist
who still managed to defend the idea of a market-oriented reform,
though in a notably cautious form.[67]

Other writers continued to advocate the need for comprehensiveness in 'perfecting' the economic mechanism. Thus, when the 1979

decisions on such perfecting were being prepared, Nikolai Fedorenko, Petrakov and others published an article which outlined four main directions of reform.[68] (1) The plan should be balanced on the basis of goal-programmes. (2) Financial planning should be coordinated with physical planning. (3) Stable five-year normatives should be established. *Khozraschet* associations should be the basic organisational unit and customer satisfaction, not gross output, should be their success indicator. (4) The wage fund should be dependent on value added, and enterprise management should have more decision-making powers over its use.

These, naturally, are much more cautious proposals than the sketches of a *khozraschet*-economy put forward some ten years earlier. Even then they were not included in the 1979 decisions,[69] and were duly repeated in a book published just before *perestroika* in 1985.[70] The goals enumerated in this book edited by Fedorenko and Petrakov for 'improving' the economic mechanism are characteristic of the pre-Gorbachev ideological climate: 'securing an increased role for the Communist party of Soviet Union', 'strengthening of centralised planning', 'uniting national, collective and personal interests on the basis of the priority of all-people's interests' and 'securing an organic linkage of branch and regional aspects of planning and management'. Not only is the conservatism of the goals enumerated evident; the economists' language had also been deformed by Sovietese–Bureaucratese.

The economists did have scores of detailed proposals in areas like pricing and efficiency calculations. They also promoted a large number of economic experiments for testing various reform proposals. The range of such experiments ranged from the ridiculous to the radical. Many *khozraschet* experiments on different levels of the economy are an example of the latter. The number of economic experiments kept growing until there were some forty experiments going on in the country in 1984. In addition to those, a so-called 'large-scale experiment' was started in 1984. Its openly admitted purpose was finally to implement the 1979 decisions.[71]

The use of experiments was meant to remedy the economists' deficient understanding about how various proposals might work in practice. It was generally acknowledged that existing 'work on a descriptive analysis of the national economy is clearly insufficient' and that this leads to impracticable and contradictory proposals.[72] But neither was the use of experiments a panacea. The enterprises and branches willing to experiment were often the best ones. On the one hand, they still had to work in the old environment, but on the other hand, they were often given privileges in resource allocation. In such conditions the results of experiments could never be generalised. They became more and more an end in themselves, a make-believe play with possible and impossible reform ideas.

During the Brezhnev years, academician Zaslavskaya says in a book published in 1989:

many became convinced in their feelings and soon also in their understanding that society had strayed from the correct path, was not functioning as it should, and could not continue as it was. Everybody was waiting for an upheaval. During sad, hopeless and desperate moments we said that our generation would hardly live to see the 'daybreak', that we would have to die in the darkness. During our best moments, though, we thought that there were healthy forces in our society, that it could return to the correct path, and we dreamed of participating in social renewal.[73]

Such emotionally laden, even messianistic hopes were soon to be focussed upon Mikhail Gorbachev.

5   Not of mathematics alone

Schools of economic thought

The mathematical economists were always a small minority among Soviet economists. What made them special was the fact that they had a consistent, even if partial and seriously flawed, theory of the socialist economy. This can not be said of their colleagues in political economy and applied economics. By the early eighties, however, it was generally recognised that the optimal planning approach was in crisis. The reformist aspirations of the Sofeists had been frustrated. The use of mathematical methods in planning and management had proved to be a typical Soviet campaign with many words and much expense but with few practical results other than limited mechanising of planning calculations. Instead of being a part of an economic modernisation programme, mathematical planning methods helped to shore up the existing economic system by curbing the information overload which otherwise would have overburdened planners. Viewed from this perspective, computerising the economy actually proved harmful.[1]

Optimal planning had thus become one of the victims of the conservatism of the Brezhnev era. Not all the fault could be laid at the door of politics. The fundamental optimal planning approach itself badly needed a reconsideration. It had remained an abstract theoretical construction. No empirical breakthroughs had been achieved in such crucial matters as the determination of the optimality criterion for national economic planning.[2] A few economists continued to argue for centralised planning through computers and shadow prices, but nobody was able to show how that could be done in practice. Scientific centralism remained a fantasy – a dream for some, a nightmare for others.

As a theoretical concept, the optimality approach was interpreted in widely differing ways. While Stanislav Shatalin argued that it showed the necessity of guiding the economy on the basis of a central optimal plan for the whole economy,[3] Viktor Volkonskii continued to interpret the optimality results as a paradigm for market-oriented reform.[4] The issues of centralisation versus decentralisation, planning and markets, continued, then, to be contested within SOFE. The optimal planning framework gave more insight into prices, efficiency and opportunity cost than any other approach within Soviet economic thought, but still its framework was increasingly admitted to be flawed. After several years of intense debate, most of the above criticism of SOFE is now accepted by leading Sofeists.[5]

As a strategy for economic reform SOFE was handicapped by its fundamental normativeness. Its more technical recommendations were derived within models of optimal socialism, and the second-best problems of applying them in imperfect reality were too often sidestepped. In 1983 leading Sofeists admitted this and argued that the time had come for a 'serious and many-sided study of the real economic development processes of the socialist economy'.[6] In 1983 the party also made its dissatisfaction with the economists known. In a Central Committee Plenum both Yuri Andropov, the Secretary General, and Konstantin Chernenko, who was soon to become his successor, claimed that social scientists had neglected the study of 'the society in which we live and work'. In the sixties, it was said, the party had placed much hope in mathematical economics and sociology, 'but so far we have just not received the necessary concrete studies of social phenomena and current economic problems'.[7]

Fedorenko, the director of TsEMI, was later retired and the institute split into two. SOFE had failed to achieve its original utopian goals. But that failure was only relative, as none of the competing schools in Soviet economics had done any better. SOFE's leading competitors for pride of place in Soviet reform economics are analysed in this chapter. They are: the Soviet political economy of socialism; the work of the Novosibirsk Insitute of Industrial Economics; Soviet organisational theory; and Soviet studies of foreign countries. The survey is not exhaustive. It is Moscow-centred and neglects all agricultural economics as well as most applied research. Still, especially from the vantage point of knowing who the main proponents of reform in the Gorbachev period have been, it is representative.

The political economy of socialism

In an earlier chapter we left the political economy of socialism (PES) in the early sixties. PES was in a sorry state. Born and developed as an integral part of Stalinist ideology, it had concentrated upon extolling the virtues of Soviet development and leadership policies. As a typical quasi-science, PES had no scholarly methods for distinguishing between true and false propositions. This, together with the abstractness and shallowness of the 'economic laws' it had proposed, made PES incapable of offering relevant policy recommendations when these were requested. This had left it open to repeated criticism by various party functionaries. Still, as became evident in the early seventies, the latter have in general seemed to prefer an ideological PES to one that consistently tried to study existing reality. Finally, in early 1984, the Party Central Committee balanced its earlier criticism of the sociologists and mathematical economists by adopting a resolution that was very critical of the work of the Academy of Sciences Institute of Economics in the field of political economy.[8] Once again, PES was condemned as being too abstract, mediocre and out of touch with contemporary problems.

It would be both tedious and unrewarding to try an overview of PES during the seventies and eighties. Fundamentally, very little changed until the last two or three years of the eighties, especially when portrayed against the backdrop of the ideological and practical needs of *perestroika*. On the contrary: the conservative ideological backlash already described perhaps centred on sociology and philosophy, but was also strong in the politically sensitive field of political economy. The smallest ideological deviations were searched for by party officials. Many of the radicals of the sixties suffered. Gennadi Lisichkin wrote four different doctoral dissertations, but was each time prevented from defending them.[9] Otto Latsis had problems with the KGB,[10] and many others, among them Nikolai Petrakov, were unable to publish all they had written. It was a small wonder that Stanislav Shatalin was able to publish his 1982 monograph, which contains fundamental criticism of PES.[11]

Most published PES is devoid of any interest. It seems appropriate to concentrate upon just two political economists, who were both born during the Stalinist revolution, studied – one in Moscow, the other in Leningrad – during the last years of Stalin's rule, and later rose to leading positions within the party and state apparatus. Vadim Andreevich Medvedev was born in 1929, graduated from Leningrad State University in 1951 and pursued an academic career in Leningrad until 1968. Then he changed over to a party career, serving as deputy chief of the Central Committee Department of Propaganda in 1970–8 and Rector of the Central Committee Academy of Social Sciences in 1978–83. After a short period as chief of the Department for Science and Educational Institutions of the Central Committee, he was made a Central Committee member and Secretary in 1986. He was for two years responsible for party relations with other communist parties of the Soviet bloc. Finally, in 1988, he became a full member of the Politbureau and Chairman of the Ideological Commission of the Central Committee. Medvedev was thus formally the main ideologist of the Soviet Communist Party, and he was therefore forcefully criticised by conservatives at the 1990 congress of the party.

Medvedev has been – if one neglects Andrei Gromyko, the long-time Foreign Minister, who had a doctorate in economics but was primarily a diplomat – the first economist member of the Politbureau since Bukharin, Sokolnikov and Voznesenskii, who were all executed under Stalin. He is, one should emphasise, a scholar with real credentials within PES. His election as a corresponding (non-voting) member of the Academy of Sciences was justified on academic grounds. Politically, he seems to occupy a place in the middle ground of the present Politbureau.

Leonid Ivanovich Abalkin, our second example, was born in 1930. He graduated from the Plekhanov Institute of National Economy in Moscow in 1952 and has pursued an academic career since. In the late seventies, he worked under Medvedev in the Central Committee Academy of Social Sciences. In 1986 he was appointed the new head of the Academy of Sciences Institute of Economics. His task was to transform this bastion of conservative PES into a supporter of perestroika. In 1989 Abalkin was made Deputy Prime Minister, responsible for economic reform within the Soviet government. Abalkin has been involved in policy formulation since the seventies.[12] He has reputedly been one of Gorbachev's close advisors since his ascension to power. Ideologically, he has been probably the dominant political economist in the country since the early seventies.

It is intriguing to note that the political position of leading Soviet academic economists has during the Gorbachev years become incomparably stronger than it ever was before. Academician Abalkin is Vice Prime Minister and academician Shatalin became in March 1990 a member of Gorbachev's presidential council. Corresponding member of the academy Medvedev has been a member of the Politbureau, and Petrakov, another corresponding member of the academy, was made in 1990 a personal adviser to Gorbachev. Other economists, among them academician Bogomolov, corresponding-member Bunich and Professor Popov, are active in parliamentary politics. While Soviet economic bureaucracies continue to be dominated by non-economists, the political process involves perhaps more leading professional economists than in any other country.

Vadim Medvedev first caught wider attention with his 1966 book on the law of value and material incentives.[13] At the time it was something of a novelty to treat these themes together. Though Medvedev's book was published after the 1965 reform decrees, it had been for the most part written before them. It is not one of the great reformist books of the sixties. Still, well in line with the mildly reformist mainstream of the decade, Medvedev both warned against belittling the role of markets and the law of value and, at the same time, argued for the priority of planning. The existence of society-wide interests in addition to personal and collective ones gives the society its socialist character, Medvedev argued. On this basis he criticises Liberman for allegedly wanting to abolish all obligatory plan targets. Those, Medvedev asserted, are necessary for assuring the priority of society-wide interests. In this way Medvedev condemned in 1966 what was to become the defining feature of the 1968 Hungarian economic reform, the absence of obligatory plan targets.

Mevedev is thus methodologically an economic centralist. He is, however, not a proponent of the command economy. Rather his centralism is of the indirect, rationalising variety. In socialism, he wrote in 1966, commodity–money relations serve social goals because they are planned. Supply is planned, prices are set centrally and even demand is strongly influenced by governmental policies. During the seventies this view of commodity–money relations as 'planned socialist markets' became generally accepted in PES.[14] Abalkin, in particular, wrote much on the theme.[15] He has been even later much concerned with the characteristics of socialist markets.

The idea of planned socialist markets is an extreme instance of a wider argument which claims that 'socialist markets' are generally in some fundamental sense different from 'capitalist markets'. This kind of thinking has clearly made the acceptance of markets easier to many in the USSR. There is, however, a deep theoretical problem involved. This idea regards markets as a technical device which can be used and moulded as deemed necessary. Thus there have been arguments to the effect that socialist markets would only use positive sanctions, would be stable and free of arbitrage, traditionally defined as antisocial speculation in Soviet ideology. In short, socialist markets would make use of all the 'socially positive' functions of markets and leave their 'negative' properties – bankruptcies, unemployment, instability, rent-seeking and so on – to capitalism.

This is a naïve and mechanistic view of markets. According to an alternative view, which seems to be better founded, there cannot be capitalist or socialist markets. There are only markets which function with differential efficiency in different environments. By excluding negative sanctions like bankruptcies socialist markets condemn enterprises to dependence upon the budget or other financiers, and society to inefficiency. By condemning arbitrage Soviet ideology deprives markets of the so-called law of one price, one of the crucial efficiency properties of the market mechanism. The list could be continued. It was only in 1989 that Leonid Abalkin seemed for the first time to accept this argument.[16] It is possible to point to the specific features of the socialist market, he now wrote. 'But they are not determined by the market itself, but by its being a part of the socialist economic system.'

The idea of planned socialist markets has been dominant in Soviet PES since the sixties. There has been a small minority of economists like Stanislav Shatalin who have continuously argued that real markets cannot be planned.[17] This is the difference between markets and the 'commodity–money relations' of indirect centralisation. These are, as has been emphasised above, two different approaches which cannot be combined. In fact, Nikolai Petrakov[18] pointed out Medvedev's inconsistency. On one hand, Medvedev had accepted the existence of the law of value, profits and production for markets; on the other hand he wanted in one way or another to subject them all to administrative planning. This, Petrakov emphasised, is a contradiction. Still, such criticisms did not prevent the idea of 'planned socialist markets' from spreading.

Medvedev's 1966 book was relatively free from scholastic theorising for its own sake. Its approach was quite empirical, and Medvedev even used some elementary algebra. This was not a common feature in the PES of the sixties. Abalkin also favours empiricism over scholasticism. In 1971 he openly criticised the scholastic abstractness of PES. In his view, that was the main reason why PES had not been able to support the 1965 reforms with relevant proposals.[19] After some initial work on the economics of the 'world socialist system', Abalkin made the study of fundamentals of economic policy his speciality.

In his early work on socialist economic integration Abalkin tried to balance the Soviet long-term goals of joint planning and general political, economic and cultural uniformity between the socialist societies with an emphasis on the necessity to pay due attention to the sovereignty of the socialist states 'for the time being'.[20] In the distant future, Abalkin argued, all property in all the socialist countries would be in the same hands. Markets would be needed neither nationally nor internationally.[21] The transition to communism – as outlined in the 1961 programme of the Soviet Communist Party – would have taken place everywhere. That, however, was a matter for the future. It was only natural, Abalkin thought, that inside a single socialist state, the USSR, such processes were much further developed than between socialist countries of different levels of communist development. Either abstracting from agriculture or thinking with justification that there is no essential difference between state and collective farms, Abalkin argued that the uniformity of property was already a fact in the Soviet Union. There was only economically monolithic state property. That, he argued, made any market regulation of the economy both unnecessary and impossible.

This was to become a key argument in Abalkin's thinking until the late eighties. The monopoly of state ownership – itself understood as an axiom – necessarily implies centralised planning, he argued in a book published in 1970.[22] The state combines both political and economic power and is therefore necessarily the one and only centre of authority in the country. Such power cannot be shared with markets or any other possible centre of economic power, Abalkin argued.

This is an open attempt at apology for the totalitarian unity of economic and political power in traditional Soviet socialism. The phenomenon itself – the unwillingness of the totalitarian state to share its power with markets – is accurately described. In 1970 Abalkin clearly applauded it. In the late eighties he and other Soviet reformists advocated the introduction of markets and pluralism of ownership as a necessary part of democratisation. The linkage between ownership and power was again emphasised, but with a different sign.

Starting from monolithic state ownership is not the only possible way of finding arguments for traditional Soviet socialism. Another way of putting the argument, also used by Abalkin, is to proceed – in the same way as Medvedev did in 1966 – from the asserted primacy of alleged national interests, existing separately from and above individual and group interests. A variant of this argument was used by Abalkin as recently as 1987.[23]

In a 1971 book Abalkin defended the absolute primacy of state ownership in an even more explicit way. To give up state ownership, as some unspecified 'right-wing opportunists' had proposed, would in fact mean abandoning socialism, he then argued.[24] Still, Abalkin was not a conservative. His arguments have to be seen in their context. Abalkin has never stood out as an outright centralist among his fellow political economists. True, he has regarded planning as the 'mode of motion' of the socialist economy, but commodity–money relations are according to him its form. Neglecting the former takes one to market socialism, neglecting the latter to 'military-bureaucratic management' and an 'administrative regime'. In this way Abalkin presents himself as a man of moderation, a proponent of indirect centralism.

But what should indirect centralism mean in practice? As so often, Abalkin's remarks are again very cautious. He never tied himself to a particular framework or set of proposals. Furthermore, he has always shunned the doctrinal bickering so typical of many Soviet political economists. Such debates at least present an opportunity of seeing what a particular economist is against. Abalkin, however, has never engaged in such quibbling. To understand his interpretation of indirect centralism, one must start with what he says on the role of economic science in socialism.

Economics, as Abalkin sees it, has a special pragmatic responsibility in society. Researchers create some of the preconditions for successful policies. Whenever there are serious economic problems, something is probably wrong with the underlying economic principles as well, he conjectures. Decision-makers should listen to expert opinion – as Abalkin also advised Mikhail Gorbachev at the party conference of 1988 – but neither should scholars live in a social vacuum. The growth of knowledge is not a matter of 'proclaiming truths', but of 'advancing hypotheses and testing them empirically'.[25] Such testing – which was traditionally, one should emphasise, totally alien to PES which had always abhorred any infections of empiricism and had much preferred to proclaim truths – has many forms, Abalkin added. Modelling and experimenting are among them, but so also is learning from the experience of the New Economic Policy. Abalkin admitted that NEP as a period of transition from capitalism to socialism had primarily been a time of overcoming capitalism. This is the only content given to the New Economic Policy by Stalinist ideology. But NEP had also, Abalkin went on to argue, been a period of learning to master socialist economic principles, among them the use of commodity–money relations. In this respect NEP still had contemporary relevance. Although in a characteristically cautious way, Abalkin had thus joined those reformists who saw NEP as a model for the Soviet future.

This 1971 reference to NEP remained just a hint of how far Abalkin's reformism might reach in favourable circumstances. The core of his published thinking was different: a strong emphasis upon the primacy of state ownership and central planning together with indirect centralisation. This is worth emphasising for two reasons. Abalkin, with such ideas, was in the early seventies a relatively reformist political economist of the younger generation. In addition, it is only against this background that we can appreciate the profundity of theoretical change brought about by the *perestroika* period. Around 1970 Abalkin was praising the monopoly of state ownership and state power as the essence of socialism. Eighteen years later he set out only two criteria for the socialist character of institutional arrangements: they should enhance productivity, generate full employment and provide social guarantees, and exclude the exploitation allegedly imposed by private ownership over the means of production on wage-labour.[26] In the late eighties Abalkin argued for markets under socialism because they set the consumer free to choose and thus provided the necessary basis for personal development, a civil society independent of state power and democracy in general.[27] He had in mind not only the markets for consumer goods: the existence of markets for means of production, services, labour power and finance in no way contradicts socialism, Abalkin now argues.

The deepest change has taken place in his understanding of socialist property. In the sixties and early seventies, as seen above, Abalkin regarded the monopoly of state property as a historic achievement of socialism on the road to communism. In the *perestroika* period he started off by sharing – together with others such as academicians Shatalin and Bogomolov as well as Mikhail Gorbachev – the idea of state property as 'nobody's property', a system of organised irresponsibility.[28] Later he changed his mind: property always belongs to somebody, the one who can actually exercise property rights. In the case of state ownership the real owner, then, is the administrative apparatus.[29] Within the Marxist discourse this conjecture has important and somewhat obvious class theoretical implications, which Abalkin has elected to bypass publicly. Still, the inference is evident. Not only is the creation of an alternative centre of economic power – markets – possible, but it is also a necessary precondition for breaking the economic power monopoly of the apparatus. At the same time

Abalkin has demonstrated how this monopoly should also be attacked from other directions. Thus, there should be alternative proposals for policy decisions, not only prepared by the bureaucracy but also by the Academy and other institutions. And naturally, there should be a spectrum of different ownership forms, only excluding the pure capitalist one, private ownership with the employment of non-family labour. Deputy Prime Minister Abalkin oversaw in Autumn 1989 the preparation of a government proposal for a law of property with only this limitation.[30]

Another important theme to which Abalkin has returned repeatedly concerns the equilibrium of the economy. Here his views have been remarkably consistent. As early as 1971 he opposed the Stalinist dogma according to which excess demand, allegedly by 'driving production forward', is and should be a permanent feature of the socialist economy. He was not the first one to oppose this conception launched by Stalin himself in 1931. Still, his explicit linking of general excess demand to the preponderance of administrative management methods is notable.[31] Abalkin understood well that as long as the economy is plagued by excess demand, both goods and means of production have to be rationed. If that is not done by markets, it has to be done by a bureaucracy. Furthermore, Abalkin regarded the – as yet modest – increase in the savings of Soviet households in the sixties as evidence of the existence of such excess demand in the market for consumption goods.

It is debatable whether there was much actual excess demand in Soviet consumption goods markets as a whole in the sixties. There is, however, no doubt that the excess demand for resources – investment goods, raw materials and labour – within the state sector is an endemic property of traditional socialism. Abalkin did not have a theory of why this was so. He seemed to imply that it was simply a consequence of the Stalinist dogma mentioned. Even so, he had accurately perceived an existing problem which became a crucial issue when the equilibrium of the Soviet economy deteriorated seriously from the late seventies onwards. As early as 1981 Abalkin emphasised the existence of a dilemma.[32] On one hand, the presence of disequilibria required the use of administrative methods of rationing. Markets for most commodities, especially investment goods, did not exist. Existing markets usually had fixed prices incapable of matching supply and demand. With severe disequilibria any attempt to introduce markets and free prices would probably induce inflationary spirals. Therefore, commodities had to be allocated by bureaucracies using their own criteria of priority. This is, of course, the essence of traditional central planning, which is thus reinforced by the existence of excess demand. But, on the other hand, excess demand is not only the cause but also the result of the traditional economic system. The latter had, after all, brought the disequilibria about. Balanced development, Abalkin argued, was only possible within a reformed economy.

This, then, is Abalkin's reformist dilemma: disequilibria seem to make reforms both impossible and necessary. To break the deadlock Abalkin proposed the implementation of a programme of balancing at the same time as the introduction of economic reforms. This was not to be. On the contrary, by attempting growth acceleration together with reforms, the Gorbachev regime drove the Soviet economy into its worst disequilibrium and crisis in decades. Abalkin was surely not the only economist who understood well and immediately the incompatibility of growth acceleration and *perestroika* reforms. As we saw in chapter 2, academician Anchishkin warned against measuring reform success by growth rates as early as in 1967. Abalkin gave the economists' protests the best possible visibility by voicing them at the 1988 party conference. Still, it took more than a year before the government was ready to act. By this time the crisis was so deep that Deputy Prime Minister Abalkin could only propose a programme which at least temporarily repealed several of the decentralising decisions already taken.[33] The path outlined by academician Abalkin in 1981 no longer seemed open for Deputy Prime Minister Abalkin in 1989.

Abalkin has never shown much interest in the traditional debates or, indeed, in the traditional debating habits of the Soviet political economy of socialism. He has been willing to concede that PES already basically knows what the economic laws of socialism are. He has even gone as far as to accept the infamous 'law' according to which the output of capital goods should always increase faster than that of consumer goods. Whether he really believes in such laws or not, his point has been that economists should not waste time arguing about them. Their primary task, Abalkin has long claimed, is to study the economic mechanism, the concrete way in which economic laws are used in planning and management. This proposal is naturally in clear conflict with the way in which traditional political economists wanted to see the tasks of PES. For them, PES should stick to scholarly analysis of economic laws (as seen in chapter 1). What is more, Abalkin has argued that through such studies of the economic mechanism PES 'becomes more and more a theory of rational socialist economising'. In this way he had linked himself in 1973 to the same wide neoclassical mode of thinking about the socialist economy into which Bukharin, Voznesenskii and the optimal planners had also, each in their different ways, belonged.[34] Abalkin did not want to be a scholastic, he wanted to be a rationaliser.

In the 1973 book Abalkin had also, for the first time, outlined his own programme for the new phase of economic reforms which he saw approaching. The state, he argued, had to decide in a direct way about the main proportions of the economy. The geographical location of production, the wage and price systems to be used and a unified technological and financial policy should also be decided centrally. Keeping decisions over such matters in the hands of the state would prevent existing disequilibria from worsening, Abalkin argued, thus showing once more his concern for the way in which disequilibria lead to a command system.

A perfect centralisation, even using modern computers, was a utopia, Abalkin argued. There always had to be a degree of inbuilt self-regulation. Its limits, however, are still an open question, Abalkin admitted exactly in the same way as Katsenelinboigen and others had done a couple of years earlier.[35] Without originality, he supported all the standard Soviet reformist solutions ranging from the formation of associations to *khozraschet* on various hierarchical levels of the economy. When confronted by an interviewer in 1989 with the fact that the one Soviet ministry which had in principle been working on *khozraschet* since the early seventies had not done better than others, Abalkin referred both to its monopoly position and to the existence of disequilibria, and seller's markets.[36] This, too, is a measure of learning.

In many respects Abalkin's reform proposals of the seventies are in the reformist mainstream already discussed and therefore not of great interest. More original is his strong emphasis on the sociopsychological aspects of *perestroika* – a term which he had used already in 1973.[37] On the one hand, there exists a psychological barrier against reforms formed by the traditional modes of thinking. As we have seen above, Nikolai Petrakov was also worried about this in 1970.[38] On the other hand, and this was more important for Abalkin, a powerful 'human factor' based on a 'feeling of being the master' could be mobilised by creating conditions for 'real participation in production management'. The psychological barrier against reform should be neutralised and public opinion drawn onto the side of reform by three means: a wide availability of (truthful) information, the possibility of critical discussion and participation in management.[39] Some twelve years later, this was to be a crucial part of Gorbachev's early domestic policies.

The 1973 book just discussed is the most interesting of Abalkin's stream of publications. By then he had developed a position that has been often repeated since. New ideas were primarily added in a 1981 book, which is in many ways a companion volume to the 1973 monograph.[40] Both books argue for the practical usefulness of PES, oppose 'market socialism' for its alleged neglect of the assumed need for political guidance of the economy, argue for equilibrium as a necessary precondition for decentralising 'most'[41] economic decisions and also repeat many of the same concrete proposals. In 1981 Abalkin also used growth projections to argue that Soviet production could potentially grow by some 7 per cent per year. Laconically, he suggested comparing this with the growth rates actually achieved. When such a comparison is made, the result is, of course, that the gap between potential and actual growth rates had widened dramatically in the seventies. Abalkin did not have to say it; his every reader knew the basic facts.

Having thus substantiated the argument for further reforms Abalkin pointed out that partial reforms give temporary results, 'but mobilising deep-lying reserves and possibilities ... demands an integrated perestroika of all elements of the economic mechanism. This task is naturally much more complicated [than partial reforms] but the effect of such a perestroika is also more impressive and lasting.'[42]

Concepts like perestroika, glasnost and the human factor were thus integral parts of reformist PES years before Gorbachev came to power and made them the basis of his policies. This is an important part of the intellectual preparation for perestroika too often neglected by observers. Still, Abalkin's published writings from the seventies and early eighties do not add up to a coherent programme for economic reform. They are silent or very vague about how markets are created, about finances and price formation, foreign trade and the ownership structure. As just seen, early Abalkin had been clearly conservative concerning ownership issues. He did not return to the question until 1988. Abalkin was very conscious of the deterioration of economic equilibrium in the USSR and knew that any decentralising reforms are very difficult to implement in an excess demand economy. Still, it was Stanislav Shatalin who in 1981 proposed a ten-year programme for economic stabilisation.[43] Among the measures advocated by

Shatalin were some which have been adopted in 1988–9. They include the sale of housing stock to the population and charging a price for some of the services in education and medicine, which, so far, have been available free of charge.

The consistency of Abalkin's thinking up to the late eighties is remarkable. So also are his cautious and modest way of argumentation and reluctance to engage in polemics – often vitriolic in PES – with fellow economists. The same is also largely true of Vadim Medvedev. He has restated his fundamental centralism several times over the years. State ownership had to be given absolute primacy, he argued in 1976[44] adding also that socialism has to be analysed primarily as an administratively planned system based on 'scientifically substantiated commands [! – P.S.] from the centre on all aspects of enterprise activity'.[45] In the 1981 edition of the 1976 monograph the term command was substituted by the more neutral term signal.[46] Commodity–money relations, Medvedev has repeated over the years, are superficial by comparison with basic administrative planning. Their temporary necessity is caused by such factors as the continued existence of non-state ownership in agriculture and of small-scale industry as well as by remaining deficiencies in computing.

Fundamentally Medvedev was a centralist, even a proponent of command economy, in the sixties. He was still one in the eighties. He explicitly argued in 1980 that the scope of commodity–money relations would get narrower as society matures towards communism.[47] In this 1980 book, which is a sadly typical treatise of the Brezhnevite ideology of developed socialism, Medvedev also argued for state control over the way in which human needs change over time. The new Soviet man should thus to a degree be a creation of the state. Such views seem a far cry from the humanistic socialism which Mikhail Gorbachev wants to create.

But, on the other hand, Medvedev has also argued that as long as commodity–money relations are necessary, they have to be used, and used in a better way than before. In particular, Medvedev was not only one of the foremost proponents of the ideology of developed socialism but is also an expert on the failures of the 1965 Kosygin reform. He has devoted many pages to analysing it. The reform failed, he admits. The consequences of that failure can be seen, Medvedev says, in the way in which efficiency growth first slowed down and then turned negative in the seventies. He has published calculations which show this.[48] Still, he argued in 1981 – as a man in his position would do – that any talk of an economic crisis in the USSR was mere capitalist propaganda without any true foundations.

Medvedev has put forward several reasons for the failure of the 1965 reform. First of all, it did not address the basic problem of disequilibrium. Here Medvedev shares Abalkin's basic concern. But there had also been too little real enterprise independence[49] and various mistakes in government policy.[50] In general, Medvedev argued in his 1983 book, the lessons of the 1965 reform had been studied all too little in the USSR. This is certainly true, but it is also true that the Soviet Union cannot have many better experts on this particular failure that Medvedev himself is.

As a rationalising centralist Medvedev has been, especially in his 1976 book, a strong advocate of the use of optimal planning techniques. In the early seventies party publications defended these methods against the vehement attacks of Gosplan planners. Both Medvedev himself – as a deputy chief of the Central Committee Department of Propaganda – and V. S. Dunaeva, an economist working in the Central Committee Academy of Social Sciences[51] tried to show how some of the new concepts introduced by the optimal planners could be reinterpreted and integrated into PES. In 1974 the then chief of the Central Committee Department of Science, the arch-conservative S. P. Trapeznikov, even said that the existing level of PES was so low that attempts to create a new PES – as had been done by the Sofeists – were totally understandable, even if they had also failed.[52] When the future of economic research was discussed in the Academy, Pyotr Fedoseev, the conservative philosopher and deputy chairman of the Academy of Sciences, poured a veritable shower of scorn over the conservatism of political economists. Fedoseev's programmatic statement, almost certainly prepared with the assistance of the Central Committee Department of Propaganda and thus Medvedev, is worth citing at some length, as his attack sums up well the real mediocrity of conservative PES. Medvedev must certainly have agreed, whether he had written the text or not:

there are still a certain number of economists who have not been able to reorient themselves in the new circumstances ... Some of these 'theoreticians' often take a dogmatic attitude toward the work that is done by economists belonging to different streams within our economic theory and practice. Hearing the word 'goal', they are ready to shout: 'that is teleologism'; the term 'consumption' they immediately associate with vulgar political economy; and anyone who mentions 'utility' is at once condemned as 'resurrecting the work of Boehm-Bawerk, the theory of marginal utility', and so on.

Such an approach is, in our opinion, not constructive and indeed hinders the development of economics. . . . It must be understood that certain categories, only used for the purpose of apology for capitalist relations by bourgeois economists, have an important role in the planning and in managing the economy of the new society.[53]

One should not, however, reach the conclusion that the party economists were willing to accept all the conclusions drawn by the SOFE group. As a offer of truce, Dunaeva's book set tough conditions. In particular, Sofeists had to accept the existence of all the economic laws declared by PES. All decentralising interpretations of the optimal planning paradigm were also to be abandoned.[54] Medvedev has been also a rationalising centralist, not a proponent of markets. He has complained about the lack of interest shown by the political economists in developing the correct Marxist interpretation of optimising in the socialist economy. At the same time he has repeatedly rejected such market-oriented interpretations of the optimal planning approach as Volkonskii in particular has advocated.

Medvedev's interpretation of Kantorovich and Novozhilov is strictly in the indirect centralisation tradition. He argues that developing optimal planning and management means strengthening, not weakening centralism.[55] Even capitalism, he has claimed, is progressing because of the various regulations that constrain markets, not due to any free play of market forces. Seen from this perspective of state-monopoly capitalism there would thus be no sense whatsoever in trying to constitute free markets in socialism. Competition as such is alien to socialism, Medvedev argued in 1976, as all enterprises are owned by the state, which also determines the volume of their production, proceeding from an optimal plan.[56] Commodity–money relations have to be developed, but they must also be submitted to central planning. Socialism, seemingly by definition, precludes the selling and buying of labour power, private production as well as any uncontrolled markets for the means of production.[57]

To conclude, Medvedev has been rightly worried about the declining efficiency growth of the Soviet economy. Many of his books contain discussions on current technological developments, as befits one who used to teach at the Leningrad Institute of Rail Transport as well as the more prestigious Leningrad Technological Institute. As early as 1981 he wrote that a 'serious *perestroika* of the economy and methods of management [as well as] the very psychology of economic behaviour is needed'.[58] But, he also added, those changes were not needed because what existed was 'mistaken or bad, but because the objective conditions of economic development are changing'.

Medvedev's 1983 book[59] has been called the original reform programme of *perestroika*.[60] While it is clearly an exaggeration to say that the book was written 'in a liberal spirit' – it is not about a reduction in the role of state *vis-à-vis* society – it is true that the book contains most of the ingredients of Gorbachev's early policies. In particular, there is a strong emphasis on the democratisation of management and on organisational change in general. It is also obvious that book was intended as a programmatic statement. Medvedev was clearly hurrying to finish the monograph, and relied upon his earlier books to the extent of lifting whole central passages from them. And, of course, just having been moved from the Academy of Social Sciences to the position of chief of the Central Committee Department of Science and Educational Institutions, he was in a political position to make a statement that would be listened to. During the Andropov interlude such statements were in demand. His proposals were not, however, wholly his own. He had been working with Abalkin, whose approach in the seventies was clearly more decentralising than Medvedev's, for many years. He was apparently also well connected with academician Abel Aganbegyan, who thanks Medvedev in the foreword to his 1979 monograph on enterprise management.[61] It is therefore no wonder if Moscow reform economists 'tend to look upon Medvedev as "their man" in the political leadership'.[62] He was after all the first economist in the Soviet Politbureau since Voznesenskii.

But if Medvedev's 1983 book is taken as the original reform programme of *perestroika*, we should note that it has both decentralising and centralising features. Thus, Medvedev proceeds – as he has always done – from the primacy of state ownership and national interests. He even thinks that the scope of planning tends to broaden, primarily to cover demographic processes and the mobility of labour. He advocates supporting private plots, but only so that their linkages with the socialist sector may be strengthened. He emphasises the importance of preventing their transformation into genuine private production for markets. Furthermore, he argues for creating new inter-branch management bodies after the model of the agro-industrial complex. At the same time he calls for 'preserving branch management to the degree it is necessary and still has a positive effect on the economy' – a true politician's statement. Medvedev is very explicit about the damage caused by disequilibria to consumers, technical progress and the possibilities of decentralisation. He advocates using prices and other demand constraining measures for attaining equilibrium. At the same time he strongly supports centralised price setting. Medvedev also rejects the Hungarian economist Janos Kornai's arguments on the deep changes in the whole economic mechanism needed for attaining equilibrium. He is absolutely against using the threat of unemployment as a disciplining device. Real participation in decision-making is to Medvedev the right way to nurture 'the feeling of being the master of production, to root responsibility and social identification with its results [to develop] a conscious relation to work and social property'. Without that, the transition to intensive growth, 'justly called the second industrialisation of the country', would be impossible.

But probably more important than these particular issues is the fact that Medvedev called openly as early as 1983 for the creation of a new conception of the economic system of socialism. It would have to meet two crucial demands, both by and large defined as negations of traditional PES.[63] The new conception should be based on the experience of different socialist countries and thus avoid the earlier absolutism of Soviet experience as the guideline for the rest of the world to follow. Also, it should not stop at abstract generalities. The new conception of socialism should be concrete enough to allow for the derivation of policy principles. Scholars should thus be able to play a genuine policy-forming role.

Developing the new conception of socialism is the main task Medvedev had as Chairman of the CPSU Ideological Commission since 1988. In his maiden speech in this new capacity Medvedev referred to the new conception as being basically that of Lenin in relation to the New Economic Policy.[64] This proposition, widely discussed in the USSR before and after Medvedev's speech, is meant to have three important ideological implications. First of all it searches for a true Leninist legitimation for the policies of *perestroika*. The Lenin now referred to is not the believer in the Kautsky-Lenin single factory image of the socialist economy. Nor is he the Lenin of War Communism, but that of the early twenties, who had in one of his last writings mentioned the need for 'a change in our whole view of socialism'.[65] Unfortunately he never said what the new view might be; but change from the single factory image can hardly be in any other direction than towards decentralisation and markets. Gorbachev has used this perspective when he has alleged that *perestroika* means fulfilling Lenin's testament.[66]

The second ideological message contained in the parallel between *perestroika* and the Lenin of the early twenties is that Stalinism is a deviation from the true socialist principles of Lenin's last writings. This was argued by a few reformists like Gennadi Lisichkin in the sixties, but now it has become the official party line. Finally, the new approach is meant to defend Lenin and the founding Marxists against accusations of being the fathers of Stalinism and the command economy.

The Medvedev–Gorbachev interpretation of the relationship between Marxism, Lenin, Stalin and Soviet society is of course neither the only possible one nor intellectually the most compelling one. On the one hand, its mere existence shows the degree to which the USSR is still an ideological state. On the other hand, it at least admits the existence of historical alternatives, something which the rigid historical schemes of Marxism–Leninism, with its objective laws, has always attempted to deny. In this sense it is not only concerned with the correct model of socialism but is also philosophically directed against the very foundation of PES.

Even before becoming the Communist Party ideology chief Medvedev had the opportunity of shaping PES in an official capacity.[67] Political economy textbooks have always had a disproportionally important position in the USSR. They have been both regarded as a crucial way of educating young people and stating the commonly accepted view on various theoretical issues. Even if there has not been an official monopoly textbook of PES since the early sixties, any textbooks to be used still have to be accepted by the relevant ministry.

Because none of the existing university textbooks were regarded as satisfactory, the Ministry of Higher Education took the somewhat exceptional step of organising an open competition for PES textbook manuscripts in 1983–6. None of the manuscripts submitted corresponded with the new requirements of the Gorbachev period. Consequently, the ministry appointed a group of prominent economists to write the new textbook. Medvedev was the nominal head of the team, while Abalkin and Abel Aganbegyan reportedly did most of the work. The manuscript was widely discussed in Soviet economic journals. It was received with mixed feelings. While progress was noted – especially as far as the treatment of capitalism was concerned – many commentators were disappointed by the relative proportion of new and old. Abalkin, who has defended the book – since published[68] – as a compromise, has in spite of that argued that no further textbooks should be written, as that might give the opponents of *perestroika* an opportunity to disseminate their views.[69]

Such a relic of the old ways of ideological policing is bound to fail under *glasnost*. In fact, while the writing of the Medvedev textbook was in progress, various authors from TsEMI were producing their own monograph-length view on the foundation of PES.[70] The writing of another textbook, this time especially for the students of economics faculties, is under way with heavy participation from Sofeists. Academician Shatalin, who has been in various ways campaigning for the comeback of SOFE, has argued that in this textbook SOFE should be presented as the core of PES.[71] Others disagree. A. Ryvkin, in particular, has claimed that he has been able to detect the rise of a new economic mythology, based upon SOFE and guiding many people's thinking about economic *perestroika*. The normativeness of SOFE, Ryvkin argues, makes it totally inappropriate for tackling the tasks ahead.[72]

Whatever one thinks about the relative merits of PES and SOFE, a conspicious feature of present-day debates in Soviet theoretical political economy is the fact that they have been almost exclusively carried on by economists who rose to prominence in the sixties. This is an advantage to the extent that such people have the experiences of the failed reforms and conservatism of the sixties and the seventies fixed in their minds. But it is much more a weakness, because they are carrying a huge burden of outdated doctrine. Sooner or later, a generational change is going to take place. Whether that will mean a renewal of Marxism, as Soviet ideologists now want, or its rejection as has happened in Eastern Europe – remains to be seen. One thing, however, has hopefully been made clear by the preceding discussion. The Soviet political economy of socialism is not in a position to be a guideline in reforming socialism in the direction of a market economy. It is fundamentally a quasi-science, an ideology developed to justify the existing institutions of traditional Soviet socialism. As such it has a conservative influence upon people's thinking. Even in the hands of reformists political economy will not give impulses to change, but it can itself be remoulded to give ideological legitimation to new institutions as long as such ideology is deemed necessary. Because of its quasi-scientific scholasticism, political economy may actually have a considerable flexibility. Abalkin had no great problem in evolving from an apologist of state property to a critic of ministerial ownership. If an ideological justification for private property under socialism were needed, it could be delivered easily. One only needs to condemn ministerial property as exploitation and argue that joint stock companies are, as voluntary associations of free individuals, the most socialist of all possible institutions.

The Novosibirsk Institute of Industrial Economics

The Siberian Branch of the Soviet Academy of Sciences was founded in the late fifties to serve several purposes. It was to help in opening up the riches of Siberia and the Soviet Far East as the new frontier. It was also intended to serve as a model for overcoming the traditional gulf between Soviet fundamental research on one hand and industrial innovation and university education on the other hand. The branch was not situated in a big city, but in a specially built academic town, Akademgorodok, outside Novosibirsk. The town was complete with institutes, housing, services, a university and facilities for experimental production. And, finally, because the branch was new, well-equipped and far from Moscow, it also served as the base for directions of research not favoured in the old centres of Moscow and Leningrad. Genetics, cybernetics and mathematical economics were all strongly represented from the very beginning.

Over the years the original attraction of Akademgorodok started to fade.[73] The drawbacks of a relatively small and tightly-knit community far from Moscow soon caused return migration to Moscow. Among prominent economists, Leonid Kantorovich returned quite early, V. L. Makarov (the present head of TsEMI), Abel Aganbegyan and Tatyana Zaslavskaya only recently. These are the names that have made Novosibirsk economics famous. Abroad, the Novosibirsk Institute of Industrial Economics (IEiOPP – the Institute for the Economics and Organisation of Industrial Production, as the institute is officially called) has been known primarily for three reasons. Two of them are leaked documents. The first dates from 1965.[74] In a confidential speech Abel Aganbegyan, then one of the angry young men of Soviet economics, painted a depressing picture of the true state of the Soviet economy. Standards of living were declining, industrial structure was outdated, unemployment a reality and the quality of plans dismal. There were, Aganbegyan argued, three reasons for this state of affairs. The burden of military outlays was huge, agriculture neglected and – what is most important – the economic system antiquated. It was both extremely centralised and undemocratic. Aganbegyan's analysis was at the time the most outspoken yet to come from a Soviet economist.

The other leaked Novosibirsk document attracted even greater attention. In 1983 the Western press published a paper by academician Tatyana Zaslavskaya, prepared, as was soon found out, for a Novosibirsk conference.[75] The 'Novosibirsk report' was seen as a sensation and was taken to imply that Yuri Andropov, then the Communist Party Secretary General, had authorised a radical search for alternative solutions for the Soviet economy. In actual fact, Zaslavskaya had only little to say in her paper about the form of a possible future economic reform. As an economist-cum-sociologist she was more interested in a description of the existing Soviet social structure and its implications. The 'Novosibirsk report' made three important points which had not been touched upon before in Soviet debates. It is important to note that they were not scholastic arguments, but based on empirical social research. Zaslavskaya argued that Soviet society should be described as consisting of 'class-groups' with potentially conflicting interests. It was not homogenous. Neither were existing interests automatically harmonious or subordinated to some putative social or society-wide interests, as political economists like Abalkin and Medvedev argued. The basis for genuine political struggle therefore existed in Soviet society. Secondly, Zaslavskaya argued that the opposition to economic reforms was concentrated on the ministerial level of the administrative hierarchy. The highest level of the social hierarchy as well as enterprise managers and skilled workers were either proponents or supporters of reform. To eliminate ministerial resistance they would have to join forces. Finally, Zaslavskaya concluded that the traditional economic system had been suitable for the commandeering of an uneducated and passive population but was not appropriate for managing modern working classes with their own goals and interests.

Zaslavskaya's findings, which were presented in more detail later, are actually quite controversial. They neglect the immensely important regional and national dimensions of Soviet society. Furthermore, Zaslavskaya simplifies matters by failing to pay sufficient attention to the fact that people will have different interests *vis-à-vis* various facets of distinct reform alternatives. A market creating reform is a different matter from indirect centralisation. People will have different attitudes towards the possibilities and responsibilities, even threats, created by change. Zaslavskaya's 1983 arguments were thus quite crude, but they were a surprise, as it was at that time not even generally understood outside a narrow circle of specialists that empirical studies of social structure are being carried out in the USSR. And what was even more important, they showed that economic reform, even in the Soviet Union, is envisaged as a matter of political struggle, coalition formation and neutralising of opponents. This was one of the lessons learned from 1965.

Aganbegyan and Zaslavskaya are two of the reasons which have made the name of the Institute of Industrial Economics. The third reason is the journal it publishes. The fame of Novosibirsk economics as practically oriented, empirically based and at least potentially reformist has been much strengthened by *EKO*, the popular Soviet economic monthly published since 1967. *EKO* has much the largest printing of any economic journal in the USSR, it has published more reformist articles during the past twenty years than anybody else, and its articles, whether practical or theoretical, are accessible and lively. By no means all the articles have been written in Novosibirsk. Some of the important reformist statements have been in fact by Moscow-based scholars. But still it is the background of empirical Novosibirsk economic and sociological research that has provided many of the arguments for reform used by Aganbegyan and Zaslavskaya in the eighties.

This orientation has been made possible by the responsibility the Institute has for studying the economic and social problems of Siberia and the Soviet Far East. Most of the results concerning Novosibirsk industry or Altai agriculture are easily generalisable to the USSR as a whole. Moscow institutes have usually been prevented from doing, or at least from publishing, such research. This helped Aganbegyan and Zaslavskaya to play an important role during early *perestroika*, when Aganbegyan became known as Gorbachev's chief economic adviser and Zaslavskaya was also reputed to be a member of Gorbachev's informal 'kitchen cabinet' or brains trust.[76] It is still uncertain to what degree such a kitchen cabinet really existed. Zaslavskaya has stated that she met Gorbachev only rarely, and Aganbegyan has recently emerged as a critic of the way in which economic policy was elaborated in the early *perestroika* years.[77] Still, there is no doubt that there was an influence. This was especially clearly seen in the ill-fated marriage of growth acceleration and reform.

The modelling of Soviet long-term development has traditionally been an important part of Novosibirsk research. The Novosibirsk analyses on the reasons for growth slowdown have had an important role in Aganbegyan's advocacy of economic reform.[78] His repeated arguments for the policy of *uskorenie*, growth acceleration, in the early eighties were clearly influenced by the work by Boris Lavrovskii, a Novosibirsk economist, on investment, capacity utilisation ratios and related matters.[79] Lavrovskii argued that the growth slowdown was caused by bottlenecks due to insufficient investment and excessively high capacity utilisation ratios. Another Novosibirsk economist, Konstantin Valtukh, presented calculations which told of a deterioration in Soviet productive capacity and advocated sharply increased investment.[80] This is also the background for Aganbegyan's concern for the technological level of Soviet industry. As Aslund has pointed out, Gorbachev's important June 1985 speech on scientific-technical progress follows closely Aganbegyan's line of argument.[81] Aganbegyan later confirmed that he was involved in preparing the early Gorbachev policies on technology and growth acceleration.[82] These policies both failed to reach their objectives and actually contributed to the deterioration of economic equilibria which by 1989 threatened the future of Gorbachev's reforms.

The third main area in the work of the Novosibirsk institute is multi-level planning models.[83] In this area IEiOPP, like TsEMI, is a follower of the optimal planning approach, and the work of the institutes has in some respects been competitive. Of more importance, probably, is the fact that there is a common theoretical background for the modelling work in both institutes. Perhaps even more explicitly than in Moscow, the conclusions drawn in Novosibirsk from the optimal planning algorithms diverge. At the one extreme, there is Konstantin Valtukh, who has been arguing since the sixties for a centralising interpretation of optimal planning and computers.[84] In the seventies, he emerged as a critic of the market-oriented SOFE of Petrakov and others, and has in the eighties repeatedly argued for the need to increase centralised investment. In 1989 he condemned outright the political decision to favour consumption at the expense of investment.[85] An intermediate position has been taken by David Kazakevich, whose mainstream interpretation of the optimising approach was sufficient to raise the conservative wrath of the Gosplan journal in 1981.[86]

The radical wing of the Novosibirsk institute was, until his death in 1987, occupied by Raimundas Karagedov. During the seventies he emerged as the most prominent – perhaps even the only prominent – proponent of a Hungarian-style economic reform in Soviet economic discussion. As early as in 1974 he argued that the new Hungarian system had proven its feasibility, enriched socialist economic theory and had both a future and an importance which 'reaches beyond the frontiers of that country'.[87] Two years later he pointed out one important reason why the Hungarian reform had survived while the Kosygin reform had failed. The latter had only changed the means by which enterprises are guided. The former was better integrated: it also changed the economic mechanism itself. In general, Karagedov argued, one cannot at the same time both decentralise and increase the degree of centralism, as Soviet theories of indirect centralisation had claimed. Two institutions cannot have the same decision-making powers at the same time. Either the enterprise or the planners have to take the genuine resource allocation decisions.[88] This is the simple point that Soviet theories of indirect centralisation have consistently overlooked. Trying to have the enterprise itself find ways of making the decisions that the centre wants it to make – the central goal of indirect centralisation – does not really mean increasing enterprise authority.

Karagedov made no secret of his preference for the Hungarian model even at a time when the Hungarian economy was drifting into increased difficulties, which were used by conservative Soviet economists as arguments against a market-oriented reform.[89] Aganbegyan noted this preference in his preface to Karagedov's 1979 monograph, but also added that this view neglected the importance of 'direct centralised management as the leading link in the economic mechanism of socialism'.[90] Aganbegyan was in the late seventies himself surely more radical than the average Soviet economist. This was seen in his insistence upon full *khozraschet* for enterprises, not for the monopolistic ministries. He also took a positive attitude to East European reforms, understood the necessity of price reform, argued for increased foreign trade as well as for a market for the means of production, and furthermore emphasised the role of credits in financing.[91] But still he distanced himself from the Hungarian model and was not in 1979 ready to abolish all obligatory plan indicators, as Karagedov was. Such disagreements within the Novosibirsk institute did not prevent Karagedov from emerging as a central Novosibirsk spokesman on economic reform in the early eighties. He directed the surveys made of Siberian enterprises which participated in the so-called Andropov economic experiment started in 1984, and underlined very explicitly the partiality and therefore insufficiency of this experiment.[92] He also outlined a short sketch of a comprehensive economic reform.

Karagedov knew both Western economic theory and Hungarian literature exceptionally well. His 1979 monograph is a tour de force, a survey of relevant Western literature on welfare economics and market failures. He was also the first one to present the views of Janos Kornai, the noted Hungarian economist, on the shortage economy, for Soviet readers.[93] He had shown as early as the late sixties that he did not believe in the direct applicability of simple theorems of market optimality. He also knew that the Hungarian reform model had not succeeded in rationalising enterprise behaviour, as soft budget constraints were still present in the system. Still, Karagedov's point of reference for the future Soviet economic reform remained the original Hungarian model of 1968. The Hungarian reform had abolished obligatory plan targets, simplified the ministerial system and liberalised a part of the price system. Following the Hungarian model, Karagedov attacked the position of the ministries and proposed a three-tier system consisting of a ministry of industry, a few subordinate ministries for the large industrial complexes such as energy and transport, and enterprises with wide-ranging powers of operational decision-making. No obligatory plan indicators would be used in his preferred economic model. The formation of medium-size and small enterprises – among them cooperatives and those 'based on personal initiative' – would be encouraged to create conditions for competition. The possibility of bankruptcy would exist.[94]

Unfortunately, Karagedov's proposals were left on a very general level. As happened with other economists of the late seventies and early eighties who had been convinced of the importance of changing the system of branch ministries, his short discussions tended to concentrate on organisational matters. The more narrowly economic issues tended to be relatively neglected. Thus, Karagedov said that the *khozraschet* rights of the enterprises should be created on all dimensions of their activity, including investment and foreign trade. On the other hand he is against leaving 'the most important goals of state economic policy' dependent upon the market. There should still be direct planning and administrative control over investment, income formation, foreign trade, currency and finance. Furthermore, the rights of enterprises should be greatest in consumer goods production, less in other areas. What all this might mean in practice, Karagedov left open. In Hungary, a small country with relatively few state enterprises, an attempt to combine markets and planning in very much the same way as Karagedov proposed for the USSR had in practice led to general informal control of enterprises by the centre. Such an outcome would have been impossible in a huge country like the Soviet Union, but Karagedov neglected the possible consequences of the size difference for the theoretical Hungarian model.

The Novosibirsk record on reformism is thus heterogeneous. Not only were different views in existence within the institute, but Aganbegyan also seems to have acted – as surely did other institute directors as well – as a filter for those opinions that were allowed to be presented outside the institute. Thus, in the early seventies Stanislav Menshikov, a leading Soviet econometrician of the world economy, who at that time worked at the Institute of Industrial Economics, forecast that by the early nineties Japan would have surpassed the USSR in per capita production levels: 'I was not believed and my naive proposal to inform our highest establishments, to warn of such a danger was answered with the words, "That's all right, we'll manage somehow"'.[95] Such judiciousness was no doubt strengthened by the contemporary attacks, mentioned earlier, on other Soviet forecasts of growth slowdown.

We may note finally that due to its policy orientation the Novosibirsk institute also became involved in preparing projects and policies which in retrospect appear mistaken or at least debatable. Building BAM, the Baikal–Amur railroad, is one example, the abandonment of 'unviable' Russian villages another. Scholars may not have been the originators of such projects and may have resisted many of them, in particular the scheme for diverting Siberian rivers. Still, the opponents of the Gorbachev policies of modernisation have argued that people like Aganbegyan and Zaslavskaya are not 'morally entitled' to lead *perestroika* because of their alleged earlier support for 'antiscientific and antipeople' policies.[96]

Theorists of management

Karagedov's writings show on the one hand the Hungarian influence and on the other the importance attached to organisational reform. The ministerial branch management system, one of the defining features of the Soviet economic system, has been under attack since the fifties for creating branch autarky, serious problems in inter-branch coordination and technical progress, as well as immensely powerful vested interests. The 1965 reform was generally thought to have failed because it did not reform the administrative system above the level of the enterprise. Zaslavskaya's 'Novosibirsk report' of 1983 identified branch ministries as the conservative guardians of the existing system. Abalkin has more recently argued that due to their concrete economic power ministries are the real owners of the means of production in the Soviet Union.[97] A young scientist has even identified the bureaucracy as a parasitic class which has sabotaged and will continue to sabotage all attempts at economic reform.[98]

Theories of indirect centralisation had contributed to illusions about the possibility of increasing enterprise authority while at the same time maintaining centralisation. Most reformers of the sixties and seventies wanted, while preserving the hierarchical subordination of enterprises, to extend economic methods of management beyond enterprises to ministries and in some cases also to regional organs. The mistake of these proposals – common to the Sofeists, a political economist like Abalkin and a management specialist like Pavel Bunich – is easy to identify. Ministries do not constrain enterprise independence because they rely on administrative methods of management, but because they are hierarchically superordinate to enterprises and responsible for the performance of the branch as a whole. Whether such interference uses bureaucratic or economic (*khozraschet*) methods, is secondary. This was beginning to be understood in the late seventies, as Aganbegyan's opposition to ministerial *khozraschet* shows. Still, Karagedov's simple insight – power over a decision cannot reside in different hands at the same time – was not generally accepted. The old mistake of the indirect centralisation approach was once more repeated in the 1987 Law on the State Enterprise, which once again sought both to increase enterprise authority and to preserve the traditional hierarchical subordination.[99]

As Shatalin and others pointed out in a paper published in 1987, the medicine prescribed by the economists' proposals for ministerial *khozraschet* is worse than the disease.[100] Giving ministries further economic rights, while conserving their hierarchical status and position as a monopoly producer, means unleashing huge monopoly powers. Other proposals for attacking the position of ministries have been developed in Soviet management science. Itself only a loosely defined and heterogeneous field of study, management science has had in the USSR a history which in many ways parallels that of economics.[101] It also went through an innovative decade in the 1920s, was suppressed during the Stalinist decades, re-emerged in the fifties and developed into competing schools in the sixties. Given the role that the state management apparatus has within a hierarchically organised society it is not surprising that the boundary between management science and economics is uncertain. It would therefore be rather pointless to try a separate overview of the reform ideas of Soviet management scientists. Rather we will concentrate our discussion on two prominent management scientists who have made and continue to make an important contribution to Soviet reform debates. They are Boris Kurashvili and Gavriil Popov.

Boris Kurashvili is a legal scholar with the Institute for State and

Law of the Academy of Sciences in Moscow. He outlined in five
articles during 1982–5 the first published radical programme with
some degree of detail for Soviet economic reform.[102] Like Karagedov's, Kurashvili's proposals are largely based on the Hungarian
model, though Kurashvili has adapted his programme more specifically to the particular needs of the Soviet economy. He does not
believe in the possibility of marginally changing the branch management system, but proposes its wholesale substitution by a system
based on large production complexes.

Instead of some fifty all-union branch ministries existing in the
early eighties, Kurashvili's reform, as outlined in 1985, would leave
only seven. There would be separate ministries for fuel and energy,
communal economy and communications, transport, supply, planning and the defence sector; the rest of the economy would be
managed by a single ministry of the economy. The fuel and energy
complex and the defence industries would be managed in the traditional centralised way. The degree of centralism would be least in the
part of economy under the ministry of the economy. The latter would
engage in forecasting and aggregative planning, check the consistency of enterprise plans and guide the economy with economic
instruments, e.g. taxes, credits and pricing rules. Enterprises under
the ministry of the economy would have full *khozraschet* and wide
autonomy. They would plan their production pattern themselves. No
obligatory plan indicators would be given to these enterprises from
above.

Simultaneously with the reorganisation of the ministries, their per-
sonnel would be drastically reduced. This would not only economise
on resources but would also limit the physical scope of the ministries
for petty tulelage of enterprises. Not all power taken from the
ministries would be given to enterprise managers. Questions of
wages and employment would be decided on a self-management
basis. Employees would also select – subject to state confirmation –
the enterprise manager. Basic production assets have to remain state
property as this is one of the defining characteristics of socialism.
Kurashvili argued in 1989 that a democratic socialism is fully attain-
able without privatisation of enterprises, on the basis of leasehold.[103]

The differentiated approach to the economy makes Kurashvili's
programme well adapted to Soviet realities. Any Soviet government
will probably want to have basic energy production, transport
and the defence industries under central control. Kurashvili's programme meets this requirement of realism. On the other hand – and

understandably, coming from a legal scholar – the programme has very little economic detail. Kurashvili does not discuss the specific issues of foreign trade, agriculture and finance. Apart from some centrally set prices, he argues for contract pricing closely controlled by the state, but does not delve into the pricing principles to be used. He is conscious of the perils of monopoly, but does not focus on possible measures to further competition. He is not terrified by the prospect of unemployment, but does not explicitly discuss its relation to the self-management he proposes. His arguments on increasing the economic role of the regions remain inconclusive. And, finally, as already noted, Kurashvili does not propose any new pluralism of ownership forms: the creation of new enterprises remains 'basically' the prerogative of the ministry of the economy.

If Kurashvili's background as a management theorist is that of a legal scholar, Gavriil Popov, a professor of the Moscow State University, is an empiricist, who has been long involved in practical consultancy work.[104] Over the years, he has developed a consistent view on the organisational problems of the Soviet economy.[105] At an early stage he explicitly abandoned the Kautsky–Lenin single factory image of the socialist economy, and he has been a longstanding and trenchant critic of the Soviet branch-based management model. At the same time, however, he has supported the view that market mechanisms are only a temporary expedient in socialism. In general, he argued in 1974, the trend is towards less market, and it would therefore 'be a fundamental mistake to transform necessity into an aspiration and, proceeding from the temporary need for widening the sphere of value parameters, to propose a theory of real socialism, allegedly only possible as a market economy'.[106]

The Gavriil Popov of the seventies and the early eighties was a moderate reformer, who was inclined to look for solutions in reorganisations. Thus, in 1982 he argued for creating a new coordinating management level of super-ministries above the level of existing branch ministries.[107] The proposal was criticised by the more radical Karagedov and Kurashvili for actually increasing the problems of hierarchy by further complicating it.[108] This duly happened when the Gorbachev administration tried to solve the problems of interministry coordination by creating a new administrative level of Bureaus of the Council of Ministers above the level of the branch ministries. Such bureaus never had the powers that the superministries proposed by Popov would have had.

Popov's other proposals from the early eighties are more radical.

Thus, he advocated what amounts to private investment in the Soviet motor industry by selling to citizens securities which give the right to receive a car in the future. This proposal was finally accepted in 1989. Popov also argued in the early eighties in favour of ending the obligation on enterprises to find alternative employment for people they make redundant, and proposed the introduction of unemployment benefits.[109] Finally, in 1984, he emerged as a radical reformer by proposing a Hungarian-type reform for the USSR, involving the abolition of all enterprise plan targets set from above.[110] The enterprise plan would in his proposal be based simply on customer orders. Within enterprises, work would be divided among largely self-managing contract brigades. Price-setting would be decentralised to inter-enterprise contracts. The enterprise wage fund would be formed as a residual. This, Popov argued, would constitute true socialist distribution according to labour.

Gavriil Popov was thus already in 1984 approaching the leasehold solution which was in 1989 made the centre-piece of the Soviet economic reform. He has remained a foremost debater on Soviet history and the future of *perestroika* ever since. In 1988–9 he emerged as the foremost economist among the burgeoning radical opposition in the Soviet parliament. In 1990 he was elected as mayor of Moscow and after the July 1990 Communist Party Congress he became one of the prominent members of the Democratic Platform group to leave the Communist Party. The fact that he has increasingly tended to concentrate upon the politics of reform can be explained both by his background in management science and the particular interpretation of Soviet society that he has made extremely popular in the USSR (to be discussed in chapter 6).

Specialists on foreign countries

The USSR, as befits a superpower, maintains a large network of research institutes concentrating on the politics, societies and economies of foreign countries. The researchers in such Academy of Sciences institutes as The Institute for the Socialist Economic World System (IEMSS, under academician O. T. Bogomolov), The Institute for The World Economy and International Relations (IMEMO, under several directors, among them the later member of the Politbureau, Aleksandr Yakovlev, and the Deputy Speaker of the parliament, Evgenii Primakov) as well as The Institute for the Study of the USA and Canada (under academician Georgi Arbatov) have made important public contributions to Soviet debates on economic and political reform. This is especially true of IEMSS. Its director, academician Bogomolov has emerged as the most radical of top-ranking Soviet economists. Among the former or present researchers of his institute Gennadi Lisichkin and Otto Latsis have been highly visible reformers since the sixties, while Nikolai Shmelev (who has more recently worked at Arbatov's institute) has been the most debated economic writer of the *perestroika* period.

IEMSS has the task of analysing developments in other socialist countries, among them China as well as Hungary, where economic reform and debate on institutional change has gone much further than in the USSR. Analysing such developments offers an obvious basis for reform proposals for the Soviet Union. The interest of IEMSS scholars in comparative studies of socialism has taken another form, too. Several of them – Ambartsumov, Lisichkin, Latsis and Shmelev among them – were already discussing the mixed economy of the New Economic Policy of 1921–8 as an alternative model of socialism in the early eighties, when it was less than fashionable to do so.[111] Nikolai Shmelev caused a sensation when his *Novyi Mir* article of 1987 – reportedly the most read Soviet publication of the year – dismissed the whole rationale of collectivisation.[112] Gennadi Lisichkin used – somewhat surprisingly – the example of Poland in arguing for the efficiency of private small-scale agriculture.[113] Anatoli Butenko, another IEMSS scholar, criticised the 1961 party programme for seeing socialism as immature communism. This view, Butenko argued, had long legitimised the absolute priority of state ownership and served as a foundation for attacks against collective farm autonomy and private plots.[114]

IEMSS scholars have thus been prominent in promoting the pluralism of ownership forms. They have certainly not had a monopoly of such proposals. Leonid Abalkin's programme statement for a November 1986 conference on economic reform referred briefly to the need for it.[115] Still Bogomolov and his colleagues have emerged as the most outspoken proponents of ownership reform. In a series of articles and interviews in 1987 academician Bogomolov emphasised the need to introduce both private and cooperative enterprises into Soviet economy. He also drew attention to the multiple nature of property rights and in particular distinguished between the right to decide upon the use of an asset (the right of the *vladelets*, the possessor) and the right to derive income from an asset or to dispose of it (the rights of the *sobstvennik*, the owner proper).[116] Such distinctions are crucial for the leasehold or *arenda* proposal, which became the centrepiece of Soviet economic reforms in 1989.

Academician Bogomolov may in 1987 also have become the first to argue for outright privatisation of production assets in the Soviet press.[117] By 1989 such advocacy had become an almost daily occurrence. While Abalkin, the Deputy Prime Minister for economic reform, still rejects the private employment of non-family labour as exploitation, a group of radicals argue openly for private property. Among economists they include Bogomolov,[118] the agrarian academician V. A. Tikhonov,[119] Gavriil Popov[120] and Gennadi Lisichkin.[121] Some have joined Western neoconservatives in arguing that state owned enterprises are always less efficient than cooperatives and private enterprises.[122]

The issue of ownership reform is thus one in which Soviet specialists on foreign countries have used their expertise to push through radical proposals. The sequencing of the reform is another example of such influence. Academician Bogomolov, referring to the experience of Hungary and China, has long argued that a radical reform of Soviet society should start, as had been done in those countries, from agriculture.[123] This proposal is based on three seemingly indisputable facts: the existing resources are used exceptionally badly in agriculture; due to the importance of local factors, central commandeering is especially unsuitable to agriculture; and a rapid growth in agricultural production creates the necessary social support for reforms by increasing consumption levels. Other factors, however, have tended to invalidate the argument in the eyes of other economists. Soviet agriculture is notably more dependent on industrial inputs than either the Chinese or Hungarians were at the time the reforms were started; a large part of produce losses takes place outside agriculture proper, especially in storage and processing; rural infrastructure is totally inadequate and geared towards existing large-scale farming; and the enterprising strata of peasants was totally destroyed during forced collectivisation and the decades after it. Finally there has been much argument about the inclinations of Soviet, especially Russian, peasantry. While some argue that the individualistic practices of family farming would be just as applicable in Russia as in other countries, others claim in the Russian nationalistic vein that the collectivist traditions of the Russian countryside make any Westernising reforms impossible and indeed harmful.[124] A third view, the most pessimistic one, would say that after collectivisation the Soviet countryside has become *sui generis*, a demoralised and destroyed landscape with little innate power of development.

What is good for China and Hungary may thus not be good for Russia. Some aspects of the differences between the USSR and other socialist countries have long been emphasised in Soviet discussion. In particular, it has been traditionally argued that the huge size of the country, its superpower status, the importance of extractive industries as well as existing national divisions make a higher degree of centralisation necessary in the USSR than in smaller and more homogeneous socialist countries. This argument has contributed to what Hewett has called The cafeteria model of learning from other countries. Soviet economists have often argued for taking a little from the Hungarian experience, something from the GDR, something else from Bulgaria and so on.[125] Not only does such an approach neglect the fact that the resulting mixture is quite probably inconsistent; there has also been too little emphasis on learning about the crucial issues of systems design and strategy. Borrowing too easily concentrates on the more technical details of management and policy without a thorough consideration of why other countries have done what they did. This means that one easily borrows mistakes as well as successes. Many examples of this are pointed out in East European analyses of current Soviet reform efforts.[126]

One should finally emphasise that learning from other countries influences Soviet reform discussions in many ways that are difficult to pin down. For example, there is the possibility of an echo effect. People have for centuries used foreigners' opinions as a mirror for looking at their own society. The economist who is in words condemning the sovietologists' talk about an economic crisis in the USSR – or the views of the non-Bolshevik Soviet economists of the twenties on agricultural institutions – may in fact have wanted to make such interpretations better known in the USSR. Until *glasnost*, after all, any open advocacy of such views was impossible. It has been argued that after the Chinese reforms were started in 1979, Soviet conservatives cited Western appraisals of them to show the negative consequences of any change in a centrally managed economy, Soviet reformers to show the inevitability of reforming the centralised system in any country, including the USSR.[127]

In the same way, a discussion of Western welfare systems may have implied recommendations for the USSR and a description of democratisation in post-Franco Spain may have sought to chart the contours of future change in the Soviet Union. Discussions of the successes and failures of Third World industrialisation have had a direct relevance to the assessment of the over-all qualities of the Soviet model.[128] Finally, one should remember that even those economists who never wrote a word on foreign countries had information and opinions about them, even personal experience of them. Such influences are impossible to trace.

Furthermore, there is a complication which may be even more serious in the case of institutes involved in foreign policy issues than generally. As academician Bogomolov recently pointed out, during the Brezhnev years, when the possibility of open debate was small, an overwhelming part of those policy proposals which now seem relevant, could only be voiced in mimeos of extremely limited circulation.[129] Such memoranda are not available to an outside observer, and any speculation on their contents would be vain.

6   The age of *perestroika*

Stages of economic reform

In previous chapters, we have let the Soviet economists with their conflicting views and proposals occupy the scene. It is time to bring order into the discussion by offering a framework in which to situate the proposals aired during the last thirty years. At this point, a comparison with East European reform concepts is also useful. By setting Soviet discussions against the framework to be proposed and contrasting them with East European concepts, we can assess the degrees of radicalism and consistency in Soviet proposals. By doing this in the context of *perestroika* we hope to be able to provide an answer, even if only a tentative one, to the question posed in the first pages of the book: is the Soviet economics profession capable of meeting the challenge posed by the reform effort? Is the crisis of *perestroika*, so evident by 1989, due to following or to ignoring the advice of the economists? Is there any connection between *perestroika* and Soviet economics?

The Kautsky–Lenin single factory image of the socialist economy lies at the roots of Soviet economic thought. After the revolution, it was reconfirmed in the 1919 programme of the Bolsheviks and later formed the backbone of Stalinist economic thinking. As Gavriil Popov points out, Stalinist thinking on socialism had so much in common with the image of future society displayed in the 1919 programme that there was no perceived need to change the party programme until 1961.[1] More controversially, Popov thinks that the single factory model was also basically implemented in practice. This may or may not have been the case – we will come back to this issue – but either way our thesis stands: the single factory image was the model towards which the society was thought to be developing. It was the predominant normative model of socialism. Both the classical and the neoclassical approaches to the economics of socialism shared it. They only differed concerning the goals and ways in which the factory

130

should be managed. The classical approach saw the economy as a wealth-creating machine while the neoclassical approach concentrated on issues of efficiency.

The single factory model has important implications. First of all, it implies homogeneous ownership forms. Anything other than state ownership of the means of production is a relic which should disappear in time. This view was reconfirmed in the 1961 programme of the Soviet Communist Party. Second, the single factory model implies hierarchical planning and management from a single centre. There are higher bodies – usually branch ministries – to which enterprises are subordinated. Branch ministries, for their part, have their superiors in the planning commission, other central economic institutions and finally at the level of the highest political leadership. Third, though the factory may use money and prices as passive instruments of measurement and accounting, there does not seem to be any need for markets and active money. Fourth, there is no distinction between economic and political power, the state and civil society, the nuts and bolts of the mechanism and independent consumers. Fifth, there are no fundamental differences between industry and other sectors of society. They should be all basically organised in the same way.

If one accepts the single factory image as the underlying Stalinist normative model, one must also admit that the Khrushchevian changes did not touch upon the fundamentals of the model. As Anatoli Butenko, the reformist philosopher, has argued, the model was restated in the 1961 Party Programme as the proper set of characteristics of communism, which was thought to be achievable within one generation.[2]

This does not mean that the model had been absolutely immune to change. Various *economic policy changes* are possible and even unavoidable within the model. They range from shifts in investment allocation to the manipulation of wage scales and minor price changes. Sometimes such policy changes, especially those in investment allocation, are meant to reflect major evolution in leadership priorities and the environment of the economic system. Other policy changes are routine everyday decisions with little actual effect on the outcomes of the system. One can also think of changes in the fundamental underlying *goals* of the system. Whether forced growth, full employment or relative equity of open income distribution are pursued or not, is an important factor independent of the policies by which one tries to attain such goals. There may also be changes in the *techniques* of the system. A substitution of calculating plans with abacuses by the use of computers is an example of that. A change in techniques does not necessarily change in any way the functioning of the system. It may, however, have a perceptible effect on the outcome of the system if it is connected with goal alterations and policy changes of sufficient depth. Arguably, this is what the proponents of the neoclassical efficiency approach were originally aiming at. Their proposed strategic goals were efficiency and rationality instead of forced growth and arbitrariness. These goals were to be pursued both by changes in policies and planning techniques. By the mid-sixties, however, it was seen that mere change in policies and techniques was not sufficient for realising the change in goals. A reform of the economic system would be needed for that.

There are many ways of partitioning an economic system. Probably the simplest way to do so is to follow the economics textbooks by saying that an economic system consists of the decision-making system, the information system and the incentive system. In the single factory image the decision-making system is that of a hierarchy; the information system consists predominantly of vertical flows and incentives are tied to fulfilling given plans. A change in any of these parts of the economic system is an economic *reform*. A comprehensive reform changes all of these parts, a partial reform only one or two of them.[3] A reform may also be partial in the sense that its changes do not encompass all of the parts of the system as a whole. One might argue that the 1965 Kosygin reform aimed at changes in three areas: in decision-making, information flows and incentives. Still, it was a partial reform in that it tried to change only the enterprise level of the economic system.

Neither are the economic system, goals, policies and techniques independent of one another.[4] To a degree, the economic system has come about for the purpose of reaching given goals, while given policies serve – within the system – to maintain the system. Thus, it is apparently impossible to perform a market-oriented economic reform without relaxing the goals of absolute full employment and relatively equal open income distribution. The share of investment in national income is not only an issue of growth versus current consumption. Given the inefficiencies of the traditional system, a high share of investment is needed to keep the economy going. In an attempted transition to a market based economy large investments, in fact, only serve to conserve the old centralised system as long as they are channelled through industrial ministries.[5]

Socialist economic reforms are often discussed in terms of their effect on the degree of centralism in the system. Logically, an economic reform may imply either decentralisation or centralisation, and both kinds of possible reforms of the Soviet economy have been discussed in the literature.[6] Here, however, we adopt a different perspective. However much reform discussion, legislation and outcomes may have varied over time and place during the post-Stalinist period, an observer willing to abstract from the mass of interesting detail can in retrospect see a striking pattern.[7] Starting from the single factory model, reform discussions have gone through stages which have in fact meant incorporating more and more features of the capitalist market economy into the normative image of socialism. This dynamism is propelled by a search for economic efficiency.

The first stage – or actually pre-stage – of economic reform discussion attempts to rationalise the single factory model. Historically, the contrast between the classical and the neoclassical approaches to the economics of socialism is the core of this stage. The decades-long quest for better performance indicators or rules for centralised price setting also belongs to this stage. So does the original Kantorovich–Novozhilov interpretation of optimal planning as a basis for indirect centralisation. The perceived rationale of this approach, as seen in chapter 2, was to increase the degree to which the centre's preferences are implemented in the economy. The theory of optimal planning was not about marketisation or even about decentralisation in the real sense of giving enterprises a greater degree of freedom. Computers were supposed to simulate markets, to derive the set of optimal prices then to be handed down to the enterprises. The only freedom that the enterprises were to have was to search for themselves for the decisions the centre wanted them to make.

Relative to traditonal arbitrariness, such guidance might well enhance productivity, especially if it were linked to changes in the goals and policies to be pursued. It would, however, not abandon the single factory image of the economy. The only thing really to change in this respect is the way in which the enterprises are made to do what the centre wants them to. They are still seen as workshops in a single factory.

There are many reasons why such Stage 1 reform proposals have been found unsatisfactory. The expected reductions in bureaucratic costs are illusory, as the derivation of optimal shadow prices involves generally collecting and processing just as much information as the derivation of a plan in the traditional form of obligatory enterprise targets. Second, as was soon found out in the USSR, no plan can be more optimal than the information it is based upon, and in the indirect centralisation model enterprises continue to have many reasons for concealing their real production possibilities and resource needs. Third, the models involved in the original Kantorovich–Novozhilov approach were based on extremely crude assumptions about enterprise goals and worker motivation. They analyse optimal price setting in a static framework immensely better than traditional Soviet political economy could ever do, but do not even attempt to discuss the dynamic issues of entrepreneurship, genuine uncertainty and new information so crucial in market competition. Fourth, the models of indirect centralisation still leave enterprises subject to ministries, which are certain to continue their notorious petty tutelage of producers as long as they have both the possibility to do so and the responsibility for the development of 'their' branch as a whole. The main advantage expected from indirect centralisation, a more stable environment for the enterprises, therefore fails to materialise and indirect centalisation keeps collapsing back into the traditional command system. All in all, it is clearly not a feasible model of the socialist economy.

Some of these problems were addressed in the second stage of reform discussions. The huge size of the planning task and the existence of uncertainty were taken to imply that the centre should concentrate on deriving an aggregated plan which would then be disaggregated in inter-enterprise contracts. This was the approach proposed by SOFE in the late sixties. Another variant of the same idea proposed, as has been seen above, that the centre should only plan 'the most important' elements of production, give these goals to producers in the form of state orders, and let enterprises agree among themselves about everything else to be produced. In addition to state orders or an aggregative plan, enterprises would be guided by stable normatives and prices. In the state order variant, that part of inputs needed to meet state orders would continue to be centrally distributed. Otherwise wholesale trade of capital goods would take over.

The state order variant of Stage 2 was first advocated by Vasili Nemchinov in 1964. Later, it was developed by Nikolai Petrakov and other Sofeists. In the early eighties it became the favoured variant proposed by reformist economists. The economic reform programme accepted by the CPSU Central Committee in June 1987 was based on this thinking.

Proposals of the Stage 2 kind are supposed to have several advantages. Even in the aggregative planning version the state retains effective control over the basic proportions of the economy. In the state order version control over a definite element of production is of an immediate kind. Opting for it could be argued, for instance, on the basis of defence needs or existing disequilibria which allegedly make complete marketisation impossible.[8] The information overload on planners would be reduced, thus allowing for more consistent and rational plans. In the traditional system, as Petrakov has quipped, 'everything is planned! Still, there is no order.'[9] By attempting to plan a smaller proportion of total production, more order would be created. In fact, it has been often argued, the preferences of the planning centre would be better implemented in this system than under the traditional system.

Stage 2 is no longer in the single factory image. In fact Stage 2, especially in the aggregative planning version, can best be compared with a capitalist corporation. Ownership is still homogeneous and the basic hierarchy remains. Control over sub-units is exercised by a variety of means, including physical planning for a proportion of production. Other elements of sub-unit activity are monitored less closely, and there even may be markets and a degree of competition within the corporation.

The aggregative planning variant of the Stage 2 proposals was the one more frequently proposed in the seventies. Still, it was the state order variant which was finally selected in 1987. It was understood from the beginning that much depended on the way in which the two tracks, state order production and the rest of the economy, were to be delineated. Originally both planners and enterprise managers preferred to have as high a share of state orders in total production as possible. For the planners that maintained the illusion of managing the whole economy, for the managers it secured supplies of inputs not otherwise obtainable in an excess demand economy. Reformist economists protested, arguing that state orders had simply become another form of the traditional central command system. As the share of state orders started to decline, another problem emerged. What could the enterprises do with their non-state order production, as no market institutions for selling it existed?

But separate from this issue of the share of state orders, the model itself has serious problems. Three of these are paramount. Stage 2 still leaves the enterprise in a subordinate position *vis-à-vis* the ministries. They continue to have both the opportunity and the need for petty tutelage. Furthermore, because there is only one owner, the state, it is in practice difficult to create meaningful competition. Finally, sometimes, as in China after 1984, the system is implemented in a form which makes the enterprises produce the same commodities for both state orders and markets. As the same commodity will consequently have two widely differing prices, enormous possibilities for arbitrage, inflation and corruption are opened up. It is unclear whether such dual-track systems with both (in practice, obligatory) state orders and (in theory, freely) marketable production are feasible over a longer period of time. The Soviet experience after 1987 casts serious doubt; so do Chinese developments since 1984.[10]

One way of addressing the problem of missing competition is seen in a NEP-type or liberal reform variant of Stage 2.[11] In this arrangement a large part of the economy, especially basic industry, would continue to be centrally managed in the traditional way. At the same time – and this is the speciality of the NEP-model – private and cooperative production is encouraged in agriculture, services, small-scale construction and handicrafts. A proportion of such production would complement centralised state industry, a proportion would compete with it. The liberal solution would in fact mean legalising substantial parts of the existing second economy. Joint ventures with foreign companies would represent another part of the non-state fringe. One segment of centrally managed state industry would encounter competition from domestic, another from joint ventures. Elsewhere, import competition would be encouraged.[12]

In the Soviet context, the New Economic Policy of 1921–8 is the historical model for such proposals. In modern times, the liberal approach has been supported also by some of the proponents of goal-programme planning. This approach was partially accepted in the August 1988 Law of Cooperation as well as by legislation allowing family farming. But – and this is more important – the liberal model is also the way in which the Hungarian economy has actually functioned since the 1968 reform. There, it has improved the quantity and quality of market supply but has failed to check the deterioration of over-all efficiency and competitiveness in the economy. The Hungarian developments – as well as the brief Soviet experience of cooperatives – show how easily the non-state fringe and the unreformed state sector come into conflict. The fundamental problem is that the non-state sector is intended to stay relatively small and the state sector relatively large. Being able to rely on such political goals, state enterprises will use their political influence to have all possible restrictions placed on the fringe even before the competition becomes real. The fringe which is outside the centralised supply system has severe problems in securing the necessary inputs. It has but few opportunities for productive investment. As it can have no certainty about the role it will be allowed to play in the politically ever uncertain future, it engages in highly profitable arbitrage, tax evasion and the laundering of money from the second economy. This invokes the wrath of the population and more governmental restrictions on non-state activities duly follow. This process is shown up in stark relief in the history of Soviet cooperatives after 1988.

This is not how the theoretical Hungarian model, logically the Stage 3 of reform discussions, was supposed to function. What later became known as the theoretical Hungarian model was first proposed by Wlodzimierz Brus, the Polish economist, in 1961.[13] This is a model of a 'planned economy with a built-in market mechanism'. Enterprises, though remaining state property, would be freed of all obligatory plan targets. The centralised distribution of the means of production would also be abolished. In fact, enterprises would be free to market their production and buy their inputs where best they could. To ensure the efficiency of markets, a significant proportion of prices, at least, would be decontrolled. The centre would only directly decide upon net investments for reasons of growth, structural change, employment and stability.

The theoretical Hungarian model was supposed to embody both genuine markets and competition. Consequently, information would be used efficiently, production would be geared towards demand, and innovation would pay. In theory, Stage 3 would function similarly to state owned enterprises in a capitalist market economy. In the end, however, this is not the way things have worked out in practice. Why not?[14]

The fundamental problem with the theoretical Hungarian model is that it creates commodity markets, but still leaves the enterprises as state property and under ministerial subordination. In the same way as in Stages 1 and 2, as long as this subordination continues and ministries have the responsibility for the functioning of 'their' branch, petty tutelage will continue, now by numerous informal ways. This is, after all, also sometimes done by government administrators in relation to state owned companies under capitalism. The fundamental difference between the two situations is in the relative size of the state sector. Such capitalist state enterprises that face private competition do not necessarily perform worse than private firms, while the share of state monopoly enterprises under capitalism is much smaller than that of the state sector in the theoretical Hungarian model.

Furthermore, there probably exists a difference in economic policy goals. A capitalist state will probably emphasise efficiency over security, while the socialist state will stress full employment.

It is therefore not surprising that the theoretical Hungarian model soon lapsed into the above-discussed liberal model, with the peculiarity that state enterprises face 'neither planning nor markets' but various stringent informal controls.[15] Furthermore, if the state decides upon net investment, too many such decisions will continue to be made on political grounds, especially if the traditional strategic goals of full employment and forced growth are still followed. Closing down enterprises, often necessary for structural reasons, will be extremely difficult, as the state will be held directly responsible for maintaining current employment. As enterprise activity continues to be constrained by political considerations and state decisions, producers cannot be made totally dependent on their financial results. Budget financing and tax tailoring will continue, thus retaining a large degree of softness in enterprise budget constraints. The sought-for rationality in enterprise response to market forces will therefore be far from satisfactory. Managers will know that the state is still present as a source of finance of last resort.[16]

In the Soviet Union, the theoretical Hungarian model has been, as was seen above, proposed by a few economists. The majority opinion, however, has been that the existing disequilibria in the economy as well as the importance of military and extractive branches make the dual-track system of state orders preferable. There was a wide consensus of economists supporting the party decision of 1987 to opt for this variant. In Hungary considerations such as the above had already by the early eighties led economists to Stage 4 of reform discussions. They argued that the umbilical cord between enterprise and state, usually but not necessarily going through ministries, had to be cut. Otherwise economic decisions would continue to be made on political grounds, enterprise budget constraints would remain soft and competition extremely weak. Formal independence of enterprises from the state administration would not be enough; a countervailing force to the ministries had to be created.

There were two main proposals for how to do this.[17] Some economists argued for self-management whereby employees would select their managers and participate directly in strategic decision-making. Having thus been made the masters of enterprises, employees would putatively have the authority to repulse any outside interference in enterprise affairs. Others pointed out that crucial power of allocation of investment remained in the hands of the state, and proposed the creation of capital markets as an alternative to state allocation. According to one proposed capital market variant Stage 4 would simulate capitalism by creating independent but still possibly state-owned possessors of assets to operate on the markets.[18] Another variant – also widely discussed in Poland – proposes allowing both domestic and foreign private investors into the economy, thus privatising large parts of existing state property and finally creating a mixed market economy with a dominant non-state sector. If the latter were to happen, as is now the politically set goal in Poland and Hungary, the transition from socialism to capitalism would techni-cally become reality. That would certainly seem to prove the argu-ment put forward by Ludwig von Mises in the socialist controversy of the twenties and thirties: the effective reform of the socialist economic system in fact entails a return to capitalism.[19]

If dual-track planning and the theoretical Hungarian model prove not economically feasible, only the self-management option could promise a feasible and possibly efficient socialist alternative to a return to capitalism. It is therefore not surprising that after the Soviet 1987 reform programme had failed, the search turned to the leasing of enterprises as a possible form of self-management. There have already also been proposals both for simulating capitalism on capital markets and for wide-ranging privatisation. Before turning to these debates we should look at Soviet economists' attempts at diagnosing the existing state of the Soviet economy.

Where is the Soviet Union?

There has been within the Soviet Union, during the *glasnost* period, an increasingly wide-ranging discussion on the socioeconomic nature of the USSR. Not surprisingly, the various characterisations already well known within Western – especially Marxist – literature have probably all been aired in one form or another during these debates. The history of Soviet society and its roots in Russia and Marxism have also been widely discussed. As a leading Western specialist on Soviet history has pointed out, as interesting as these debates have been, many of the published contributions have been derived from Western literature and important periods of Soviet history – such as the New Economic Policy period – are still often handled in a partisan spirit.[20] The deficiencies in the education of historians, as well as the still existing limitations on the use of archives, are handicaps which can be overcome only slowly.

Most of the discussion on the nature and history of Soviet society has been carried on by philosophers, political scientists and journalists. There have been surprisingly few attempts at an economic analysis of any scholarly depth of the principles of the Soviet system. In fact, only two seem worth taking up here. The first one is the celebrated and seemingly widely accepted image of an 'administrative system' by Gavriil Popov. The second approach, first proposed by Aven and Shironin, two young economists, and later elaborated upon by academician Stanislav Shatalin and Egor Gaidar,[21] does not accept Popov's model, but sees the USSR as a 'bargaining economy'. Similar differences of analysis, one should add, have long existed in Western literature on the Soviet Union. They are important, as the first step in reforming any system should be the formation of a conception of the system to be reformed. Without a sufficiently good understanding of the system, the possibilities of success in any attempted reform are at best fragile.

Gavriil Popov, the Moscow State University professor of management who emerged as a radical reformer in 1983–5 and has since become a leading spokesman of the emerging radical opposition, published in early 1987 a lengthy review of *Novoe Naznachenie*, a novel by Aleksandr Bek.[22] Bek, a classic writer of Stalinist war literature, had in the early sixties written a manuscript on the career of an 'Onisimov', a minister for the iron and steel industry. Partly based on a real person, the book only came out in the West in 1977,[23] and was finally published in the USSR in 1986.

Onisimov's career covered several decades. He was one of Stalin's best economic commanders, who worked extremely hard, knew in detail every single enterprise within his branch and was absolutely obedient to the will of Stalin. He kept the industry working in the most difficult of circumstances, but at the same time his obedience made him spend huge resources on a useless innovation while blocking a major real advance in technology.

Using this example, Popov, the management professor, depicted the Stalinist economic system as one based on 'the centralisation of decisions and punctual, undeviating, over-riding fulfilment of directives from Above. . . . This is a system of specific and detailed management in physical terms (*in natura*). It is a system of continuous operational management of production from the centre. This is the Administrative System.' Popov further argues that this system over time not only produces workers who shy away from risk, innovation and initiative – as had been argued by academician Zaslavskaya in her 1983 Novosibirsk report – but also causes a similar deterioration in managerial capacities. In this way it carries the seeds of its own demise. Finally he claims that the administrative system, though it did necessarily produce the reign of terror, did not end with Stalinism. Thinking so, he has repeatedly argued, was the crucial mistake made by Khrushchev. The administrative system proved to be able to live without Stalin and terror. Terror ended after 1953, but the administrative system lived on. It was transformed from a 'cult of personality type' to a 'bureaucratic socialism type' without any change in its fundamentals.[24] The Soviet Union is still a society based on a single hierarchy of state ownership, a mono-organisational society.

Popov's basic argument – though not all the conclusions he draws – seems to be widely accepted in the USSR. Mikhail Gorbachev has repeatedly spoken of an administrative-command system. Others have pursued the parallels between different command systems. Nikolai Petrakov has called the Soviet Union a feudal-command system of management[25] and argues that at the basis of the current Soviet crisis lies a swollen state, one which has taken upon itself the power over, and responsibility for, the smallest economic details.[26] In a closely related vein Nikolai Shmelev argues that the discussion over the real fundamentals of reform had not even started in late 1988. The question to be posed and answered is whether the economy should be based on power (as in a command hierarchy) or on money (as in 'any normal economy').[27]

Popov, Petrakov and Shmelev leave no doubt that they see the roots of the administrative-command system in Soviet Marxism. Popov, in particular, argues that the basic fault of Soviet socialism is the fact that it was consciously created. The ethos of the administrative system is in an authoritarian attempt to make people happy – to build socialism and communism – without letting people themselves decide what they want. Any attempts to command people, to decide their fates, have always led to tragedies, irrespective of the possibly noble motives involved, Popov argues.[28] Without quite saying it, Popov clearly accepts the traditional libertarian view, forcibly defended by Friedrich Hayek, which contrasts the natural growth of capitalism with attempts to impose artificially constructed models of an ideal society upon people. For Popov, this is primarily a criticism of Lenin and secondarily of Gorbachev, who in Popov's radical view relies too much on an attempted revolution from above without seeing that any commanding of people will just reinforce the administrative system. This is the particular and controversial conclusion which Popov draws from his model: any attempts at a revolution from above are doomed to strengthen the very system they try to remove. The same criticisms could naturally be levelled against the earlier SOFE attempts at constructing optimal socialism. Popov's individualistic approach logically condemns SOFE as another variant of totalitarianism.

Because the task ahead is to liberate the natural development of humankind from the fetters of the administrative system, Popov gives political democratisation priority over all economic reforms.[29] He is certainly right in warning about the dangers of leaving *perestroika* to be implemented by the very same institutions that have so long served the administrative system.[30] Such arguments, however, risk overlooking the fact that the administrative system is not necessarily as monolithical and obedient as Popov makes it out to be. Popov's model might, as do other variants of the totalitarian model, underestimate the degree of independence and conflict within traditional socialism. Almost all people belong in some way to one of the existing institutions, and more often than not they have found ways for promoting their interests within the system. Popov himself has recently been forced to admit that there might be a problem in linking democratisation with the increase of open income inequality necessarily brought about by a market-oriented reform.[31] Perhaps people will decline to be liberated into democracry and the market economy.

This is a real possibility. Studies reported by academician Tikhonov say that only one in five qualified Siberian agricultural workers want to become the possessors of the land they till.[32] In Western Ukraine only one in ten agricultural workers wants to become an independent peasant.[33] Though others have cited less disturbing studies, Tikhonov, an outspoken opponent of collectivisation, concludes that perhaps people have to be economically forced into economic freedom: 'the present system may be razed with the help of the same methods which created it'. It is not only the agrarian workers who have adapted themselves to Soviet realities. According to another study, in the mid-eighties only a fifth of managers interviewed in a relatively high-technology branch could be characterised as consistent supporters of the reform. Most of them wanted more power but no responsibility.[34] The first experiences of *perestroika* in 1986–7 further diminished the level of support for reform among the population.[35] By Autumn 1989 the dissatisfaction had grown to threatening proportions, and Popov's political conclusion about the priority of democratisation was coming under increasing challenge. Perhaps people should really be forced into freedom.[36]

The sociological background for such political conclusions has been stated in Soviet studies.[37] Many social groups have carved themselves social niches which make them at least suspicious of and sometimes openly opposed to radical economic reforms. They may well decline liberation from the administrative system. In this view any reform measures need to be based on a detailed analysis of the structure of social interests instead of libertarian generalisations. At least before 1988, academician Zaslavskaya has argued, such analysis had never been performed, and the economic results of existing reforms were meagre, to say the least.[38] It is as if the demolishers of the administrative system did, after all, believe in its efficiency: the system works through commands from above; therefore it can also be changed by commands from above. This is Tikhonov's explicit conclusion; the same attitude is also reflected in the Gorbachev leadership's deep belief in the priority of reform legislation. The fundamental diagnosis of Soviet society as an administrative system is shared with Popov, while the practical conclusion is diametrically opposed.

But, as already mentioned, the administrative system is not the only possible interpretation of Soviet society. Perhaps, after all, the Soviet economy has not been one of commands but one of bargaining. Instead of the picture where all power and instructions flow from top to bottom, a bargaining model of the Soviet economy argues that though the command picture may have been correct about Stalinism, things have changed since then.[39] For decades now, no Soviet Onisimov has been able to know intimately the enterprises of his branch. There are too many of them, and the attempts at rationalising administration and developing planning technologies – described in previous chapters – have not produced the results expected. The real economy does not function according to the rules of the single factory image, the bargaining model argues. True, the superior echelons have powerful means at their disposal in implementing their goals. They manage supplies, distribute money, assign plans and decide upon managerial careers. But neither are the enterprises powerless. They have the best possible information concerning local production possibilities, can put more or less effort into plan fulfilment, and often engage in second economy activities. Within the enterprise, workers have parallel leverage *vis-à-vis* the management. To some degree, the same is true about ministries versus planners and even about planners against the political leadership. Soviet regions have been in some cases governed as relatively independent fiefs. In this perspective, the USSR is not an administrative system.

In principle this is well known. But in fact, the proponents of the bargaining model argue, the implicit if not explicit dominance of the command economy model in Soviet thinking has prevented the study of how bargaining takes place in practice. The single factory image may have been the goal, but it was never successfully implemented. Therefore economists, not knowing how the system actually functions, propose reform measures without being able to foresee how the economy will react to them. From this perspective the economists' complaints (recorded in chapter 1) about conservative bureaucrats declining to accept their reasonable proposals are unfounded: a consistent reform strategy has to take into consideration the feedback arising in reform implementation. This has not been the case in Soviet reforms. The proponents of the bargaining model argue that the economists do not even have the necessary knowledge and conceptual framework to do that.

This argument, which is theoretically compelling, can be supported not only by examples from recent Soviet reform experience; Hungarian and Chinese reform experiences also give plentiful examples of bargaining within the reform process. Aven and Shironin use both kinds of examples. Hewett has argued that this is exactly the crucial lesson of socialist reform processes which has been ignored both by Soviet economists and Soviet leaders.[40]

Some prominent Soviet economists, Shatalin and Zaslavskaya among them, prefer the bargaining model to the administrative system model. Still nobody can claim to know in any detail how the economy actually functions. Pressed hard, the advocates of the administrative system model would also concede the existence of bargaining. Nor does the bargaining economy model claim that power is equally distributed within the hierarchy. Still, the reform perspectives offered by the models are contradictory. While the Popov model can be used both to support libertarian and revolution from above conclusions, the bargaining model essentially claims that the situation is much more complicated. A careful analysis of interests, their conflicts and possible coalitions would be needed for any reform programme to succeed. There is some consistency in the fact that in 1990 Popov is both a leading opposition politician and the mayor of Moscow, while Shatalin, a supporter of the bargaining model, has become a member of Gorbachev's presidential council.

It is not important in this context which of the models – if any – is the appropriate one. The lack of in-depth studies of Soviet polity, economy and society makes choice largely an arbitrary matter of preference, and one way to interpret the first years of the Gorbachev regime would be to say that it has been wavering between the different approaches. But clearly it has not been served in the best possible ways by scholars who have too often rested content with general propagandistic declarations on the necessity of *perestroika*, democratisation and *glasnost*. If the basic mode of functioning of the existing economy is still a matter of contention, the case is hardly any better concerning many other, more specialised aspects of the economy. This is easily shown with a few examples.

The first example concerns the reasons for Soviet growth deterioration. By the early eighties there could be no doubt about the slowdown of the Soviet economy. Though the fact was admitted, it was interpreted in widely differing ways. The published opinions of Soviet economists differed on whether this had been caused by such factors fundamentally exogenous to the economy as changes in demography or in the availability and costs of energy and raw materials, or whether the reason should be sought for within the economy, in such endogenous factors as a deterioration in the supply of effort, a decline in investment or a slackening in technical progress. To a degree, such disagreements are inevitable in any country, as existing information can more often than not be interpreted in various ways. The peculiarity of the Soviet case lies in the absence and unreliability of crucial statistics. There is simply no basis on which to resolve such disagreements.

The disputes start with the size and growth rates of national income. While official statistics claim that Soviet national income had grown about ninety times from 1928 to 1985, the independent calculations of Khanin, an economist, and Seliunin, an economic journalist, gave a growth multiplier of only seven.[41] As seen above, Khanin had already referred to such results in the late sixties. Then they were suppressed, but under *glasnost* they have been widely debated as the interpretation of Soviet economic history was seen to be crucial for the possible legitimacy of the Stalinist system as a vehicle for growth and industrialisation. Few believe any longer in official growth figures. It is a good indicator of the existing range of uncertainty that in response to such criticisms Soviet statistical officials have referred to the high authority of the CIA, whose calculations give results between those of the official figures on one hand and Seliunin and Khanin on the other.[42] A Soviet official publicly using the CIA as an arbiter would have been unthinkable just a few years earlier, and such willingness reflects the ultimate recognition of the state of Soviet statistics.

The issue at hand is primarily that of the prices used in statistical aggregation. They fail to reflect relative scarcities and utilities, are deformed by arbitrary taxation, and the allegedly constant prices used in growth measurement contain an unknown amount of hidden inflation. The unreliability of the price basis also figures in another debate, that concerning the relative share of investment in national income. According to official – and CIA – figures the Soviet share is well in line with the international average. Vasili Seliunin has, using a different price basis, estimated that the real investment share is about 40 per cent.[43] That is an internationally exceptionally high figure and Seliunin has consequently argued for reduced investment, especially in the energy sector and agriculture.[44] Others have strongly disagreed, arguing that the actual share of investment in national income is around 20–25 per cent and the Soviet economy is seriously undercapitalised.[45] Among those disagreeing with Seliunin's proposal is none other than Grigori Khanin, the economist who earlier cooperated with Seliunin on the criticism of official growth statistics.[46] The share of military expenditure is hardly less contested, and this issue has also been debated in the Soviet press.[47]

Furthermore, the share of investment in national outlays is a different thing from real growth in productive capacity. In the mid-seventies the USSR tried – as did other socialist countries at the same time – to improve the efficiency of investment by cutting down its growth rate. The result, research conducted in Aganbegyan's institute claimed, was a worsening of bottlenecks, which decreased capacity utilisation ratios and slowed down the rate of growth of economic activity.[48] The commissioning of new productive capacities declined, production capital aged and consequently the productive potential of the country deteriorated. The traditional economic model simply needs huge investments to keep running, and a cut in investment growth threatened the renewal of productive capacity. Consequently, Novosibirsk researchers like Valtukh and Lavrovskii have called for increased investment as the only way of modernising the Soviet economy. With more political weight, the same line has been supported by the lobbyists for the energy sector and agriculture. Machine building, which, since the late seventies, has been increasingly seen as the key to economic modernisation, technical progress and long-term economic growth.

Mikhail Gorbachev had early accepted the view, strongly argued by, among others, academician Aganbegyan, that an acceleration of economic growth (*uskorenie*) is a necessary precondition for solving Soviet economic problems.[49] The extremely ambitious five-year plan for 1986–90 foresaw an acceleration of economic growth implemented through, among other things, a small increase in the share of investment in national income as well as a strong reorientation of investment towards machine building.[50] This policy was mistaken for several reasons, the most important of which has already been touched upon. Given the absence of new mechanisms for investment allocation, any attempt at accelerating growth by reallocating investment will necessarily strengthen the power of the ministries. *Uskorenie* is in clear conflict with *perestroika*.

Another aspect of the relationship between *uskorenie* and *perestroika* must also be pointed out in this connection. There was another view on the decline in the rate of commissioning of new productive capacities. Several economists, most notably V. K. Faltsman of TsEMI, argued that the problem was not in bottlenecks that could be opened by new investment but in the increasing costliness of adding to capacity.[51] If this explanation is accepted – and there are strong grounds for doing so – increasing investment outlays will rather worsen than solve Soviet economic problems. Hidden inflation and other reasons leading to increasing costliness should be tackled first. A stepping up of investment will otherwise only waste money. This, in retrospect, is clearly what happened in 1985–9. Contrary to plan, nominal investments increased hugely and were directed more and more to the energy sector and agriculture.[52] The most powerful ministries once again won the struggle over resource allocation in relation to the expressed goals of the politicians. The major goals of the five-year plan were missed. There was no notable technical progress in machine building[53] and as hidden – and increasingly also open – inflation accelerated, the deterioration of productive capacity continued.[54]

This brings us to our third example of the degree of uncertainty concerning the state of the economy. The economists knew of existing hidden inflation and of the troubled financial state of the economy as a whole. Some of them, like Abalkin, had been worried about it when matters were still relatively well under control. By the eighties hidden inflation and disequilibria were among the problems of the

Soviet economy most frequently discussed by the academic economists. At the same time the statistical, planning and financial authorities continued to deny the existence of any inflation in the USSR.
They proceeded as if the statistics they used gave a truthful picture of
the economy. To maintain illusions during the first Gorbachev years
they even engaged – as the newly appointed head of the statistical
office admitted in early 1990 – in statistical falsification to give a rosier
picture of the economy.[55] The economists presented different
estimates on the rate of inflation and tried to alarm the authorities in
various ways. The mechanisms of inflation were explained in the
press in some detail.[56] Neither was there any doubt about the
existence of excess supply of money.[57] A fourth of budget incomes, a
leading authority told us in late 1987, consists of borrowing.[58] It took
the financial authorities another year to admit the existence of a
budget deficit. As seen above, the first programmes for balancing the
economy were presented by the academic economists as early as
1981–2. By 1986–7 all the reform proposals of the academic economists emphasised the need to equilibrate the economy.

Relative to the financial authorities, who continued to offer reassur-
ances that credit expansion was under control,[59] the academic economists had a much more realistic picture of the financial state of the
country. Still their estimates for the rate of hidden inflation and the
scale of monetary overhang – accumulated cash reserves of the
population – varied widely. This cannot have increased the authorities' confidence in such calculations. Furthermore, as Lev Braginskii,
a leading academic financial specialist points out, there are only a
very few financial experts in the country.[60] Academician Aganbegyan
argues that the issues of anti-inflationary policy and money supply
are in general not understood by economists and officials.[61] This
seems to be confirmed when even a noted specialist bases his analysis
of the financial ills of the USSR on a confusion between economic
stocks (wealth) and flows (income).[62] An extreme example was
offered in Autumn 1989 by academician Abalkin, who explained the
absence of a governmental proposal for an inheritance tax by the
alleged fact that no competent person had been found to write one.[63]

Where is the Soviet Union going?

Even this short review of four issues shows that the understanding of
Soviet economists concerning the nature and state of their economy is
deficient. The prevailing view on the economic system in existence is

open to serious counterarguments; there is no consensus on the size and rate of growth of the economy; the share of investment and military expenditure in national income is unknown; the deterioration of productive capacity is explained by widely differing reasons; and the extent and causes of inflation are hotly debated. These are only some examples of the existing range of uncertainty. Such conflicts of scholarly opinion do, of course, exist in all countries. What makes the Soviet case peculiar is the absence and unreliability of relevant statistics as well as the traditional Marxist–Leninist doctrine of a single truth. The decision-makers are not only not accustomed to receiving independent advice but they have also been socialised into believing in the objectivity of Truth. To the extent that the politicians still maintain this frame of mind, conflicting analyses and recommendations coming from the economists must be especially disturbing. In this light one can understand those who maintain that a primary condition for successful economic reform in the USSR is unanimity of leading academic advice.[64]

Another aspect of confusion was added to the discussion by the difficulty of anticipating popular reactions to proposed policy measures. The issue of price reform is the prime example here. It has been clear to the economists, at least since the early days of optimal planning theory, that sensible economic decisions can only be based on equilibrium prices. SOFE had argued this since the sixties concerning both investment and consumption goods. The economic arguments for equilibrium prices are compelling and well understood. There is however a political problem involved. The prices of many basic consumer goods are below production costs. They not only fail to reflect relative scarcities but also have to be heavily subsidised from the budget. As such prices are also often below market equilibrium levels, they lead to queuing, retrading, rationing and black markets. The argument for raising such prices is certainly strong. The negative effect on consumers' monetary purchasing power can be compensated using cash transfers.

The strategies for price reform proposed by the economists always left much unclear. Opinions differed concerning the degree to which price reform would mean a centralised recalculation of prices or a liberalisation of price formation.[65] The former proposal is in the spirit of indirect centralisation, the latter in that of market creation. Some economists, Shatalin and Petrakov among them, have also argued for a currency reform that would eliminate at least a large part of the accumulated cash reserves by households and enterprises. Estimates varied, but the size of this monetary overhang – purchasing power ready to enter the market – threatens to make any equilibrating by price increases very difficult.[66] The larger the overhang, the greater the danger of unleashing an inflationary spiral when allowing even minor price increases.

Others have disagreed with the proposals on price and currency reform. Nikolai Shmelev has argued that any increases of retail prices would endanger the political support of the reformers.[67] Recurring rumours of a forthcoming currency reform have caused some panic amongst the Soviet population. Finally in the fall of 1988 Stanislav Shatalin, making a spectacular self-criticism, publicly apologised for his earlier proposals for price increases and currency reform.[68] The tenor of public discussion changed abruptly. The politicians have repeatedly postponed the reform of retail prices. In Autumn 1989 *Kommunist* could only publish an article putting forward the simple case for equilibrium prices by explicitly saying that it only represented the author's personal opinion.[69] Assumed political realities had overwhelmed economic logic. Economically irrational prices continue to disorientate decision-making.

The issue, however, is still alive. As consumer goods markets continued to deteriorate the Soviet government announced in May 1990 a reform package, which contained sharp price increases. The reaction of the population was such that panic buying emptied shop shelves of almost all that had still been available. The popularity of the government hit bottom. One of the consequences was that a policy of pre-announced price increases lost any political chance that it otherwise might still have had. Trying to plan a possible sequencing of economic reforms, reformers had to look for variants that would not start with higher prices.[70]

Such uncertainty, ambiguity and vacillation evident in the economists' diagnoses and proposals cannot have strengthened their credibility with the politicians and the general public. Still, one has to remember that their understanding of the economy has been much better than that of the economic authorities, and their willingness to propose policy measures much greater than that of the politicians to adopt them. In 1985, Gorbachev's economic agenda still seemed to be based only on policy changes. The goal of growth acceleration was supposed to be reached by a mobilisation of effort (the so-called human factor), shifts in investment priorities and by re-equipping the economy. All of these measures had been earlier advocated by the economists. Changes in the economic system proposed by the government were minor. A July 1985 decree extended the principles of the economic experiment started by Yuri Andropov to all Soviet industry. Various bodies were created to supervise economic complexes. It was only at the XXVIIth Party Congress in April 1986 that Gorbachev announced that he aimed at a radical reform of the economic system. Various commissions for economic reform had existed since 1982, and in late 1985 a new one, headed by the then Gosplan chief Talyzin, was founded. It soon established a scientific section chaired by academician Aganbegyan. Other members of the scientific section included the directors of key Academy research institutes Leonid Abalkin (Institute of Economics), Oleg Bogomolov (IEMSS), Valeri Makarov (TsEMI, after Fedorenko), Aleksandr Granberg (the Novosibirsk IEiOPP, after Aganbegyan), Aleksandr Anchishkin (the Institute for Forecasting, IEiP NTP, separated from TsEMI) as well as such prominent economists as Tatiana Zaslavskaya (IEiOPP, later the director of a public opinion research institute in Moscow), Nikolai Petrakov (TsEMI), Stanislav Shatalin (IEiP NTP), Gavriil Popov (Moscow State University) and Ruben Evstigneev (IEMSS).[71]

Gosplan and the Talyzin reform commission prepared a joint blueprint for reform strategy in 1986. Dissatisfied both with it, and with the fact that the report was not published, Aganbegyan and other academic economists prepared a reform outline of their own for a November 1986 conference.[72] Among the authors were Aganbegyan, Abalkin, Bunich, Petrakov, Popov and Shatalin. According to published reports, the blueprint was generally accepted by the thousand participants of the conference. It clearly reflected the majority view of reformists both within the Academy and outside it. A high degree of specialist consensus had been reached. This proposal, 'the 1986 concept', served as the basis for preparing the economic reform decree of June 1987 and the more detailed legislation following after that.[73] It therefore has a key position in the assessment of Soviet reform economics.

Fundamentally the November 1986 concept still continued within the Soviet tradition of indirect centralisation. It had five main elements. First of all, a transition to dual-track planning was envisaged. Part of production ('the most important and especially scarce goods') would be based on state orders, which would be binding for both sides. Increasingly, however, enterprises would be able to decide upon production themselves on the basis of users' orders and ensuing contracts. Small-scale investment could also be locally decided. Only those inputs needed to meet state orders would be centrally distributed. Basically planners would regulate the economy by economic means, by setting prices and other normatives. Centralism would also prevail in policies on technical progress, economic structure, investments, finance and incomes.

Second, the enterprises would have more autonomy than ever before. Within the limits set by state orders and normatives, the enterprise would decide upon output and product mix, customers and suppliers, the structure of wages and the magnitude of investment. Inputs for non-state order production would circulate through trade. Incomes were to be dependent on the economic results of the enterprise. Competition and the possibility of closure would be real. The ministry would not be responsible for the economic results of an individual enterprise; this was assumed to put an end to petty tutelage from above. The access of enterprises to foreign markets would be made easier.

Third, the increasing authority of the enterprise would be redistributed, as the traditional one-man rule of the director would be moderated by self-management on the part of the labour force. Fourth, regional authorities would have new powers and an independent financial status. Fifth, cooperatives and individual production would be encouraged.

Though this concept did become the basis of Gorbachev's economic reform, the economists did not write the whole reform legislative programme or oversee its implementation. As early as early 1987 Abalkin characterised the draft Law on the State Enterprise – the centrepiece of 1987–8 reform legislation – as a compromise.[74] The draft law was further changed in a centralist direction before being accepted.[75] Many academic scholars criticised the draft in public for permitting the continuation of the old centralism, especially if the share of state orders in total production were to remain high.[76] Indirect centralisation was supposed to be based on stable and uniform normatives. The continuing habit of using normatives tailored for each enterprise and changed indiscriminately came under protest as early as early 1987.[77] There were also complaints about the detrimental effects of post-reform attempts at fulfilling a five-year plan which had been written for different conditions.[78] The proposal to start a new five-year plan in 1988 was, however, not heeded.[79]

This, Aganbegyan said later in a wide-ranging criticism of economic decision-making during the early Gorbachev years, was only the visible tip of the iceberg. While scholars participated in the writing of basic reform legislation, all detailed decrees were written by the bureaucracies they affected.[80] Not surprisingly, much smaller changes in power and responsibility were decreed than the economists had advocated. This fact, and inconsistencies in reform design as well as numerous mistakes in economic policies were, according to Aganbegyan, criticised by the economists in numerous working groups and meetings. The economists are not, Aganbegyan seeks to prove, responsible for the state into which the economy had slid by 1989. In particular, they had, according to Aganbegyan, opposed many of the decisions that contributed to the worsening shortages on the consumer goods markets.

Writing in late 1988, Aganbegyan still thought that the conceptual basis for reform created in November 1986 remained valid.[81] We have already seen that there are important reasons to think otherwise. Most of the objections raised against the general schemes of indirect centralisation are also valid in relation to the 1986 concept. The goal of stable and uniform normatives is illusory, while enterprise-specific normatives are just another form of traditional central management. Enterprises cannot be independent as long as they are subject to ministries, and the 1986 concept maintained this subjection, though it wanted to make it looser.[82] Indirect centralisation does not lead to the creation of markets, if essentially centralised price formation is retained, as the 1986 concept wanted.[83] In fact, the 1986 concept does not even use the term market, but talks of commodity–money relations as instruments of the mechanism of planned management.[84] The proposed wide use of contract pricing under conditions of soft budget constraints, excess demand and monopolistic supply is a recipe for inflation. True enough, the importance of competition was mentioned in the 1986 concept, but there were hardly any concrete proposals for creating it. At the same time a further centralisation of enterprises into associations was proposed. Another inflationary element was the direct link proposed between enterprise output (measured in current prices) and the wage fund. The more authority enterprises were given on pricing, the more inflationary would this link become in practice. Not surprisingly, this is exactly what happened in 1988–9. The enterprises were given more rights by relaxing centralism in planning. Without the discipline created by competition and hard budget constraint conditions, they used the shortest way to increase profits and wages – by price inflation.

This does not mean that the 1986 concept had been without any significant strengths. First of all, it argued strongly in favour of the need to balance the economy, and in particular, proposed outlines for a financial reform. The economists knew in 1986 that stable money is one of the preconditions of markets. Second, there was emphasis on the need for competition, anti-monopoly measures and a multitude of enterprise forms and sizes. There were also references to an increasing opening up of the economy. On neither of these points, unfortunately, were the proposals worked out in sufficient detail. Third, there was strong emphasis on the comprehensiveness of the reform. Proposals ranged from inter-enterprise relations to central planning, from managerial education to price and financial reform. Fourth, it was argued that all the reforms should come into force at the same time, with the beginning of the next five-year plan period.

This was not to be. Not only was the reform legislation and its implementation different from what the economists had proposed, but the 1986 concept itself soon had competitors. In fact, by 1989 it had been generally thrown out in favour of more radical approaches. Only a few of its originators any longer spoke up for indirect centralisation of the 1986 form. There was now more emphasis on the need to restart the economic reform. Indirect centralisation was increasingly seen as a dead end. We can distinguish between three alternatives to the 1986 concept put forward in the Soviet press at the end of the eighties. They are the *slavophile*, the *radical socialist* and the *westernising* concepts.

These concepts were presented with varying degrees of consistency, there was a clear evolution of general emphasis over time, and even the position of individual economists shifted. This is not surprising. The boundaries of political debate widened fast, making new proposals presentable and even potentially acceptable. With the continuing deterioration of the economic state of the country there was increasing pressure for more radicalism. And, finally, as the previous pages should have made clear, the 1986 concept was the summation of decades of Soviet economic reformism. It was the concept whose fundamentals had been in existence since the sixties. When it turned out to be deficient, the reformist economists had to grope their way towards new approaches. As Gavriil Popov put it in 1988: 'The theoretical, scientific capital, with which we started *perestroika* in 1985, has been in fact exhausted. It was enough for starting the work. But during these years we devoted too much time in popularising the basic ideas [of *perestroika*] instead of advanced theoretical studies.'[85]

The slavophile concept does not exist as a concrete proposal crafted with professional competence. In essence, it is a spiritual rejection of economic rationality and markets. In 1986 an engineer called Mikhail Antonov attracted attention with his criticism of Soviet economic theory.[86] Existing applied economics, he argued, was worthless, the political economy of socialism an apology, and SOFE based on wholly false foundations. What was needed was a proper Russian form of economising, based on the allegedly ancient traditions of collectivity and spirituality, he argued. The economists have rejected such arguments as mere slavophile sentimentality,[87] while Antonov and others have continued their attacks on the reform economists. These are presented as lackeys of capitalism and imperialism, who already in the Brezhnev era had tried to destroy the Russian village and are now busy selling Russia to foreigners. Abalkin, Aganbegyan, Shmelev and Zaslavskaya are the agents of a new comprador class, Russian servants of imperialist capitalism, trying to benefit from this.[88]

Not surprisingly, the negative programme of the slavophiles is relatively better developed than any positive one. They are against markets, cooperatives, private property and unemployment. They oppose in particular the export of raw materials and energy, an opening of the economy and joint ventures with capitalist firms. Such feelings seem to have had some success in fomenting local opposition to proposed special economic zones in Russia.

The slavophile's only economic proposal seems to concern the use of 'ancient Russian' collective forms in industry and especially in agriculture.[89] Recently they have joined forces with another current opposed to *perestroika*, the conservative defenders of the working class. Of older origins, this opposition has become more active recently.[90] It may still become a political force. As presented by A. A. Sergeev, a political economy professor at the Trade Union University, its economic programme seems to consist of centralism, collectivism, full employment, stable prices and an opposition to entrepreneurship.[91] Sergeev was reportedly strongly applauded at the November 1989 conference on economic reform.[92]

The radical socialist solution has quite wide support among professional economists. It wants to enhance the socialist character of *perestroika* by basing it on self-management and the leasing of enterprises. This current grew from several sources. Among them are the traditional socialist ideals of self-management, contract brigades in Soviet industry, experiments in Soviet agriculture and general assessments of the failures of earlier Soviet reform attempts.

Insistence on the socialist character of self-management has made leasehold (*arenda*) ideologically easy to accept as the alternative to introducing private property.[93] Only the most conservative political economists have seen it as an assault on state property and the unity of the socialist economy.[94] In leasehold, the state remains the owner of the means of production, which are entrusted to the work collective as the lessee. Leasehold can also be used as a transitional phase to an employee buy-out. Recent legislation enumerates various possible lessors and lessees, but the basic principle is simple: workers of a factory or farm – or of a workshop within one of these – are put in possession of it through leasehold. *Arenda*, Vadim Medvedev emphasised in his first speech as the CPSU Central Committee Secretary for Ideology, is the natural way to overcome the alienation of workers from the means of production.[95] It creates 'a feeling of being the master of production', thereby providing efficient incentives, and is thus allegedly hugely productive. In this view self-management on the basis of state ownership is the long-sought-after real socialism and the transition to *arenda* is the essence of revolutionary *perestroika*.

In a formal sense, elements of self-management had always existed in Soviet industry through brigades of different kinds. Both a 1983 law and the 1987 Law on the State Enterprise tried to boost self-management. Though the independence of brigades has usually remained nominal, there have been grassroots attempts at reviving the brigades on an autonomous basis. As seen above, Gavriil Popov proposed as early as in 1984 the brigade contract, within the framework of autonomous enterprises, as the model for reforming the economy.[96]

In Soviet agriculture, collective farms have always been theoretically self-managing. The Akchi experiment of the sixties, which had tried to turn this theory into reality, was resurrected in 1986. Writing in *Literaturnaya Gazeta*, Belkin, a noted economist, and Perevedentsev, an equally well-known demographer, advocated Akchi as the model for the future Soviet farm sector.[97] By this time various new leasing and self-management experiments had been going on for several years, and Gorbachev has since promoted various forms of agriculture *arenda*, including family farming. Other officials have been less enthusiastic, and the practical results have been mixed at best.[98] Leading agricultural economists have argued that if it is impossible to abolish collective and state farms, they should be made into voluntary organisations of independent leasehold collectives.[99]

Experiments in the leasing of service (and at least one industrial) enterprises were started in both the Baltic republics and Georgia under Andropov.[100] The goal was to experiment with the widest possible enterprise autonomy compatible with state ownership. Wider publicity for the leasing of industrial enterprises was first given in early 1988. At the time it was still regarded as something exotic.[101] As already mentioned, the political leadership embraced the idea in 1988. In spring 1989 *Voprosy Ekonomiki* – now edited by Gavriil Popov – called *arenda* the basis of radical *perestroika*,[102] and in November 1989 a law on *arenda* was passed. The change in favour of leasing had been extremely fast.

A reconsideration of the experience of earlier reform attempts had contributed to this turnabout. On one hand, several leading TsEMI economists have argued that the basic mistake of the traditional reform concept of indirect centralisation had been its neglect of democratisation. Centralism remains a worthy goal, a defining feature of socialism, they asserted, but central management had to be under democratic control. Otherwise the tools of indirect centralisation would only be used to further the group interests of the planners. They do not coincide with the interests of the society.[103] Calling for a democratic socialism, these economists have criticised both the supporters of traditional central management and those proposing a market based model.[104] In the age of large-scale production any harking back to free competition is an anachronism, these Sofeists argue. Neither do they like all the properties of markets. Unemployment, in particular, has in their view no place in socialism.

These Sofeists defend democratic state ownership, democratic centralism as well as the development of socialist competition and 'commodity–money relations' – but only on this basis.[105] This would be real socialism and an economically efficient system.[106] Academician Fedorenko also, whose reform proposals had for many years been notably cautious, emerged under *glasnost* as a proponent of self-managing socialism based upon the *arenda* of state owned assets.[107]

Arenda thus had support at the highest political level, had been allegedly successfully tested experimentally, and was proposed by leading economists on the theoretical grounds of its socialist character. Furthermore, by 1988 economists like Pavel Bunich and Gavriil Popov had started to argue for *arenda* as the only possible solution for the blind alley into which the 1987 reform programme was heading.[108] The petty tutelage of enterprises by ministries had by no means ended. On the contrary, the continuing practices of tailoring enterprise-specific normatives and pre-empting production through state orders showed that the planning system based on normatives was not bringing the results expected. It was a blind alley.

But neither were the existing leasehold arrangements in industry satisfactory. True, in less than two years the number of state enterprises on leasehold had grown to more than a thousand,[109] but *arenda*, as it has been introduced in practice, was in most cases only nominal, a change in the way in which ministries tax 'their' enterprises.[110] Ministerial *arenda* soon lost much of its credibility and some economists, among them Viktor Volkonskii, a radical reformer since the sixties, wanted to abandon the whole idea of *arenda* as just another variant of indirect centralisation.[111] Others wanted to save the idea of leasehold by stripping it of its ministerial framework. Proponents of *arenda* such as Popov and Bunich argue that the subordination of leasehold enterprises to ministries has to be abolished. Popov proposes making the republics the owners of enterprises instead of ministries.[112] Free from ministerial subordination, enterprises on *arenda* would become the free agents of a market economy. In fact, Popov clearly implies, *arenda* should not be seen as a permanent state but as a basis for transition from state ownership to group and private ownership.

This proposal is logical, if the ministries are seen as the bastions of the old system of power and management. It is also in line with Popov's theory of the administrative system, which emphasises the need for democratisation on the basis of republican and other elected political institutions. Finally, it may become politically inevitable with the development of popular movements for democracy from below, especially on the republican level. The demands for economic independence of the republics have little substance without overwhelmingly republican ownership of state property.

Bunich's proposal is somewhat different. He supports the use of financial institutions as lessors, and a gradual transformation of most leasehold enterprises into collective property.[113] The issue of ministerial versus regional versus financial institution lessorship was left open in the autumn 1989 Law on Leasehold with the exception of land, which is to be leased by local soviets.[114]

If ministerial leasehold is no solution it is also recognised by the proponents of regional ownership that the latter may create new problems. Enterprise subordination would be transferred from one hierarchy (Moscow-based branch ministries) to another (the republican soviet), to one that is geographically closer and therefore in a better position to monitor enterprise activities. Ministerial petty tutelage will often simply be exchanged for regional control. Neither is it clear that increasing pressure by democratically elected soviets will make enterprise decision-making economically more rational. Every economic system faces decisions that have to be made on political criteria, but contrary to what many Soviet reformists profess to believe, there is no reason to suppose that a blending of political and economic decision-making either within an enterprise or in the economy at large would somehow inevitably lead to a more efficient economy.[115] This was in fact partly admitted when the election of enterprise directors by the workforce, introduced in the 1987 Law of the Socialist Enterprise, was abandoned in autumn 1989. Both China and Yugoslavia offer many examples of the dangers of regional petty tutelage.

Secondly, the law on *arenda* has come into force before the proposed markets for commodities, inputs and capital have been created. In an irrational environment, plagued by disequilibria and deficits, enterprises on *arenda* will continue to be dependent upon administrative discretion. Even in the best of worlds it would be extremely difficult to envisage wage schemes linking the income of each worker to enterprise performance with any precision. The assumed incentive advantages of *arenda* will be lost when workers understand that given the existing Soviet economic system with its administrative discretion and irrational prices, enterprise performance will be measured in some essentially arbitrary way and the effort of each individual worker can only have an imperceptible (if any) effect on performance.

Third, Yugoslav experience seems to show that self-management under regional administration is an exceptionally inefficient economic system.[116] Some of the economic problems of self-management, primarily the tendency to underinvestment and wage inflation, can in principle be alleviated by linking self-management with share issues and capital markets, and this has been pointed out in the Soviet literature.[117] So far the steps taken in the USSR towards the creation of capital markets have been timid. There has been little progress towards creating institutional investors and secondary markets. At the same time there has been much ideological opposition towards a rentier class. Without sufficiently well developed secondary markets, allocation of capital between enterprises has to remain in the hands of the planners, capital assets do not receive a market valuation, and the pressure on managers of those assets to increase their value remains weak.[118] Finally, one should remember that even if there were no obstacles to developing capital markets, the maturation of these markets would take years, perhaps even decades. Thus, the efficiency properties praised in economics textbooks would only be available in the long run.

One can therefore conclude that leasehold is at best a form of transition to collective ownership. Without a market environment, self-management is not a feasible solution. Within a market environment, Western experience and theoretical research seem to show that self-managed enterprises are viable, but hardly as efficient as capitalist enterprises.[119] It is in this perspective hardly surprising that academician Abalkin has warned against excessive *arenda* optimism.[120] With an obvious glance at Bunich and Popov he has argued that the search for any single solution is illusory, reminiscent of the Krushchevian campaigns for growing maize. *Arenda*, Abalkin argues, should be seen only as one possible solution among others. At the same time he has together with the government abandoned any solutions involving 'exploitation' – hired labour by non-family members. But if private ownership in the capitalist form is ruled out, *arenda* and collective ownership have to be the main alternatives to state property.

This brings us to the third current of Soviet post-1986 reform thought, the Westernising or liberal tendency. This tendency is Westernising in two senses. It explicitly or implicitly plays down the differences between capitalism and socialism, arguing that the market economy is *the* natural economic model for any society, whoever may own the means of production. It is also Westernising in the sense of emphasising the need for opening up the economy to world markets. This tendency is liberal in the classical sense of arguing for a less pervasive state, one that would concede part of its power to markets and political civil society, one that would, furthermore, as has been increasingly argued, also privatise part of its property.

To the extent that traditional Soviet socialism identified the normative future society with homogeneous state ownership, all-encompassing planning and self-sufficiency, even the 1986 reform concept was Westernising and liberal. After all, it proposed a relaxation of all these three characteristics. Later, and especially since 1988, discussion of markets and ownership forms in the USSR has been immensely more pragmatic than ever before. Leonid Abalkin set the tone of much of this discussion when he defined the criteria for the socialist character of economic institutions in 1988 as economic efficiency, the existence of social guarantees and the exclusion of 'exploitation'.[121] But still, one can easily detect a sub-group of reform economists who have pursued the Westernising ideas since 1987 with greater consistency than others. Some of them see the causation going from marketisation to opening up, others see it sooner the other way round. Still, while the radical socialists looked for solutions in self-management and accepted markets – if they did even that – as a necessary environment for self-managed enterprises, the liberals started with an emphasis on the need for markets and on this basis – in many cases at least – arrived at an appreciation of private property as the proper ownership arrangement needed for functioning markets.

The issue was put with all necessary clarity as early as the beginning of 1987 by 'L. Popkova' in a short letter to *Novyi Mir*.[122] 'Popkova' – in reality Larisa Piyasheva, a researcher with the Academy of Sciences Institute of the International Workers' Movement[123] – presented two arguments. First, one has to choose either socialist ideology or markets. The idea of market socialism is absurd, and all attempts to combine the two are bound to fail. Second, markets are immensely more efficient than any central management could ever be.

'Popkova's' letter was a sensation, not least because of her attack on the Marxist–Leninist ideology of socialism. One critic accused her of not understanding that free markets no longer exist even in real capitalism,[124] another – a leading reformist – referred to optimal planning theories to show that indirect centralisation is indeed both possible and desirable.[125] At the same time, as we have seen above, belief in indirect centralisation with shadow prices had already turned into a consciousness of the need for market prices among former optimal planners.[126]

Piyasheva works for an institute with an international profile. So does the economist, Nikolai Shmelev, who emerged as the main spokesman of the Westernising view in 1987, when his *Novyi Mir* article was probably read and debated more than any other publication of that year.[127] He worked for many years at Bogomolov's institute on issues of East–West trade. Later he moved over to Arbatov's Institute for the Study of the USA and Canada. Shmelev's celebrated 1987 article addressed both the Soviet past and the future. He condemned collectivisation outright, arguing that it had destroyed the peasant class with its love of the land and aptitude for hard work. Markets and a strong currency, he argued, are the natural way of organising the economy, while the command economy subordinates everything to decisions made in secrecy. The result is technological backwardness and an almost total lack of planned development. Only markets could offer the solution for the USSR, as for any country. In creating them one should not be afraid of unemployment. It could not be avoided in a real market economy. A degree of unemployment would be only natural and good for flexibility and incentives.

Approving of unemployment was too much for Mikhail Gorbachev, as well as for many leading economists.[128] Socialist markets, though they exist and must be further developed, are different from capitalist markets, they argued. There neither is nor can be any markets for natural resources, labour power and capital under socialism, wrote, for instance, Abel Aganbegyan in 1988.[129] Such markets as do exist are also regulated in many ways – including centralised price setting for 'the most important goods' – and there are therefore no bankruptcies, unemployment, inflation or crises. There is a 'unity and interaction' of plan and markets. This is exactly the thinking against which Piyasheva and Shmelev have correctly argued, pointing out that the market mechanism is an organic unity from which one cannot choose only 'positive' properties.

In his 1987 article Nikolai Shmelev made two additional points which he was to develop further in later articles. One should open up the economy, especially by creating special economic zones with priority legislation for foreign investment. Furthermore, one should try by every means to protect consumption levels during the transition to the market system. The accelerated growth target of the plan should be abandoned, agriculture should be liberated from planning, and consumer goods should be imported on the basis of credit. Shmelev has also presented numerous and widely discussed concrete proposals for balancing the economy.[130] Several of them were included in the government stabilisation programme of autumn 1989. Intriguingly, he is not a proponent of private property. Competition and capital markets, he argues, are technical devices which can be used both in socialism and capitalism. 'The main thing is that the collective of the socialist enterprise should be really independent, its real owner – in a joint stock company or some other form. Don't you like the words "owner"? Then, let is be "possessor" or "user". The question is not about words.'[131] Neither does Shmelev propose abolishing all central planning, though its scope should be largely restricted to defence plants.

The distinction between radical socialists and liberals becomes blurred in the case of economists such as Bunich and Popov, who see *arenda* at least partly as a transitory form and at the same time argue for functioning capital markets. There are, however, also outright proponents of privatisation. Viktor Volkonskii, whose opposition to leaseholding we noted above, proposes the creation of a mixed economy through various holding companies to be owned by the state, republics, regions, enterprises and private citizens.[132] In 1990 this was also advocated by Nikolai Petrakov, a personal adviser to President Gorbachev.[133] Academician Emelyanov of the Agricultural Academy counters the arguments on 'exploitation' under private ownership by saying that real exploitation should not be identified with private production. 'It arises primarily when the people do the work, but the managing elite, without producing anything, decides upon the fruit of their work.'[134] Academician Oleg Bogomolov argues in the CPSU Central Committee journal that private production has to be accepted because of its economic efficiency,[135] while academician Shatalin, in 1990 a member of Gorbachev's presidential council, argues strongly both for private production, multi-party parliamentarianism and direct foreign investment. The state sector, Shatalin concludes, should be restricted to infrastructure. Even defence plants could be in private hands.[136]

Soviet arguments both for markets and private production are usually totally pragmatic. Typically, markets are defended as the normal mechanism of resource allocation, the only alternative to which – central planning – has failed beyond any doubt. The democratic character of market choice is also much emphasised. This view was underlined by Petrakov as early as in 1971. The arguments for private production are usually similar or derived from an assumed need to have competing property arrangements. There is hardly any evidence of the influence of modern economic theories of property rights. The libertarian arguments on private property as a necessary foundation of political liberty have, however, already surfaced in the Soviet press.[137]

Similarly, no detailed proposals about the technical questions of privatising state property seem to have been published. The privatisation drafts of Popov,[138] Volkonskii[139] and Seliunin, the economic journalist,[140] are all quite superficial, though they do point towards the different alternative directions already discussed in East European countries in more detail. This may be partly explained by the fact that discussing privatisation is a new matter in the USSR, partly by the opinion polls which imply that only a quarter or one-fifth of Soviet citizens would support the open introduction of private production and hired labour outside the family.[141] In the circumstances, promoting proxies for private property in the guise of cooperatives and leaseholding may well be the only politically accessible alternative.

The Abalkin reform programme

During 1987 and 1988 the economists complained repeatedly that their diagnoses and proposals were being neglected in practice. Abalkin's criticism of the state of the economy and government policies at the summer 1988 party conference, though it reflected widely shared opinion among academic economists, caused a minor sensation but no immediate policy reaction. Only in November 1988 did the government ask the Institute of Economics for a new reform programme, which was also duly submitted in January 1989.[142] Still, there was no immediate action. In spring 1989, many of the leading academic economists were elected members of the USSR Congress of People's Deputies. Though the economic discussion at the first Congress was disappointing, several of the economists were made members of the new Supreme Soviet. Pavel Bunich soon emerged as the vice-chairman of the Supreme Soviet Commission on Economic Reform and Gavriil Popov as one of the co-chairmen of the Inter-Regional Group of deputies, the radical opposition. At the same time the economic situation continued to deteriorate. The strikes of summer 1989 showed how widespread dissatisfaction had become. It was finally admitted by the political leadership that not only was the economy in need of strong stabilisation policies but that the economic reform had to be restarted.[143] In August 1989 academician Abalkin was made a vice-premier in the new government. A reform commission chaired by him quickly wrote a new reform programme, which was debated in a November 1989 conference of economists and finally accepted – in a somewhat diluted form – at the December 1989 Congress of People's Deputies.

The Abalkin programme[144] – presented to the Congress of People's Deputies by Prime Minister Nikolai Ryzhkov[145] – is a unique document. The Soviet government had never before such a detailed and coherent blueprint for economic reform. It offered both a short-term programme of economic stabilisation, a description of the economic model set as a goal, and an evaluation of alternative paths to the goal.[146] For the first time in the USSR, the Abalkin programme set denationalisation of state property through *arenda* and the selling off of enterprises to workers and collectives as a goal. It was also clearly committed to a transition to a market economy, including the introduction of markets for labour, capital and foreign exchange. This transition would be cushioned by a system of social guarantees. A centrally managed sector should remain for raw materials, fuels and defence plants, but the bulk of the economy would operate through a market only regulated by the state. The programme is far superior to the July 1987 concept of economic *perestroika*.

The discussion at the November Conference and December Congress showed that in the main the government programme enjoyed the support of the leading academic economists. The programme was received in a hostile way only by the slavophiles like Sergeev, discussed above (pp. 154–5). It is true that many of the reformist economists were worried about the effectiveness of the stabilisation programme prepared by the Planning Commission and the Ministry of Finance. There were also doubts about the step-by-step reform strategy adopted as well as about the actual content of planning for the future. Even so, such disagreements among the reformers were probably secondary in the autumn of 1989, though it is true that an economic reform can stumble on any of the numerous technical details that were to be sorted out during 1990, the short period of preparation allocated in Abalkin's programme. For a period at least, reformers generally chose to close ranks behind Abalkin's programme.

The Abalkin programme was still far less radical than the changes under way in many East and Central European countries. In principle, it still excluded the possibility of hired labour outside the family, and in seeming contradiction with Abalkin, Prime Minister Nikolai Ryzhkov strongly underlined that the government had no intention of creating genuine large-scale private production.[147] In fact, in his speech at the December 1989 Congress he ruled out any large-scale denationalisation of state enterprises, including the sale of small and medium plants. During 1989, as has been pointed out above, several economists had argued for open private production, and their dissatisfaction with that part of the government programme as presented by Ryzhkov is therefore not surprising.[148] On the other hand one can argue that the use of hired labour in cooperatives and under leasehold gives, in the best case, quite good approximations to private production. The government programme was also criticised for the fact that a sufficiently strong programme for opening-up the economy is still missing.[149] Furthermore, the anti-monopoly measures outlined remained unclear and even contradictory.[150]

There was – even in late 1989 – no reason to believe that the Abalkin programme of autumn 1989 would be the final word in Soviet economic reforms. Large-scale privatisation and a real opening-up of the economy are necessary for economic efficiency, and these issues had already been raised in Soviet discussions. Still, even the limited degree of radicalism of the Abalkin programme proved too much for the masses of practical economists and administrators upon whom its implementation depends. One could already detect clear differences of emphasis between the Abalkin programme of November and the more conservative way in which Ryzhkov presented the government programme in December.

The first months of 1990 proved fatal for the government programme. Instead of stabilising the economy as planned, the government proved unable or unwilling to prevent the equilibrium from deteriorating seriously. Rising rates of inflation and worsening shortages swept away the basis of the government programme in a few months. Gorbachev and his key economic advisers, Petrakov and Shatalin, soon made their dissatisfaction known and promised a new, more radical reform programme. The initial success of Poland's drastic stabilisation programme was studied in detail.

In the end the Soviet government and Gorbachev's presidential council were unable to decide upon a truly new reform programme. The new version, presented by Prime Minister Ryzhkov in May 1990, hardly added anything else new to the December programme but a detailed schedule for raising the prices of most consumer goods.[151] The government had earlier rejected the Polish road of a shock treatment because it lacked the popular support necessary for drastic measures.[152] Within a few days its new version of reform programme had also proved to be not feasible, as angry consumers hoarded any goods remaining in the shops and indignant politicians rejected the programme in crucial republican parliaments. A new wave of strikes threatened.

Two things proved to be the undoing of the government programme. The population declined to accept such a transition to a market economy which promised only price increases in the short run, relegating the benefits of a market economy into the future. In addition to that, several Soviet republics and regions – including the Russian republic – were no longer willing to accept the decisions made by the central government in Moscow.

In the summer of 1990 a plain struggle for power seemed to occupy most of the politician's resources. The economists, on the other hand, continued their search for solutions to the continuing dissolution of the Soviet economy. Academician Bogomolov argued that the failure of the efforts of Abalkin and the government showed that a strategy of piecemeal transition to a market economy was indeed impossible.[153] The July 1990 Congress of the Soviet Communist Party disagreed, once again calling for a gradual transition to a regulated market economy.[154] An economist spokesman of conservatives at the congress disagreed with this line, calling for workers' self-management.[155] Writing during the party congress, Nikolai Petrakov, the President's adviser, sketched a new sequence of reforms, starting with the denationalisation of state industries instead of price increases.[156] A gradual price reform could follow later, Petrakov argued. Speaking at the congress, Leonid Abalkin disagreed, stressing that price increases are inevitable in a transition to markets.[157] No trace of the relative reformist consensus behind Abalkin's programme of autumn 1989 seemed to remain.

Conceptually things may have changed to a positive direction since 1989. Not only are issues of ownership and markets discussed much more thoroughly, but the crucially difficult problems of sequencing the transitional steps to a new economic regime were also being understood much better than before. Still, from the limited point of view of a rational economic reform, things were much worse in 1990 than they were in 1989. Even if the transition is largely about diminishing the role of the state in the economy, it can only be implemented in a more or less orderly way by a strong government, following consistent policy guidelines and enjoying popular support. Exactly such a government was missing in the USSR in 1990. Without it, the chances of an economic upturn in the near future seemed slim indeed.

Notes

1 The Soviet political economy of socialism

1. *Oktyabr*, 1988:1, p. 184.
2. *Kommunist*, 1987:5, 30–9 (L. I. Abalkin and A. I. Anchishkin); *Kommunist*, 1987:6, 10–19 (A. G. Granberg and P. G. Bunich).
3. Anchishkin died prematurely in summer 1987.
4. See Pekka Sutela, *Socialism, Planning and Optimality*, Finnish Society for Sciences and Letters, Helsinki 1984.
5. See 'Yubilei uchenogo', *Ekonomika i matematicheskie metody*, 1987:6, 1139–40.
6. Ibid.
7. Ye. G. Yasin, 'Administrativanaya sistema tsen ili ekonomicheskii mekhanizm', *Ekonomika i matematicheskie metody*, 1988:2, 205–20.
8. See Kovacs, Janos Matyas, 'Reform economics: The classification gap', *Daedalus*, 1990:1, 215–48.
9. N. Maksimov, *K kritik marksizma*, Molodaya Rossiya, Moscow 1906, p. 13. Maksimov is a pen-name of Bogdanov.
10. August Bebel, *Die Frau und das Sozialismus*, Dietz, Berlin 1954, p. 605 (first published in 1878).
11. Karl Kautsky, *Erfurtin ohjelma*, Helsinki, Tammi 1974, p. 167 (first published in 1892). Compare V. I. Lenin, *Polnoe sobranie sochineniya*, 5th edn, Moscow, Politizdat (various years), vol. 33, p. 101. For a discussion see Sutela, *Socialism, Planning and Optimality*, pp. 37–40.
12. See Lenin, *Polnoe sobranie sochineniya*, vol. 4, pp. 219–29.
13. Ibid., vol. 37, p. 422.
14. N. Bukharin and E. Preobrazhensky, *The ABC of Communism*, Penguin, Harmondsworth 1969 (first published in 1919).
15. Lenin, *Polnoe sobranie sochineniya*, vol. 45, p. 376.
16. See, for instance, M. Gorbachev, 'Sotsialisticheskaya ideya i revoliutsionnaya perestroika', *Pravda*, 26 November 1989.
17. K. Marx, *Grundrisse einer Kritik der politischen Oekonomie (Rohentwurf)*, Dietz, Berlin 1968, p. 89.
18. G. G. Bogomazov, *Marksizm–Leninizm i problemy tovarnodenezhykh otnoshenii v period stroitelstva sotsializma v SSSR*, Izdatelstvo Leningradskogo Universiteta, Leningrad 1974, pp. 64–77; Silvana Malle, *The*

Economic Organization of War Communism, Cambridge University Press, Cambridge 1985, pp. 190–4.

19. See ibid. and L. D. Shirokorad, *Ideologicheskaya borba i Razvitie politicheskoi ekonomiki sotsializma v SSSR v perekhodnoi period*, Izdatelstvo Leningradskogo Universiteta, Leningrad, pp. 20–6.

20. See, for example, N. Fedorenko, 'O sozdanii i razvitii sovetskoi ekonomiko–matematicheskoi nauki', *Ekonomika i matematicheskie metody*, 1974:3, 419–31.

21. See, for instance, Strumilin's letter to leading optimal planners published after his death in *Aktualnye problemy ekonomicheskoi Nauki v Trudakh S. G. Strumilina*, Nauka, Moscow, 1977, 147–52.

22. See Sutela, *Socialism, Planning and Optimality*, p. 49.

23. For a discussion see G. A. Cohen, *Karl Marx' Theory of History. A Defense*. Clarendon Press, Oxford 1978.

24. E. A. Preobrazhensky, *The New Economics*, Clarendon Press, Oxford 1965 (first published in 1926).

25. Ilmari Susiluoto, *The Origins and Development of Systems Thinking in the Soviet Union*, Suomalainen Tiedeakatemia, Helsinki 1982.

26. I. Gladkov, 'Protiv opportunizma v teorii planirovaniya', *Planovoe Khoziaistvo*, 1933:5–6, 263–77.

27. V. V. Kuibyshev, *Stati i Rechi, T. V. 1930–1935*, Partizdat CK VKP(b), Moscow 1937.

28. A. A. Arzumanian, 'O Razvitie ekonomicheskoi Nauki i ekonomicheskogo obrazovaniya v SSSR', *Vestnik Akademii Nauk*, 1964:8, 3–12.

29. R. W. Davies, 'The socialist market: a debate in Soviet industry', *Slavic Review*, 1984:2, 201–23; Pekka Sutela, 'Economic incentives in Soviet prewar economic thought', in Stefan Hedlund, ed., *Incentives and Economic Systems*, Croom Helm, London & Sydney 1987, pp. 151–77.

30. L. Aleksandrov, 'Mechty, voploshchennye v zhizn', *Ekonomicheskaya Gazeta*, 1987:39, 15.

31. A. M. Alekseev in 'Glagoly proshlogo', *Ogoniok*, 1989:6–7, 23, 30–1.

32. I. Lapidus, *Predmet i metod politicheskoi Ekonomii*, Gosudarstvennoe izdatelstvo, Moscow – Leningrad 1931.

33. Sutela, *Socialism, Planning and Optimality*, pp. 61–5.

34. V. V. Kolotov, *Nikolai Alekseyevich Voznesenskii*, 2-e izd., Izdatelstvo politicheskoi literatury, Moscow 1976; Mark Harrison, *Soviet Planning in Peace and War, 1938–1945*, Cambridge University Press, Cambridge 1984.

35. N. Voznesenskii, *Voennaya ekonomika SSSR v period otechestvennoi voiny*, Gosudarstvennoe izdatelstvo politicheskoi literatury, 1948 (no place indicated).

36. See K. Ostrovitjanow, 'Ueber die Maengel im Unterricht der politischen Oekonomie in der Hochschule', in *Beitraege zur Geschichte der politischen Oekonomie des Sozialismus*, Dietz, Berlin 1975, pp. 295–313.

37. Gregory Grossman, 'Scarce capital and Soviet doctrine', *Quarterly Review of Economics*, 1953:3, 311–43.

38. Sutela, *Socialism, Planning and Optimality*, p. 69.
39. J. V. Stalin, *Ekonomicheskie problemy sotsializma v SSSR*, Gosudarstvennoe izdatelstvo politicheskoi literatury, Moscow 1952.
40. Yaroshenko, whose existence as a real person has been sometimes doubted, only reappeared in public view in 1989, at the age of ninety-four. See 'Kak Ya stala "poslednei Zherstvoi" ', *Pravda*, 29 September 1989.
41. 'Za polnoe preodolenie ossichok i koronnoe uluchenie raboty sovetskikh ekonomistov', *Voprosy Ekonomiki*, 1953:1, 3–13.
42. A. I. Mikoyan, *Rech na XX Sëzde KPSS*, Gospolitizdat, Moscow 1956, pp. 30–7.
43. L. F. Ilichev, *Obshchestvennye nauki i kommunizm*, Izdatelstvo AN SSSR, Moscow 1963, p. 21.
44. V. S. Nemchinov, *Ekonomiko-matematicheskie metody i modeli*, Sotsekgiz, Moscow 1962, p. 140.
45. V. S. Nemchinov, *O Dalneyshem sovershenstvovanii planirovaniya i upravleniya narodnym khoziaistvom*, 2-e izd., Ekonomika, Moscow 1965, p. 66.
46. See Gregory Grossman, ed., *Value and Plan. Economic Calculation and Organization in Eastern Europe*, University of California Press, Berkeley, 1960.
47. L. F. Ilichev, 'Nekotorye problemy razvitiya obshchestvennykh nauk', *Vestnik Akademii Nauk*, 1962:11, 7–34, cited on p. 19.
48. L. A. Leontev, 'Ot goloska starogo i trebovaniya zhizni', *Ekonomicheskaya Gazeta*, 20 November 1961.
49. L. F. Ilichev, 'XXII Sëzd KPSS i zadachi ideologicheskoi raboty', in *XXII Sëzd KPSS i voprosy ideologicheskoi raboty*, Gosudarstvennoe izdatelstvo politicheskoi literatury, Moscow 1962, 7–87, cited on p. 43.
50. *Sistema ekonomicheskikh Nauk*, Nauka, Moscow 1968.
51. See Stephen Fortescue, *The Communist Party and Soviet Science*, Macmillan, London 1986.
52. See 'Razvitie issledovanii v oblasti ekonomiki', *Vestnik Akademii Nauk*, 1970:2, 13–20.
53. See 'O rabote partiinoi organizatsii Instituta Ekonomika Akademii Nauk SSSR . . .', *Kommunist*, 1972:1, 3–5.
54. N. P. Fedorenko, 'Aktualnye problemy razvitiya sovetskoi ekonomicheskoi nauki', *Voprosy Ekonomiki*, 1973:7, 50–63.
55. *Ekonomicheskii stroi sotsializma, V trekh tomakh*, Ekonomika, Moscow 1984.
56. E. I. Kapustin, 'Ekonomicheskii stroi sotsializma', *Ekonomicheskaya Gazeta*, 1985:16, 10.

2   The mathematical challenge to orthodoxy

1. Alfred Zauberman, *The Mathematical Revolution in Soviet Economics*, Royal Institute for International Affairs and Oxford University Press, London 1975.

2. V. V. Volkonskii, *Model optimalnogo planirovaniya i vzaimosviazi ekonomicheskikh pokazatelei*, Ekonomika, Moscow 1967, p. 10.
3. Mikhail Antonov, 'Uskorenie: vozmozhnosti i pregradi', *Nash Sovremennik*, 1986:7, 3–20.
4. Susan Gross Solomon, *The Soviet Agrarian Debate*, Westview, Boulder, Colorado 1978.
5. Aleksandr Erlich, *The Soviet Industrialization Debate, 1924–1928*, 2nd edn, Harvard University Press, Cambridge, Mass. 1967.
6. Evsey Domar, *Essays in the Theory of Growth*, Oxford University Press, Oxford 1957.
7. Nicholas Spulber and Kamran Moayed Dadkhad, 'The pioneering stage in input–output economics', *The Review of Economics and Statistics*, 1975:1, 27–34.
8. Leon Smolinski, 'The origins of Soviet mathematical economics', *Jahrbuch der Wirtschaft Osteuropas*, 1971, 137–54.
9. Moshe Lewin, *Political Undercurrents in Soviet Economic Debates*, Pluto Press, London 1974; D. V. Valovoi and G. E. Lapshina, *Sotsializm i tovarno-denezhnye otnosheniya*, Ekonomika, Moscow 1972, pp. 107–9.
10. I. G. Bliumin, *Subëktivnaya shkola v politicheskoi ekonomii, vol. 2, Matematicheskaya shkola*, Vtoroe, ispravlennoe i dopolnennoe izdanie, Izdatelstvo Kommunisticheskoi Akademii, Moscow 1931.
11. See V. Kuibyshev, *Stati i rechi, Tom. V. 1930–1935*, Partizdat CK VKP (b), Moscow 1937, p. 78.
12. O. Bogomolov, 'Peremena Dekoratsii', *Ogoniok*, 1990:23, 0–2.
13. V. Yankulin, 'Otkrytie dlia fanernovo tresta', *Literaturnaya Gazeta*, 6 February 1985.
14. V. L. Makarov, 'Glubokii issledovatel', *EKO*, 1987:1, 77–83.
15. See, for instance, Don Lavoie, *Rivalry and Central Planning*, Cambridge University Press, Cambridge 1985.
16. Oskar Lange, 'Computer and the market', in Alec Nove and Mario Nuti, eds, *Economics of Socialism*, Penguin, Harmondsworth 1972, pp. 401–5 (1st edn 1967).
17. Yankulin, 'Otkrytie dlia fanernogo tresta'.
18. See Andrei Belykh, 'Mathematical economics and Soviet planning', *Carleton Economics Papers*, 89–03 (February 1989), p. 7.
19. See the papers reprinted in V. V. Novozhilov, *Voprosy razvitiya sotsialisticheskoi ekonomiki*, Nauka, Moscow 1972.
20. See Alfred Zauberman, 'Economic thought in the Soviet Union, II', *Review of Economic Studies*, 1949–50:2, 102–16.
21. K. V. Ostrovitianov, 'Ob itogakh i napravlenii raboty Institute Ekonomii Akademii Nauk SSSR', *Voprosy Ekonomiki*, 1948:1, 86–91.
22. See A. Vainshtein, 'Vecher pamiati Akademika V. S. Nemchinova', *Ekonomika i matematicheskie metody*, 1965:4, 617–21.
23. Yankulin, 'Otkrytie dlia fanernogo tresta'.
24. Aron Katsenelinboigen, *Soviet Economic Thought and Political Power in the USSR*, Pergamon, New York 1980, p. 37.

25. There is an English translation: L. V. Kantorovich, *The Best Use of Economic Resources*, Harvard University Press, Cambridge, Mass. 1965.
26. N. Ya. Petrakov, 'Beskompromissnyi boyets', *EKO*, 1987:1, 84–5.
27. G. Sorokin, 'Perspektivnoe planirovanie narodnogo khoziaistva', *Planovoe Khoziaistvo*, 1956:1, 30–47.
28. I. Bliumin and V. Shlapentokh, 'Ob ekonometricheskom napravlenii v burzhuaznoi politicheskoi ekonomii', *Voprosy Ekonomiki*, 1958:11, 79–93.
29. V. Nemchinov, 'Sovremennye problemy sovetskoi ekonomicheskoi Nauki', *Voprosy Ekonomiki*, 1959:4, 18–34, cited on p. 23.
30. V. Nemchinov, 'Ekonomiko–matematicheskie metody i modeli' (1962), in V. S. Nemchinov, *Izbrannye Proizvedeniya*, vol. 3, Ekonomika, Moscow 1967, pp. 148–50.
31. V. Nemchinov, 'Ekonometriya' (1961), in V. S. Nemchinov, *Izbrannye proizvedeniya*, vol. 3, Ekonomika, Moscow 1967, p. 135.
32. Aron Katsenelinboigen, *Soviet Economic Thought and Political Power in the USSR*, Pergamon, London, 1980.
33. L. Kantorovich, *The Best Use of Economic Resources*; V. Novozhilov, 'O Primenenii matematiki pri optimalnom planirovanii narodnogo khoziaistva' (1961), in V. Novozhilov, *Voprosy razvitiya sotsialisticheskoi ekonomiki*, Nauka, Moscow 1970, p. 238: V. Glushkov, A. Dorodnitsyn and N. Fedorenko, 'O nekotorykh problemakh kibernetiki', *Izvestiya*, 6 September 1964.
34. L. V. Kantorovich, 'Matematicheskie metody v reshenii khozyaistvennykh zadach', in *Teoriya i Praktika khozyaistvennoi reformy*, Ekonomika, Moscow 1967, 159–73.
35. A. Aganbegyan, 'Bez prava medlit', *Izvestiya*, 18 April 1968.
36. N. Fedorenko, 'Instrumenty optimizatsii planovykh reshenii', *Kommunist*, 1978:6, 31–42.
37. See Sutela, *Socialism, Planning and Optimality*, pp. 90–1.
38. Jan Tinbergen, 'The theory of the optimum regime', in Jan Tinbergen, *Selected Papers*, North-Holland, Amsterdam 1959, pp. 264–303.
39. Yuri Oleinik in *Ekonomisty i matematiki za kruglym stolom*, Ekonomika, Moscow 1965, p. 199.
40. The basic references are A. Katsenelinboigen, Yu. V. Ovsienko and E. Yu. Faerman, *Metodologicheskie voprosy optimalnogo planirovaniya sotsialisticheskoi ekonomiki*, TsEMI AN SSSR, Moscow 1966; A. Katsenelinboigen, I. Lakhman and Yu. V. Ovsienko, *Optimalnost i tovarno-denezhnye otnosheniya*, Nauka, Moscow 1969 and A. Katsenelinboigen, S. M. Movshovich and Yu. V. Ovsienko, *Vosproizvodstvo i ekonomicheskii optimum*, Nauka, Moscow 1972.
41. N. P. Fedorenko, *O razrabotke sistemy optimalnogo funktsionirovaniya ekonomiki*, Ekonomika, Moscow 1968.
42. M. Gorbachev, 'Sotsialisticheskaya ideya i revolyutsionnaya perestroika', *Pravda*, 26 November 1989.
43. V. I. Danilov-Danilian and M. G. Zavelskii, *Sistema optimalnogo perspektivnogo planirovaniya narodnogo khoziaistva*, Nauka, Moscow 1975.

44. See Janos Kornai, *Mathematical Planning of Structural Decisions*, 2nd edn, Akademiai Kiado, Budapest 1975 (1st edn 1967), pp. 417–22.
45. Volkonskii, *Model optimalnogo planirovaniya i vzaimosvyazi ekonomicheskikh pokazateley*, p. 10.
46. A. M. Matlin, 'Review of *Ekonomisty i matematiki za kruglym stolom*', *Ekonomika i matematicheskie metody*, 1965:4, 622–25.
47. A. I. Katsenelinboigen and E. Yu. Faerman, 'Tsentralizm i khozyaistvennaya samostoyatelnost v sotsialisticheskoi ekonomike', *Ekonomika i matematicheskie metody*, 1967:3, 331–46.
48. Katsenelinboigen, Lakhman and Ovsienko, *Optimalnost i tovarno-denezhnye otnosheniya*.
49. M. G. Zavelskii, 'O problemakh teorii narodnokhozyaistvennogo optimuma', *Ekonomika i matematicheskie metody*, 1978:4, 673–776.
50. A. Aganbegyan, 'O primenenii matematicheskikh metodov v ekonomicheskom analize', *Voprosy Ekonomiki*, 1960:2, 54–66.
51. V. Novozhilov and S. Gladevich, 'Khozraschetnaya sistema planirovaniya', in *Optimalnoe planirovanie i sovershenstvovanie upravleniya narodnym khoziaistvom*, Nauka, Moscow 1969, 26–40.
52. See *Diskussiya ob optimalnom planirovanii*, Ekonomika, Moscow 1968.
53. S. S. Shatalin, 'Nekotorye problemy teorii optimalnogo funktsionirovaniya sotsialisticheskoi ekonomiki', *Ekonomika i matematicheskie metody*, 1970:5, 835–48.
54. S. S. Shatalin, *Proportsionalnost obschestvennogo proizvodstva*, Ekonomika, Moscow 1968.
55. A. I. Anchishkin and Yu. V. Yaremenko, *Tempy i proportsii ekonomicheskogo razvitiya*, Ekonomika, Moscow 1967.
56. Ibid.

3 The reformist programme

1. For a thorough discussion of these concepts see Ed A. Hewett, *Reforming the Soviet Economy*, Brookings, Washington DC 1988.
2. Michael Kaser, 'The reorganization of Soviet industry and its effects on decision making', in Gregory Grossman, ed., *Value and Plan: Economic Calculation and Organization in Eastern Europe*, Greenwood Press, Westport, Conn. 1976, 213–44.
3. See Alec Nove, *The Soviet Economy: An Introduction*, rev. edn, Allen & Unwin, London 1966, pp. 161–73.
4. Pekka Sutela, 'Economic incentives in Soviet pre-war economic thought', in Stefan Hedlund, ed., *Incentives and Economic Systems*, Croom Helm, London 1987, 151–77.
5. See A. M. Alekseev in 'Glagoly proshlogo', *Ogoniok*, 1989:6–7, 23, 30–1.
6. See Eugene Zaleski, *Planning Reform in the Soviet Union, 1962–66*, The University of North Carolina Press, Chapel Hill 1967, ch. 4.
7. There is a translation in Morris Bornstein and Daniel R. Fusfeld, eds, *The*

Soviet Economy: A Book of Readings, rev. edn, Irwin, Homewood, Illinois 1966, pp. 352–58.

8. George F. Feiwel, *Soviet Quest for Economic Efficiency, Issues, Controversies and Reforms*. Praeger, New York 1967, pp. 205–22.

9. Zaleski, *Planning Reforms in the Soviet Union, 1962–1967*, p. 116.

10. Janos Kornai, *The Economics of Shortage*, 2 vols. North-Holland, Amsterdam 1980.

11. The best accounts of these discussions remain Zaleski, *Planning Reforms in the Soviet Union, 1962–1967* and Feiwel, *Soviet Quest for Economic Efficiency*.

12. V. V. Novozhilov, 'Cost-benefit comparisons in a socialist economy', in V. S. Nemchinov, ed., *The Use of Mathematics in Economics*, Oliver & Boyd, London & Edinburgh 1964, pp. 33–189 (originally published in 1959).

13. V. V. Novozhilov, 'K diskussii o printsipakh planovogo tsenoobrazovaniya', in *Primenenie matematiki v ekonomike, Vyp. 1*, Izdatelstvo Leningradskogo Gosudarstvennogo Universiteta, Leningrad 1963, pp. 46–54, especially p. 52.

14. L. V. Kantorovich, *The Best Use of Economic Resources*, Harvard University Press, Cambridge, Mass. 1965, p. 150.

15. Martin Cave, *Computers and Economic Planning*, Cambridge University Press, Cambridge 1980; William Conyngham, *The Modernization of Soviet Industrial Management*, Cambridge University Press, Cambridge 1982.

16. Vasili Seliunin, 'Planovaya anarkhiya ili balans interesov', *Znamya*, 1989:11, 203–20.

17. See the two volumes of selected works: V. V. Novozhilov, *Voprosy Razvitiya sotsialisticheskoi ekonomiki*, Nauka, Moscow 1970; V. V. Novozhilov, *Problemy izmereniya zatrat i rezultatov pri optimalnom planirovanii*, Nauka, Moscow 1972.

18. N. Ya. Petrakov, *Nekotorye aspekty diskussii ob ekonomicheskikh metodakh khoziaistvovaniya*, Ekonomika, Moscow 1966, pp. 20, 77–8.

19. V. Nemchinov, 'Sotsialisticheskoe khoziaistvovanie i Planirovanie proizvodstva', *Kommunist*, 1964:5, 74–87, reprinted in V. S. Nemchinov, *O dalneyshem sovershenstvovanii planirovaniya i upravleniya narodym khoziaistvom*, 2-e izd., Ekonomika, Moscow 1965, 49–73 and in *Kommunist*, 1987:11, 23–32. Gorbachev's endorsement is in 'O zadachakh partii po korennoi perestroiki upravleniya ekonomikoi. Doklad generalnogo sekretarya M. S. Gorbacheva na plenume TsK KPSS 25 iyunia 1987 goda', *Kommunist*, 1987:10, 5–47, especially p. 28.

20. V. S. Nemchinov, *O dalneyshem sovershenstvovanii planirovaniya i upravleniya narodnym khoziaistvom*, p. 8.

21. V. S. Nemchinov, 'Sotsiologicheskii aspekt planirovaniya', in V. S. Nemchinov, *Izbrannye proizvedeniya*, vol. 5, Nauka, Moscow 1968, p. 100.

22. See Novozhilov, *Problemy izmereniya zatrat i rezultatov pri optimalnom planirovanii*, p. 32 and more generally Moshe Lewin, *Political Undercurrents in Soviet Economic Debates*, Pluto Press, London 1974.

23. V. S. Nemchinov, *Izbrannye Proizvedeniya*, vol. 6, Nauka, Moscow 1970, p. 180.
24. For a summary and detailed criticism of these proposals, see Michael Ellman, *Soviet Planning Today*, Cambridge University Press, Cambridge 1971; Michael Ellman, *Planning Problems in the USSR*, Cambridge University Press, Cambridge 1973.
25. Ibid.
26. Gertrude E. Schroeder, 'Soviet economic "reforms": a study in contradictions', *Soviet Studies*, 1968:2, 3–16.
27. See Ellman, *Soviet Planning Today*, p. 161.
28. For a good discussion see Hewett, *Reforming the Soviet Economy*, pp. 227–45.

4 The years of radicalism and reaction

1. Nikolai Petrakov, 'Upravlenie ekonomikoi i ekonomicheskie interesy', *Novyi Mir*, 1970:8, 167–86, cited on p. 167
2. L. Abalkin, 'Ekonomicheskaya nauka i obshchestvo', *Novyi Mir*, 1971:9, 167–78.
3. Moshe Lewin, *Political Undercurrents in Soviet Economic Debates*, Pluto Press, London 1975.
4. G. S. Lisichkin, *Plan i rynok*, Ekonomika, Moscow 1966, p. 53.
5. G. Lisichkin, 'Mify i realnost', *Novyi Mir*, 1988:11, 160–88.
6. See Alexander Yanov, *The Drama of the Soviet 1960s*, Institute of International Studies, University of California, Berkeley 1984.
7. A. Birman, 'Neobratimost', *Literaturnaya Gazeta*, 11 January 1967.
8. B. Rakitskii, *Formy khozyaistvennogo rukovodstva predpriyatiyami*, Ekonomika, Moscow 1968.
9. See G. Khanin, 'Ekonomicheskii rost i vybor', *Novyi Mir*, 1967:12, 261–3 (on growth rates), 'Banki v narodnym khozyaistve', *Novyi Mir*, 1968:12, 249–53 (on competition), 'Logika ekonomicheskogo mekhanizma', *Novyi Mir*, 1970:5, 270–4 (on comprehensive reform).
10. See Boris Kagarlitsky, *The Thinking Reed: Intellectuals and the Soviet State from 1917 to the Present*, Verso, London 1988, pp. 188–201.
11. G. Popov, 'S tochki zreniya ekonomista', *Nauka i Zhizn*, 1987:4, 54–65: E. G. Yasin, 'Administrativnaya sistema tsen ili ekonomicheskii mekhanizm', *Ekonomika i matematicheskie metody*, 1988:2, 209–20; Nikolai Shmelev, 'Libo sila, libo rubl', *Znamya*, 1989:1, 128–47; L. Abalkin, 'Rynok v ekonomicheskoi sisteme sotsializma', *Voprosy Ekonomiki*, 1989:7, 3–12.
12. F. Hayek, 'Planirovanie i demokratiya', *EKO*, 1989:11, 143–55.
13. V. A. Volkonskii, 'Tovarno-denezhnyi mekhanizm v optimalnom upravlenii khozyaistvom i tsenoobrazovanie', *Ekonomika i matematicheskie metody*, 1967:4, 489–99, cited on p. 493.
14. N. P. Fedorenko, *O Razrabotke sistemy optimalnogo funktsionirovaniya ekonomiki*, Nauka, Moscow 1968.

15. N. P. Fedorenko, *Voprosy optimalnogo funktsionirovaniya ekonomiki*, Nauka, Moscow 1980.
16. E. Gorbunov and Yu. Ovsienko, 'Preodolet psikhologicheskii barer', *Novyi Mir*, 1971:2, 147–58.
17. Nikolai Petrakov, 'Upravlenie ekonomiki i ekonomicheskie interesy', *Novyi Mir*, 1970:8, 167–86.
18. B. Smekhov, 'Prostata i slozhnost ekonomiki', *Novyi Mir*, 1971:1, 148–59.
19. N. Petrakov, 'Potreblenie i effektivnost proizvodstva', *Novyi Mir*, 1971:6, 192–206.
20. Gorbunov and Ovsienko, 'Preodolat psikhologicheskii barer', p. 147.
21. See Pekka Sutela, *Socialism, Planning and Optimality*, Finnish Society for Sciences and Letters, Helsinki 1984, p. 127.
22. Nikolai Petrakov, 'Mify rynochnogo sotsializma i ekonomicheskaya realnost', *Problemy Mira i Sotsializma*, 1973:2, 33–7.
23. N. Vladova and N. Rabkina, 'Sobstvennost i Rynok', *Voprosy Ekonomiki*, 1988:10, 76–86; N. Vladova and N. Rabkina, 'Vozmozhno li kontseptsiya ekonomicheskogo sinteza', *Neva*, 1989:10, 143–56.
24. Yu. Burtin, 'Akhillesova pyata istoricheskoi teorii marksa', *Oktyabr*, 1989:11, 3–25.
25. B. Pinsker, 'Byurokraticheskaya khimera', *Znamya*, 1989:11, 183–202; Vasili Seliunin, 'Planovaya anarkhiya ili balans interesov', *Znamya*, 1989:11, 203–20.
26. O. Amurzhuev and V. Tsapelik, 'Kak pobedit diktat monopolista', *Ekonomicheskaya Gazeta*, 1989:49, 7.
27. Yu. V. Sukhotin, 'Ekonomicheskaya reforma i narodnokhoziaistvennyi optimum', in *Voprosy effektivnosti obshchest vennogo proizvodstva*, Nauka, Moscow 1970, 11–79.
28. For an analysis, see Masaaki Kuboniwa, *Quantitative Economics of Socialism*, Kinokuniya Company Ltd and Oxford University Press, Tokyo and Oxford 1989, pp. 201–20.
29. E. Yasin, 'Sotsialisticheskii rynok ili yarmarkaillyuzii?', *Kommunist*, 1989:15, 53–63 Yu. Borozdin, 'Ekonomicheskaya Reform i torarno-denezhnye Otnosheniya *Voprosy Ekonomiki*, 1990:1, 13–25.
30. Michael Ellman, *Soviet Planning Today*, Cambridge University Press, Cambridge 1971, p. 191.
31. Lisichkin, *Plan i Rynok*.
32. Ibid., pp. 13, 56.
33. Conference report as cited in Ellman, *Soviet Planning Today*, p. 19.
34. V. N. Bogachev, 'Optimalnyi plan i polnyi khozraschet', in *Voprosy effektivnosti obshchestvennogo proizvodstva*, 80–140, cited on pp. 97–8.
35. A. I. Katsenelinboigen, I. L. Lakhman and Yu. V. Ovsienko, *Optimalnost i tovarno-denezhnye otnosheniya*, Nauka, Moscow 1969.
36. N. Ya. Petrakov, *Khozyaistvennaya reforma: plan i ekonomicheskaya samostoyatelnost*, Mysl, Moscow 1971; N. Petrakov, *Nekotorye voprosy upravleniya sotsialisticheskoi ekonomikoi*, TsEMI, Moscow 1971.
37. See N. Petrakov, 'Upravlenie Ekonomiki i ekonomicheskie interesy'.
38. See Sutela, *Socialism, Planning and Optimality*, pp. 99–100.

39. A. Bachurin, 'V. I. Lenin i sovremennye problemy planirovaniya narod-nogo khoziaistva', *Planovoe Khozyaistvo*, 1969:11, 3–18.

40. N. Kovalev, 'Politicheskaya ekonomika sotsializma i ekonomiko-matematicheskie metody', *Planovoe Khozyaistvo*, 1972:5, 30–40.

41. P. Krylov, 'Tsentralizovannoe planirovanie v novykh usloviyakh', *Ekonomicheskaya Gazeta*, 1969:45, 8–9, cited on p. 8.

42. Sutela, *Socialism, Planning and Optimality*, pp. 143–4.

43. A. G. Aganbegyan, 'Prakticheskie dela ekonomicheskoi Nauki', *EKO*, 1989:9, 17–29.

44. *Problemy optimalnogo funktsionirovaniya sotsialisticheskoi ekonomiki*, N. P. Fedorenko, ed., Nauka, Moscow 1972, p. 38.

45. Martin Cave, *Computers and Economic Planning*, Cambridge University Press, Cambridge 1980; William J. Conyngham, *The Modernization of Soviet Industrial Management*, Cambridge University Press, Cambridge 1982.

46. N. Baibakov, 'Dalneyshee sovershenstvovanie planirovaniya – vazhneyshaya narodnokhoziaistennaya zadacha', *Planovoe Khozyaistvo*, 1974:4, 5–13.

47. M. Bor and S. Logvinov, 'O Knigakh 'Kompleksnoe narodnokhozyat-sitvennoe planirovanie' i 'Problemy planirovaniya i prognozirovaniya', *Planovoe Khozyaistvo*, 1975:9, 134–41.

48. N. Moiseenko and M. Popov, *Demokraticheskii tsentralism – osnovnoi print-sip upravleniya sotsialisticheskoi ekonomikoi*, Lenizdat, Leningrad 1975.

49. D. V. Valovoi and G. E. Lapshina, *Sotsializm i tovarnye otnosheniya*, Ekonomika, Moscow 1972, pp. 107–9.

50. Most of such proposals can be found in *Problemy optimalnogo funktsion-irovaniya sotsialisticheskoi ekonomiki*.

51. Gordon L. Rocca, ' "A second party in our midst": the history of the Soviet Scientific Forecasting Association', *Social Studies on Science*, 1981:2, 199–247.

52. See S. Shatalin, 'Akademik A. I. Anchishkin: vospominaniya soratnika i druga', *Voprosy Ekonomiki*, 1989:1, 26–36.

53. Ibid.

54. Aganbegyan, 'Prakticheskie dela ekonomicheskoi nauki'.

55. Conyngham, *The Modernization of Soviet Industrial Management*.

56. See *Programmo-tselevoi metod v planirovanii*, Nauka, Moscow 1982, p. 34.

57. N. Ya. Petrakov and E. Rudneva, 'O Roli, meste i funktsiyakh komple ksnykh programm v sisteme upravleniya sotsialisticheskoi ekonomikoi', *Ekonomika i matematicheskie metody*, 1978:4, 639–53.

58. V. Tambovtsev and A. Tikhomirov, *Organizatsiya upravleniya kom-pleksnymi programmami*, Izd. MGU, Moscow 1982.

59. N. Fedorenko, *Nekotorye voprosy teorii i praktiki planirovaniya i upravleniya*, Nauka, Moscow 1979, p. 16.

60. For a clear discussion of this see Yu. Sukhotin, 'O motivatsionnom aspekte khozyaistvennogo planirovaniya', *Ekonomika i matematicheskie metody*, 1983:2, 328–45.

61. Ibid.

62. A. Bim, 'Gosudarstvennyi Plan: novye zadachi, novaya model', *Kommunist*, 1989:11, 3–9.
63. E. Novikov and Yu. Sukhotin, *Kompleksnye narodnokhozyaistvennye programmy*, Nauka, Moscow 1976.
64. See, for example, Sergei Shrashko, 'Trudnye budni BAMa', *Sibirskie Ogni*, 1989:1, 132–42.
65. R. G. Karagedov, 'Sovershenstvovanie sistemy ekonomicheskogo upravleniya v vengerskoi narodnoi respublike', *Izvestiya sibirskoi otdeleniya akademii Nauk SSSR, Seriya obshestvennykh Nauk*, 1974:6:2, 21–34.
66. R. G. Karagedov, 'Ekonomicheskoe regulirovanie i politika dokhodov', *Izvestiya sibirskoi otdeleniya Akademii Nauk SSSR, Seriya obshestvennykh Nauk*, 1976:11:3, 20–30.
67. V. A. Volkonskii, *Problemy sovershenstvovaniya khoziaistvennogo mekhanizma*, Nauka, Moscow 1981.
68. N. Fedorenko, V. Perlamutrov, N. Petrakov and V. Starodubrovskii, 'Parametry upravleniya', *Pravda*, 23 March 1978.
69. See Morris Bornstein, 'Improving the Soviet economic mechanism', *Soviet Studies*, 1985:1, 1–30.
70. *Khozyaistvennyi mekhanizm v sisteme optimalnogo funktsionirovanie sotsialisticheskoi ekonomiki*, Nauka, Moscow 1985.
71. See Ed. A. Hewett, *Reforming the Soviet Economy*, Brookings Institution, Washington DC 1988, pp. 260–73.
72. *Problemy optimalnogo funktsionirovaniya sotsialisticheskoi ekonomiki*, p. 221.
73. Tatjana Saslawskaja, *Die Gorbatschow-Strategie*, Orac, Vienna 1989, p. 70.

5   Not of mathematics alone

1. Vasili Seliunin, 'Planovaya anarkhiya ili balans interesov', *Znamya*, 1989:11, 203–20.
2. See the discussion in *Problemy narodnokhoziaistvennogo kriteriya optimalnosti*, Nauka, Moscow 1982.
3. S. S. Shatalin, *Funktsionirovanie ekonomiki razvitogo sotsializma*, Izdatelstvo MGU, Moscow 1982.
4. V. A. Volkonskii, *Problemy sovershenstvovaniya khoziaistvennogo mekhanizma*, Nauka, Moscow 1981.
5. Yu. Sukhotin, V. Dementev and Yu. Ovsienko, 'Ekonomiko-matematicheskoe napravlenie: uroki i perspektivy', *Voprosy Ekonomiki*, 1989:1, 110–20; S. Shatalin, 'Teoriya optimalnogo funktsionirovaniya sotsialisticheskoi ekonomiki', *Voprosy Ekonomiki*, 1989:8, 3–13.
6. N. Fedorenko, Yu. Ovsienko and N. Petrakov, 'Planomernost i problemy sovershenstvovaniya khozyaistvennogo mekhanizma upravleniya', *Ekonomika i matematicheskie metody*, 1983:3, 397–406.
7. 'Aktualnye voprosy ideologicheskoi, massovo-politicheskoi raboty partii', *Pravda*, 15 June 1983.

8. See 'V tsentralnom komitete KPSS', *Pravda*, 24 February 1984.
9. Otto Latsis, 'Kovcheg na melkovode', *Rabochaya Tribuna*, 27 March 1990.
10. See 'Doroga k zdravomu Smyslu', *Izvestiya*, 9 April 1990.
11. Shatalin, *Funktsionirovanie ekonomiki razvitogo sotsializma*.
12. See 'Ne delit, a zarabatyvat', *Ogoniok*, 1989:1, 2, 25–7, 41 (an interview of Abalkin).
13. V. A. Medvedev, *Zabon stoimosti i materialnye stimuly sotsialisticheskogo proizvodstva*, Ekonomika, Moscow 1966.
14. For a review see *Istoriya politicheskoi ekonomii sotsializma*. Izd. 2-e, Izdatelstvo LGU, Leningrad 1983, pp. 283–317.
15. L. I. Abalkin, *Khozyaistvennyi mekhanizm razvitogo sotsializma*, Mysl, Moscow 1973.
16. L. Abalkin, 'Rynok v ekonomicheskoi sisteme sotsializma', *Voprosy Ekonomiki*, 1989:7, 3–12.
17. Shatalin, *Funktsionirovanie ekonomiki razvitogo sotsializma*.
18. N. Ya. Petrakov, *Nekotorye aspekty diskussii ob ekonomicheskikh metodakh khoziaistvovaniya*, Ekonomika, Moscow 1966, pp. 101–3.
19. L. Abalkin, 'Ekonomicheskaya nauka i obshchestva', *Novyi Mir*, 1971:9, 167–78.
20. L. I. Abalkin, *Planomernoe razvitie i proportsii mirovogo sotsialisticheskogo khoziaistva*, Mysl, Moscow 1965.
21. L. I. Abalkin and B. N. Ladygin, *Ekonomicheskie zakonomernosti razvitiya mirovogo sotsializma*, Vysshaya shkola, Moscow 1963.
22. L. I. Abalkin, *Politicheskaya ekonomiya i ekonomicheskaya politika*, Mysl, Moscow 1970.
23. L. I. Abalkin, *Novyi tip ekonomicheskogo myshleniya*, Ekonomika, Moscow 1987, especially on p. 77.
24. L. I. Abalkin, *Ekonomicheskie zakony sotsializma*, Nauka, Moscow 1971.
25. Abalkin, *Ekonomicheskie zakony sotsializma*, p. 96.
26. Philip Hanson, 'Some schools of thought in the Soviet debate on economic reform', *Berichte des Bundesinstituts für ostwissenschaftliche und internationale Studien*, 29–1989, p. 23.
27. Abalkin, 'Rynok v ekonomicheskom sisteme sotsializma'.
28. See Philip Hanson, 'Ownership and economic reform', *Radio Liberty Research*, RL 154/88 (6 April 1988).
29. See 'Strategiya obnovleniya', *Ogoniok*, 1989:6–7, 13, 18–20.
30. 'Proekt zakona o sobstvennosti SSSR', *Pravda*, 18 November 1989.
31. Abalkin, *Ekonomicheskie zakony sotsializma*, pp. 156–7.
32. L. I. Abalkin, *Dialektika sotsialisticheskoi ekonomiki*, Mysl, Moscow 1981, pp. 268–71.
33. See 'Lekarstvo byvaet i gorkim', *Argumenty i Fakty*, 1989:41, 1, 2–3 (an interview with Abalkin).
34. L. I. Abalkin, *Khoziaistvennyi mekhanizm razvitogo sotsialisticheskogo obshchestva*, Mysl, Moscow 1973, pp. 5, 261.
35. Abalkin, *Khoziaistvennyi mekhanizm razvitogo sotsialisticheskogo obshchestva*, p. 254.

36. 'Strategiya obnovleniya'. p. 19.
37. Abalkin, *Khoziaistvennyi mekhanizm razvitogo sotsialisticheskogo obshchestva*, p. 244.
38. N. Petrakov, 'Upravlenie ekonomiki i ekonomicheskie interesy', *Novyi Mir*, 1970:8, 167–86.
39. Abalkin, *Khoziaistvennyi mekhanism sotsialisticheskogo obshchestva*, pp. 216–19.
40. Abalkin, *Dialektika sotsialisticheskoi ekonomiki*.
41. Ibid., p. 316.
42. Ibid., p. 246.
43. See 'Obsuzhdenie proekta TsK KPSS', *Voprosy Ekonomiki*, 1981:1, pp. 61–4 and Shatalin, *Funktsionirovanie ekonomiki razvitogo sotsializma*.
44. V. A. Medvedev, *Sotsialisticheskoe proizvodstvo*, Ekonomika, Moscow 1976, pp. 57–9.
45. Ibid., p. 189.
46. Ibid., 2-e izd., Ekonomika, Moscow 1981, p. 188.
47. V. A. Medvedev, *Teoreticheskie problemy razvitogo sotsializma*, Mysl, Moscow 1980, p. 37.
48. Medvedev, *Sotsialisticheskoe Proizvodstvo*, 1-e izd., pp. 136–45; 2-e izd., pp. 132–50.
49. V. A. Medvedev, *Upravlenie sotsialisticheskim proizvodstvom: problemy teorii i praktiki*, Politizdat, Moscow 1983, pp. 56–63.
50. Medvedev, *Sotsialisticheskoe proizvodstvo*, 2-e izd., p. 187.
51. See V. S. Dunaeva, *Ekonomicheskie zakony sotsializma i problemy narodno-khozyaistvennogo optimuma*, Mysl, Moscow 1976.
52. S. Trapeznikov, 'Ekonomicheskuyu nauku – na uroven sovremennykh zadach kommunisticheskogo stroitelstva', *Voprosy Ekonomiki*, 1974:2, 3–18.
53. P. Fedoseev, 'Ekonomicheskaya nauka: nekotorye zadachi ego razvitiya', *Voprosy Ekonomiki*, 1974:2, 60-4.
54. Pekka Sutela, *Socialism, Planning and Optimality*, The Finnish Society of Sciences and Letters, Helsinki 1984, pp. 139–41.
55. Medvedev, *Sotsialisticheskoe proizvodstvo*, 2-e izd., p. 266.
56. Ibid., 1-e izd., p. 170.
57. Medvedev, *Razvitoi sotsializm: voprosy formirovaniya obshchestvennogo soznaniya*, p. 57.
58. Medvedev, *Sotsialisticheskoe proizvodstvo*, 2-e izd., p. 258.
59. V. A. Medvedev, *Upravlenie sotsialisticheskim proizvodstvom: problemy teorii i praktiki*, Politizdat, Moscow 1983.
60. Anders Aslund, *Gorbachev's Struggle for Economic Reform*, Pinter, London 1989, pp. 36, 112.
61. A. G. Aganbegyan, *Upravlenie sotsialisticheskimi predpriyatiyami*, Ekonomika, Moscow 1979.
62. Aslund, *Gorbachev's Struggle for Economic Reform*, p. 36.
63. Medvedev, *Upravlenie sotsialisticheskim proizvodstvom*, p. 236.
64. See 'Sovremennaya kontseptsiya sotsializma', *Pravda*, 5 October 1988.

65. V. I. Lenin, 'O kooperatsii', in V. I. Lenin, *Polnoe sobranie sochineniya*, vol. 45, Izdatelstvo politicheskoi literatury, Moscow 1966, p. 376.

66. M. Gorbachev, 'Sotsialisticheskaya ideya i revol yutsionnaya perestroika', *Pravda*, 26 November 1989.

67. Pekka Sutela, 'Reformability of the objective economic laws of socialism', in Janos Matyas Kovacs and Marton Tardos, eds., *Plan and/or Market*, Routledge, London 1991.

68. *Politicheckaya ekonomiya. Uchebnik dlya vysshikh uchebnikh zavedenii*, Politizdat, Moscow 1988.

69. See 'Obsuzhdenie v otdelenii ekonomiki AN SSSR', *Voprosy Ekonomiki*, 1988:7, 14–61, especially p. 61.

70. *Ocherki politicheskoi ekonomii sotsializma*, Pod red. N. P. Fedorenko, Nauka, Moscow 1988.

71. See 'Perestroika ekonomicheskoi teorii', *Ekonomicheskie Nauki*, 1989:1, 51–7.

72. A. Ryvkin, 'Ekonomicheskaya teoriya i realnost', *Voprosy Ekonomiki*, 1989:1, 130–41.

73. Mark Popovsky, *Upravlyaemaya nauka*, Overseas Publications, London 1978.

74. See S. F. Cohen, ed., *An End to Silence*, Norton, New York and London 1982, pp. 223–7.

75. Published in English as 'Novosibirk report', *Survey*, 1984:1, 88–108.

76. See Aslund, 'Gorbachev's economic advisors'.

77. Tatjana Saslawskaja, *Die Gorbatschow-Strategie*, Orac, Vienna 1989; Aganbegyan, 'Prakticheskie dela ekonomicheskoi nauki'.

78. See, for instance, *Puti povysheniya effektivnosti narodnogo khoziaistva*. Pod red. A. G. Aganbegyan and D. D. Moskvina, Nauka, Moscow 1987.

79. B. L. Lavrovskii, *Analiz sbalansirovannosti proizvodstvennykh moshchnostei v promyshlennosti*, Nauka, Novosibirsk 1983; A. G. Aganbegyan, *Challenge: The Economics of Perestroika*, Heinemann, London 1988. For a discussion see Pekka Sutela, 'Soviet investments and the decline of economic growth', *Nordic Journal of Soviet and East European Studies*, 1988:2, 99–115.

80. Sutela, 'Soviet investments'.

81. Aslund, 'Gorbachev's economic advisors', pp. 259–60.

82. Aganbegyan, 'Prakticheskaya dela ekonomicheskoi nauki'.

83. A. G. Aganbegyan, K. A. Bagrinovskii and A. G. Granberg, *Sistema modelei narodnokhoziaistvennogo planirovaniya*, Mysl, Moscow 1972.

84. K. K. Valtukh, *Obshchestvennaya poleznost produktsii i zatraty truda na ego proizvodstva*, Mysl, Moscow 1965.

85. K. K. Valtukh, 'Sokratit investitsii?', *EKO*, 1989:9, 69–72.

86. D. M. Kazakevich, *Ocherki teorii sotsialisticheskoi ekonomiki*, Nauka, Novosibirsk 1980; E. Lazutkin and S. Starostin, 'Teoreticheskie problemy sotsialisticheskoi ekonomiki', *Planovoe Khozyaistvo*, 1981:5, 126–8.

87. R. G. Karagedov, 'Sovershenstvovanie sistemy ekonomicheskogo

upravleniya v vengerskoi narodnoi respubliki', *Izvestiya SO AN SSSR, seriya obshchestvennykh nauk*, 1974:6:2, 21–34.

88. R. G. Karagedov, 'Ekonomicheskaya regulirovanie i politika dokhodov', *Izvestiya SO AN SSSR, seriya obshchestvennykh nauk*, 1976:11 :3, 20–30.
89. See, for instance, Tamas Bauer and Karoly Attila Soos, 'The current debate among Soviet economists over the transformation of the system of economic control', *Eastern European Economics*, 1981:3, 70–89.
90. R. G. Karagedov, *Khozraschet, effektivnost i pribyl (ocherki teorii)*, Nauka, Novosibirsk 1979, p. 6.
91. See Bauer and Attila Soos, 'The current debate among Soviet economists over transformation of the system of economic control'.
92. R. G. Karagedov, 'Pervye itogi, problemy, perspektivy', *EKO*, 1985:5, 80–99.
93. R. G. Karagedov, 'Mekhanizm funktsionirovanie sotsialisticheskoi ekonomiki', *Izvestiya SO AN SSSR, seriya obshchestvennykh nauk*, 1982:11:3, 115–28.
94. R. G. Karagedov, 'Ob organizatsionnoi strukture upravleniya promysh-lennostyu', *EKO*, 1983:8, 50–69; R. G. Karagedov, 'O napravleniyakh sovershenstvovaniya khoziaistvennogo mekhanizma', *Izvestiya SO AN SSSR, seriya ekonomika i prikladnaya sotsiologiya*, 1984:1:1, 21-33.
95. See S. Menshikov, 'Ekonomicheskaya structkura sotsializma: chto vperedi?', *Novyi Mir*, 1989:3, 190–212.
96. See Julia Wishnevsky, 'Architects of *perestroika* defended', *Report on the USSR*, 17 March 1989, 4–6; Oleg Platonov, 'O, Rus, vzmakhni Krylami! . . .', *Nash Sovremennik*, 1989:8, 111–32.
97. Abalkin, 'Strategiya obnovleniya'.
98. Sergei Andreev, 'Prichiny i sledstviya', *Ural*, 1988:1, 104–39; Sergei Andreev, 'Struktura vlasti i zadachi obshchestva', *Neva*, 1989:1, 144–73; Sergei Andreev, 'Prichiny i sledstviya: god spustia', *Ural*, 1989:6, 3–12.
99. See Richard E. Erickson, 'The new enterprise law', *The Harriman Institute Forum*, 1988:2, 1–8.
100. V. G. Grebennikov, O. S. Pchelintsev and S. S. Shatalin, 'O problemakh razvitiya sotsialisticheskoi sobstvennosti v SSSR', *Izvestiya SO AN SSSR, seriya ekonomika i prikladnaya sotsiologiya*, 1986:7:2, 7–16.
101. See Richard F Vidmer, 'Soviet studies of organization and management: a "jungle" of competing views', *Slavic Review*, 1981:3, 404–22.
102. The articles are B. P. Kurashvili, 'Gosudarstvennoe upravlenie narod-nym khoziaistvom: perspektivy razvitiya', *Sovetskoe Gosudarstvo i Pravo*, 1982:6, 38–48; B. P. Kurashvili, 'Sudby otraslevogo upravleniya', *EKO*, 1983:10, 34–57; B. P. Kurashvili, 'Sotsialisticheskie proizvodstvennye othosheniya: nekotorye aktualnye aspekty', *Izvestiya SO AN SSSR, seriya ekonomika i prikladnaya sotsiologiya*, 1985:7:2, 12–23; B. P. Kurashvili, 'Kontury vozmozhnoi perestroiki', *EKO*, 1985:5, 59–70. Also see B. P. Kurashvili, *Ocherk teorii gosudarstvennogo upravleniya*, Nauka, Moscow 1987; Ron Amann, 'Towards a new economic order: the writings of B. P. Kurashvili', *Detente*, Winter 1987, 8–10; Ed. A. Hewett, *Reforming*

the Soviet Economy, Brookings, Washington D.C. 1988, pp. 289–93.

103. Boris Kurashvili, 'Perspektivy sovetskogo sotsializma', *Vek XX i Mir*, 1989:5, 18–23.
104. Vidmer, 'Soviet science of management'.
105. See G. Kh. Popov, *Problemy teorii upravleniya*, Ekonomika, Moscow 1974.
106. Ibid., p. 108.
107. G. Popov, 'Razvitie otraslevogo upravleniya promyshlennosti', *Kommunist*, 1982:18, 48–59.
108. Karagedov, 'Ob organizatsionnom strukture upravleniya promyshlennostyu'; Kurashvili, 'Gosudarstvennoe upravlenie narodnym khoziaistvom: perspektivy razvitiya'.
109. See Philip Hanson, 'From brigade contracts to economic reform', *Radio Liberty Research*, RL 265/84, 9 July 1984.
110. G. Popov and V. Shcherbakov 'Dialektika podriada', *Pravda*, 27 June 1984; G. Kh. Popov, 'Polnyi khozraschet osnovnogo zvena ekonomiki', *EKO*, 1984:7, 20–36.
111. For references see Hanson, 'Some schools of thought in Soviet economic debates'.
112. N. Shmelev, 'Avansy i dolgi', *Novyi Mir*, 1987:6, 142–58.
113. Gennadi Lisichkin, 'Obrashchenie k realnosti', *Znamya*, 1987:12, 173–84.
114. A. P. Butenko, 'Teoreticheskie problemy sovershenstvovaniya novogo stroya: o sotsialno-ekonomicheskoi prirody sotsializma', *Voprosy Filosofii*, 1987:2, 17–29.
115. L. Abalkin, 'Proizvodstvennye otnosheniya i khoziaistvennyi mekhanism', *Ekonomicheskaya Gazeta*, 1986:46, 2, 4.
116. See Hanson, 'Some schools of thought in Soviet economic debates', p. 20.
117. O. Bogomolov, 'Skolko stoyat dengi?', *Literaturnaya Gazeta*, 16 September 1987.
118. See 'Sotsializm – 90-e gody', *Komsomolskaya Pravda*, 3 October 1989 (an interview with Bogomolov).
119. V. A. Tikhonov, 'Zhit bez illusii', *Ogoniok*, 1989:36, 1–3.
120. Gavriil Popov, 'O polze neravenstva', *Literaturnaya Gazeta*, 4 October 1989.
121. Gennadi Lisichkin, 'Dogmy i zhizn', *Izvestiya*, 25 January 1989.
122. Tikhonov, 'Zhit bez illusii; B. Pinsker, 'Biurokraticheskaya khimera', *Znamia*, 1989:11, 183–202; Vasili Seliunin, 'Planovaya anarkhiya ili balans interesov?', *Znamia*, 1989:11, 203–20.
123. See, for instance, O. T. Bogomolov, 'Mir sotsializma na puti perestroiki', *Kommunist*, 1987:16, 92–102.
124. Compare Nikolai Shmelev, 'Avansy i dolgi' with Anatoli Salutskii, 'Umozreniya i realnost', *Nash Sovremennik*, 1988:6, 136–62.
125. See, as an example, O. Bogomolov, 'Obshchee dostoyanie', *Pravda*, 14 March 1983.
126. See Tamas Bauer, 'The firm under perestroika', *Berichte des Bundesinstituts für ostwissenschaftliche und internationale Studien*, 37–1989.

127. Gilbert Rozman, *A Mirror for Socialism*, I. B. Tauris, London 1985.
128. Jerry F. Hough, *The Struggle for the Third World*, Brookings, Washington D.C. 1986.
129. 'Put k zdravomu smyslu'.

6 The age of *perestroika*

1. G. Popov, 'Programma, kotoroi rukovodstvovalsya Stalin', *Nauka i Zhizn*, 1989:7, 45–54.
2. A. P. Butenko, 'Teoreticheskie problemy sovershenstvovaniya novogo stroia: o sotsialno-ekonomicheskoi prirode sotsializma', *Voprosy Filosofii*, 1987:2, 17–29.
3. See Ed A. Hewett, *Reforming the Soviet Economy*, Brookings, Washington DC, 1988.
4. See Paul Marer, 'A conceptual framework of reform in centrally planned economies, with an application to Hungary', a paper presented at a conference on Plan and/or Market, Vienna, 26–8 June 1989.
5. See Pekka Sutela, 'The marketization of Eastern Europe' in Ronald Hill and Jan Zielonka, eds, *Restructuring Eastern Europe: Views from Western Europe*, Edward Elgar, London 1990.
6. Joseph S. Berliner, 'Planning and management', in Abram Bergson and Herbert S. Levine, eds, *The Soviet Economy: Towards the Year 2000*, Allen & Unwin, London 1983, 362–80.
7. Leszek Balcerowicz, 'The "socialist controversy" debate and the discussion of economic reform in the socialist countries', to appear in Janos Matyas Kovacs and Marton Tardos, eds, *Plan and/or Market*, Routledge, London 1991; Sutela, 'The marketization of Eastern Europe'.
8. See L. Abalkin, 'Novaya kontseptiya tsentralizma', *Ekonomicheskaya Gazeta*, 1987:50, 2.
9. Nikolai Petrakov, 'Zolotoi chervonets vchera i zavtra', *Novyi Mir*, 1987:8, 205–21.
10. Cyril Lin, 'A decade of reform in China: crossing the Rubicon', a paper presented at the Malente Symposium VIII, 16–18 October 1989.
11. Berliner, 'Planning and management'.
12. N. Petrakov and E. Yasin, 'Ekonomicheskie metody upravleniya', *Ekonomicheskaya Gazeta*, 1986:47, 12.
13. Wlozdimierz Brus, *The Market in a Socialist Economy*, Routledge & Kegan Paul, London 1972 (originally published in 1961).
14. See Janos Kornai, 'The Hungarian reform process: visions, hopes and reality', *Journal of Economic Literature*, 1986:4, 1687–737; Wlodzimierz Brus and Kasimierz Laski, 'Product market and capital market in the light of the experience of the Hungarian new economic mechanism', in O. T. Bogomolov, ed., *Market Forces in Planned Economies*, Macmillan, London 1990.
15. Tamas Bauer, 'The Hungarian alternative to Soviet-type planning', *Journal of Comparative Economics*, 1983:3, 304–16.

16. Janos Kornai, 'The affinity between ownership and coordination mechanisms', O. T. Bogomolov 1990 ed., *Market Forces in Planned Economies*, Macmillan, London 1990.
17. Kornai, 'The Hungarian reform process'.
18. Marton Tardos, 'The ownership reform in Hungary', a paper presented at the Conference on Plan and/or Market, Vienna, June 26–8 1989.
19. Balcerowicz, 'The "socialist controversy" debate'.
20. R. W. Davies, *Soviet History in the Gorbachev Revolution*, Macmillan, London, 1989.
21. P. O. Aven and V. M. Shironin, 'Reforma ekonomicheskogo mekhanizma: realnost namechaemykh preobrazovanii', *Izvestiya sibirskogo otdeleniya Akademii Nauk SSSR, seriya ekonomika i prikladnaya sotsiologiya*, 1987:13, 32–41, S. S. Shatalin and E. T. Gaidar, *Ekonomicheskya reforma: prichiny, napravleniya, problemy*, Ekonomika, Moscow 1989.
22. G. Popov, 'S tochki zreniya ekonomista', *Nauka i Zhizn*, 1987:4, 54–65.
23. Aleksandr Bek, *Novoe naznachenie*, Posev, Frankfurt-am-Main, 1977.
24. Gavriil Popov, 'Dva tsveta vremeni, ili Uroki Khrushcheva', *Ogoniok*, 1989:42, 14–17.
25. Nikolai Petrakov, 'Tovar i rynok', *Ogoniok*, 1988:34, 6–7, 22–3.
26. Nikolai Petrakov, 'Ekonomika i gosudarstvo', *Ogoniok*, 1989:10, 8, 14–15.
27. Nikolai Shmelev, 'Libo sila, libo rubl', *Znamia*, 1989:1, 128–47.
28. Popov, 'Dva tsveta vremeni, ili uroki Khrushcheva'.
29. Gavriil Popov, 'Pobeseduem v dukhe glasnosti . . .', *Ogoniok*, 1988:33, 6–7, 30–1.
30. G. Popov, 'Perestroika upravleniya ekonomikoi', in *Inogo ne dano*, Yu. Afanasiev, ed., Progress, Moscow 1988, 621–33.
31. Gavriil Popov, 'O Polze neravenstva', *Literaturnaya Gazeta*, 4 October 1989.
32. V. A. Tikhonov, 'Zhit bez illusii', *Ogoniok*, 1989:36, 1–3.
33. See academician I. Lukinov as cited in 'Temp i logika shagov reformy', *Ekonomicheskaya Gazeta*, 1989:47, 7–8.
34. See N. Ya. Petrakov and E. G. Yasin, 'Snachala – eksperiment, zatem – korennaya perestroika: mneniya, fakty, kommentarii', *EKO*, 1987:4, 18–38.
35. V. E. Bolkov, 'Khoziaistvannaya reforma v plenu otchuzhdeniya', *EKO*, 1989:3, 3–18.
36. A. Migranian, 'Dolgii put k evropeiskomu domu', *Novyi Mir*, 1989:7, 166–84.
37. T. Zaslavskaya, 'O strategii sotsialnogo upravleniya perestroikoi', in *Inogo ne dano*, 9–50.
38. See 'Narod bezmolvstvuet?', *Ogoniok*, 1988:41, 6–7, 22–4 (an interview with Tatiana Zaslavskaya).
39. Aven and Shironin, 'Reforma ekonomicheskogo mekhanizma'.
40. Hewett, *Reforming the Soviet Economy*, p. 301.

41. V. Seliunin and G. Khanin, 'Lukavaya tsifra', *Novyi Mir*, 1987:2, 181–204.
42. M. Korolev, 'Statistika znaet?', *Pravda*, 30 January 1989.
43. V. Seliunin, 'Tempy rosta na vesakh nakopleniya', *Sotsialisticheskaya Industriya*, 5 January 1988.
44. V. Seliunin, 'Cheryne dyry ekonomiki', *Novyi Mir*, 1989:10, 153–78.
45. B. E. Krasniuk, 'Mif o chrezmernoi norme nakopleniya', *EKO*, 1989:8, 3–17; K. K. Valtukh, 'Sokratit investitsii', *EKO*, 1989:9, 69–72.
46. G. I. Khanin, 'Razmyshleniya nad tsiframi 1988 goda', *EKO*, 1989:4, 116–25.
47. See Hans-Henning Schroeder, 'Versorgungskrise, rustungsabbau und konversion in der UdSSR. Part 1, Versorgungskrise und Ruestungslast-debatte', *Berichte des Bundesinstituts für ostwissenschaftliche und internationale Studien*, 56–1989.
48. Pekka Sutela, 'Soviet investments and the decline of economic growth', *Nordic Journal of Soviet and East European Affairs*, 1988:2, 99–115.
49. See, for instance, A. G. Aganbegyan, *Sovetskaya ekonomika – Vzgliad v Buduschchee*, Ekonomika, Nauka, 1988; Abel Aganbegyan, *Challenge: The Economics of Perestroika*, Heinemann, London 1989.
50. Hewett, *Reforming the Soviet Economy*, pp. 306–22.
51. See Sutela, 'Soviet investments'.
52. V. Loginov, 'Plany i realnost', *Voprosy Ekonomiki*, 1989:4, 21–32.
53. A. G. Aganbegyan, 'Reshitelnee vesti perestroiku ekonomicheskoi nauki i praktiki', *Ekonomika i matematicheskie metody*, 1989:2, 197–201.
54. Khanin, 'Razmyshleniya nad tsiframi 1988 goda'.
55. 'Panel on Soviet economic performance', *Soviet Economy*, 1987:1, 3–39; B. P. Orlov, 'Illuzii i realnost ekonomicheskoi informatsii', *EKO*, 1988:8, 3–20; V. Kirichenko, 'Vernut doverie statistike', *Kommunist*, 1990:3, 22–32.
56. V. D. Belkin and V. V. Ivanter, *Planovaya sbalansirovannost: ustanovlenie, podderzhanie, effektivnost*, Ekonomika, Moscow 1983; A. Melkov and V. Perlamutrov, 'Bank – eto ne sobes', *Pravda*, 30 September 1987.
57. A. G. Aganbegyan, 'Programma korennoi perestroiki', EKO, 1987:11, 3–19.
58. V. Belkin, 'Rubliu upravliat proizvodstvom', *Izvestiya*, 12 December 1987.
59. V. V. Demenchuk, 'Usilit bankovskoe vozdeistvie na ekonomiku', *Ekonomicheskaya Gazeta*, 1986:35, 6–7.
60. Lev Braginskii, 'Kuda nesti meshok s dengami', *Ogoniok*, 1989:42, 9–11.
61. Aganbegyan, 'Reshitelnee vesti perestroiku ekonomicheskoi nauki i praktiki'.
62. V. N. Bogachev, 'Yeshche ne pozdno', *Kommunist*, 1989:3, 31–41.
63. 'Ne delit, a zarabatyvat', *Ogoniok*, 1989:41, 1, 2, 25–7 (an interview with Leonid Abalkin).
64. G. Zoteev and E. Hewett, 'Protsess ekonomicheskikh reform i ego katalizatory', *Kommunist*, 1989:13, 50–60.

65. Anders Aslund, *Gorbachev's Struggle for Economic Reform*, Pinter, London 1989, pp. 128–36.
66. S. S. Shatalin, 'Sotsialnoe razvitie i ekonomicheskii rost', *Kommunist*, 1986:14, 60–70; Petrakov, 'Zolotoi chervonets vchera i zavtra'.
67. Nikolai Shmelev, 'Novye trevogi', *Novyi Mir*, 1988:4, 160–75.
68. S. Shatalin, 'Khochu priznat svoyu oshibku', *Sotsialisticheskaya industriya*, 30 October 1988.
69. E. Yasin, 'Sotsialisticheskii rynok ili yarmarka illuzii?' *Kommunist*, 1989:15, 53–62.
70. 'Another version of a plan for market economy', *Moscow News*, 15 July 1990 (an interview with Nikolai Petrakov).
71. Aslund, 'Gorbachev's economic advisors'.
72. The papers of the conference were published in *Ekonomicheskaya Gazeta*, 1986:46, 1986:47 and in a revised form together with summaries of discussion in *Reforma upravleniya ekonomikoi, problemy i poisk*. Pod red. A. G. Aganbegyan, Ekonomika, Moscow 1987.
73. Hewett, *Reforming the Soviet Economy*; Aslund, *Gorbachev's Struggle for Economic Reform*.
74. 'Uchenye obsuzhdayut proekt zakona SSSR o gosudarstvennoi predpriyatii', *Voprosy Ekonomi*, 1987:5, 70–92.
75. See 'Formy khozrascheta i proforma biurokratii', *Moskovskaya Pravada*, 14 May 1989 (an interview with P. G. Bunich).
76. 'Uchenye obsuzhdayut proekt zakona SSSR o sotsialisticheskoi predriyatii'; 'Korennoi vopros perestroiki', *Pravda*, 13 June 1987.
77. N. Ya. Petrakov and E. G. Yasin, 'Ekonomicheski metody tsentralizovannogo planovogo rukovodstva', in *Reforma upravleniya ekonomikoi: problemy i poisk*, 68–97.
78. Pavel Bunich, 'The reform and parodies on it', *Moscow News*, 1987:40, 12.
79. 'Formy khozrascheta i proforma biurokratii'.
80. A. G. Aganbegyan, 'Prakticheskie dela ekonomicheskoi nauki', *EKO*, 1989:9, 17–29; Aganbegyan, 'Reshitelnee vesti perestroiku ekonomicheskoi nauki i praktiki'.
81. Aganbegyan, 'Reshitelnee vesti perestroiku ekonomicheskoi nauki i praktiki'.
82. B. Milner and V. Rapoport, 'Razvitie organizatsionnykh struktur upravleniya', *Ekonomicheskaya Gazeta*, 1986:47, 13–14.
83. Petrakov and Yasin, 'Ekonomicheskie metody upravleniya'.
84. L. I. Abalkin, 'Teoreticheskie osnovy perestroiki khoziaistvennogo mekhanizma', in *Reforma upraveleniya ekonomikoi, problemy i poisk*, 30–55.
85. G. Kh. Popov in 'Perestroika upravleniya ekonomikoi: problemy, perspektivy', *Ekonomika i matematicheskie metody*, 1988:5, 890–924, cited on p. 891. Also see O. M. Yun in ibid., p. 900.
86. Mikhail Antonov, 'Uskorenie: vozmozhnosti i pregrady', *Nash Sovremennik*, 1986:7, 3–20.
87. D. M. Kazakevich, 'Ekonomicheskaya teoriya, ekonomiko–matematicheskie metody i planovoe upravlenie', *Ekonomika i*

matematicheskie metody, 1987:1, 132–41; V. P. Chichkanov, 'Emotsii vmesto analiza', *EKO*, 1989:4, 104–15.

88. Julia Wishnevsky, 'Architects of perestroika defended', *Report on the USSR*, 17 March 1989, 4–6; A. Salutskii, 'Poiski istina i "Pop-nauka"', *Ekonomicheskie Nauki*, 1989:10, 78–85; Oleg Platonov, 'O, Rus, vzmakhni krylami', *Nash Sovremennik*, 1989:8, 111–32; Mikhail Antonov, 'Vykhod est!', *Nash Sovremennik*, 1989:8, 71–110, 1989:9, 139–58.

89. Anatoli Salutskii, 'Umozreniya i realnost', *Nash Sovremennik*, 1989:6, 136–62.

90. Valeri Vyzhutovich, 'Diktatura zdravogo smysla', *Izvestiya*, 8 December 1989. Also see Yitzhak M. Brudny, 'The heralds of opposition to *perestroika*', *Soviet Economy*, 1989:2, 162–200.

91. A. Sergeev, 'Iz segodnia zavtra ili pozavtra?', *Ekonomicheskie Nauki*, 1989:9, 121–31; 'Zavtra ili pozavtra', *Nash Sovremennik*, 1989:10, 102–9 (an interview with A. Sergeev).

92. Anatoli Salutskii, 'Moskva, kolonnyi zal . . .', *Literaturnaya Rossiya*, 8 December 1989.

93. Boris Kurashvili, 'Perspektivy sovetskogo sotsializma', *Vek XX i Mir*, 1989:5, 18–23.

94. A. Eremin, 'Sobstvennost: ekonomicheskaya osnova sotsializma', *Ekonomicheskaya Gazeta*, 1989:32, 8.

95. 'Sovremennaya kontseptsiya sotsializma', *Pravda*, 5 October 1988.

96. G. Popov and V. Shcherbakov, 'Dialektika podryada', *Pravda*, 27 June 1984.

97. V. Belkin and V. Perevedentsev, 'Drama Akchi', *Literaturnaya Gazeta*, 1 April 1987.

98. Karl-Eugen Waedekin, 'The reemergence of the kolkhoz principle', *Soviet Studies*, 1989:1, 20–38.

99. Don Van Atta, 'Theorists of agrarian *perestroika*', *Soviet Economy*, 1989:1, 70–99.

100. Aslund, *Gorbachev's struggle for Economic Reform*.

101. See, for instance, L. Nikiforov, 'Obshchee i lichnoe: novye formy', *Ekonomicheskaya Gazeta*, 1988:8, 10.

102. 'Arendnyi podryad – osnova korennoi perestroiki ekonomiki', *Voprosy Ekonomiki*, 1989:3, 35–53.

103. Yu. Sukhotin, V. Dementyev and Yu. Ovsienko, 'Ekonomiko-matematicheskoe napravlenie: uroki i perspektivy', *Voprosy Ekonomiki*, 1989:1, 110–20.

104. Yu. V. Sukhotin, V. E. Dementyev and Yu. V. Ovsienko, 'O metodologii sovremennykh podkhodov k perestroike upravleniya economikoi', *Ekonomika i matematicheskie metody*, 1988:3, 389–402; B. Rakitskii, 'Revolyutsionnyi khararkter ideologii perestroiki', *Voprosy Ekonomiki*, 1988:10, 3–14.

105. Yu. V. Ovsienko and V. L. Perlamutrov, 'O demokraticheskom mekhanizme sotsialisticheskoi ekonomiki', *Ekonomika i matematicheskie metody*, 1989:2, 202–10; Yu. V. Shukhotin and V. E. Dementyev, 'K

voprosu o sotsialisticheskom kharaktere perestroiki', *Ekonomika i matematicheskie metody*, 1989:4, 581–89; Yu. V. Sukhotin, 'Izvyani teorii – zigzagi praktiki', *EKO*, 1989:7, 3–17.

106. V. Pugachev, 'Kontseptsiya optimizatsionnogo khoziaistvennogo mekhanizma', *Voprosy Ekonomiki*, 1989:1, 120–9.

107. N. P. Fedorenko and V. L. Perlamutrov, 'Khozraschetnye otnosheniya – dinamika i perspektivy', *Voprosy Filosofii*, 1987:2, 3–16; N. P. Fedorenko and V. L. Perlamutrov, 'K teorii vedeniya obshchestvennogo khoziaistva pri sotsializme', *Voprosy Filosofii*, 1988:3, 26–38; *Ocherki politicheskoi ekonomii sotsializma*, Pod red. N. P. Fedorenko, Nauka, Moscow 1988.

108. P. G. Bunich, 'Novye tsennosti', *Oktiabr*, 1987:12, 144–57; Gavriil Popov, 'Pobeseduem v dukhe glasnosti', *Ogoniok*, 1988:33, 6–7, 30–1.

109. M. Krushinskii, 'Klyuchevoe slovo reformy', *Izvestiya*, 2 December 1989.

110. P. Bunich, 'Bez Polumer!', *Ekonomicheskaya Gazeta*, 1989:20, 14–15; A. N. Tolstikov, 'K realnomu khozraschetu cheres Arendu', *EKO*, 1989:7, 19–27.

111. V. Volkonskii, A. Vavilov and E. Saburov, 'Povorot "vsyo vdrug" ', *Sotsialisticheskaya Industriya*, 15 September 1989.

112. Gavriil Popov, 'O polze neravenstva', *Literaturnaya Gazeta*, 4 October 1989.

113. P. Bunich, 'Bez Polumer!'; 'Filosofiya Arendy', *Pravda*, 2 December 1989 (an interview with P. G. Bunich).

114. 'Osnovy zakonodatelstva soyuza SSR i soyuznykh respublik ob Arende', *Ekonomicheskaya Gazeta*, 1989:49, 14–15.

115. Compare N. Ya. Petrakov, *Demokratizatsiya khoziaistvennogo mekhanizma*, Ekonomika, Moscow 1988; G. Kh. Popov, *Puti perestroika*, Ekonomika, Moscow 1989.

116. Harold Lydall, *Yugoslavia in Crisis*, Oxford University Press, Oxford 1989.

117. V. A. Volkonskii in 'Arendnyi podriad – osnova korennoi perestroiki ekonomiki'.

118. Hanson, 'Some schools of thought in the Soviet debate on economic reform', p. 13.

119. Jacques H. Dreze, *Labour Management, Contracts and Capital Markets*, Basil Blackwell, Oxford 1989.

120. 'Strategiya obnovleniya', *Ogoniok*, 1989:13, 6–7, 18–20 (an interview with L. I. Abalkin).

121. Leonid Abalkin, 'Obnovlenie sotsialisticheskoi sobstvennosti', *Ekonomicheskaya Gazeta*, 1988:45, 10–11.

122. L. Popkova, 'Gde pyshnee pirogi?', *Novyi Mir*, 1987:5, 239–41.

123. See 'The market instead of socialism', *Komsomolskaya Pravda*, 25 May 1989, as translated in *BBS Survey of World Broadcasts*, SU/W0082 A/4–5, 23 June 1989.

124. T. Valovaya, 'Trudnyi put poznaniya', *Ekonomicheskaya Gazeta*, 1987:35, 9.

125. O. Latsis, 'Zachem zhe pod ruku tolkat?', *Novyi Mir*, 1987:7, 266–8.
126. S. Kirillov, 'Rol ekonomiko–matematicheskikh metodov v teorii tsenoobrazovaniya', *Ekonomischeskie Nauki*, 1986:12, 28–37; E. Yasin, 'Ekonomicheskaya nauka i ekonomiko–matematicheskie metody', *Ekonomicheskie Nauki*, 1987:2, 48–55.
127. Nikolai Shmelev, 'Avansy i dolgi', *Novyi Mir*, 1987:6, 142–58.
128. 'O zadachakh partii po korennoi perestroike upravleniya ekonomikoi. Doklad Generalnogo Secretarya TsK KPSS M. S. Gorbacheva na Plenume TsK KPSS 25 iyunya 1987 goda', *Ekonomicheskaya Gazeta*, 1987:27, 2–9.
129. Aganbegyan, *Sovetskaya ekonomika – vzglyad v budushchee*, pp. 183–97.
130. Shmelev, 'Novye trevogi'; Nikolai Shmelev, 'Ekonomika i zdravyi Smysl', *Znamia*, 1988:7, 155–84; Shmelev, 'Libo sila, libo rubl'.
131. Shmelev, 'Libo sila, libo rubl', p. 131.
132. Volkonskii, Vavilov and Saburov, 'Povarot "vsyo vdrug"?'
133. 'Another version of plan for market'.
134. See 'Obmeniaemsia mysliami pered sëzdom', *Sotsialisticheskaya Industriya*, 20 May 1989.
135. O. Bogomolov, 'Meniayushchisya oblik sotsializma', *Kommunist*, 1989:11, 33–42.
136. 'Akademik S. Shatalin: izderzhki neizbezhny, no . . .', *Literaturnaya Gazeta*, 11 October 1989.
137. A. P. Butenko, 'Kakim byt sotsializm?', *Pravda*, 8 August 1989; B. Pinsker, 'Biurokraticheskaya khimera', *Znamya*, 1989:11, 183–202.
138. Popov, 'V Polzu neraventsva'.
139. Volkonskii, Vavilov and Saburov, 'Povorot "vsyo vdrug"?'
140. Vasilii Seliunin, 'Planovaya anarkhiya ili balans interesov?', *Znamia*, 1989:11, 202–20.
141. Sergei Shishko, 'Eta "strashnaya" chastnaya sobstvennost . . .', *Nedelia*, 1989:52, 9.
142. Yu. P. Chaplygin, 'Ekonomicheskaya reforma: v poiske putei razvitiya', *Izvestiya Akademii Nauk SSSR*, 1989:3, 5–23.
143. Ed. A. Hewett, 'Perestroika and the Congress of People's Deputies', *Soviet Economy*, 1989:1, 47–69.
144. *Radical Economic Reform: Top-Priority and Long-Term Measures*, All-Union Conference and Workshop on Problems of Radical Economic Reform, November 1989 (mimeo). The materials were also published in *Ekonomicheskaya Gazeta*, 1989:43–7.
145. 'Effektivnost, konsolidatsiya, reforma – put k zdarovoi ekonomike. Doklad N. I. Ryzhkova na vtorom sëzde narodnykh Deputatov SSSR', *Izvestiya*, 14 December 1989.
146. For a discussion see Ed A. Hewett, '*Perestroika*-plus': the Abalkin reforms', *Planecon Report*, 1989:48–9, 1 December 1989.
147. 'Sut Zamysla', *Pravda*, 29 December 1989 (an interview with Prime Minister N. I. Ryzhkov).
148. Larisa Piyasheva, 'Liubov k traditsiyam', *Moskovskie Novosti*, 1989:49, 10.

149. I. Ivanov, 'Dykhanie mirovogo Rynka', *Ekonomicheskaya Gazeta*, 1989:49, 8.
150. O. Amurzhuev and V. Tsapelik, 'Kak podedit diktamonopolista', *Ekonomicheskaya Gazeta*, 1989:49, 7.
151. 'Ob ekonomicheskom polozhenii strany i kontseptsii perekhoda k reguliruemoy rynochnoy ekonomike. Doklad N. I. ryzhkova na tretei sessii verkhovnogo Soveta SSSR', *Pravda*, 25 May 1990.
152. 'Reforma: vtoroe dykhanie', *Rabochaya Tribuna*, 11 April 1990.
153. 'Peremena dekoratsii', *Ogoniok* 1990:23, 0–2 (an interview with Oleg Bogomolov).
154. 'K guamannomu. demokraticheskomu sotsializmu', *Pravda*, 15 July 1990.
155. A. V. Buzgalin, *Pravda*, 8 July 1990.
156. 'Another version of plan for market'.
157. L. I. Abalkin, *Pravda*, 7 July 1990.

Select bibliography

Abalkin, L. I., *Ekonomicheskie zakony sotsializma*, Nauka, Moscow 1971.
Khoziaistvennyi Mekhanizm razvitogo sotsializma, Mysl, Moscow 1973.
'Rynok v ekonomicheskoi sisteme sotsializma', *Voprosy Ekonomiki*, 1989:7, 3–12.
Aganbegyan, Abel, *Challenge: The Economics of Perestroika*, Heinemann, London 1989.
'Prakticheskie dela ekonomicheskoi nauki', *EKO*, 1989:9, 17–29.
Antonov, Mikhail, 'Uskorenie: vozmozhnosti i pregrady', *Nash Sovremennik*, 1986:7, 3–20.
Aslund, Anders, 'Gorbachev's economic advisors', *Soviet Economy*, 1987:3, 246–69.
Gorbachev's Struggle for Economic Reform, Pinter, London 1989.
Aven, P. O. and Shironin, V. M., 'Reforma ekonomicheskogo mekhanizma: realnost namechaemykh preobrazovanii', *Izvestiya sibirskogo otdeleniya akademii nauk SSSR, seriya ekonomika i prikladnaya sotsiologiya*, 1987:13, 32–41.
Belkin, V. D. and Ivanter, V. V., *Planovaya sbalansirovannost: ustanovlenie, podderzhanie, effektivnost*, Ekonomika, Moscow 1983.
Bogomolov, O. T., 'Mir sotsializma na puti perestroiki', *Kommunist*, 1987:16, 92–102.
Brus, Wlodzimierz, *The Market in a Socialist Economy*, Routledge and Kegan Paul, London 1972.
Cave, Martin, *Computers and Economic Planning*, Cambridge University Press, Cambridge 1980.
Conyngham, William, *The Modernization of Soviet Industrial Management*, Cambridge University Press, Cambridge, 1982.
Ekonomisty i matematiki za kruglym stolom, Ekonomika, Moscow 1965.
Ellman, Michael, *Planning Problems in the USSR*, Cambridge University Press, Cambridge 1973.
Fedorenko, N. P., *O razrabotke sistemy optimalnogo funktsionirovaniya ekonomiki*, Nauka, Moscow 1968.
Fedorenko, N. P. and Perlamutrov, V. L., 'K teorii vedeniya obshchestvennogo khoziaistva pri sotsializme', *Voprosy Filosofii*, 1988:3, 26–38.
Hanson, Philip, 'Some schools of thought in the Soviet debate on economic reform', *Berichte des Bundesinstituts für ostwissenschaftliche und internationale Studien*, 29–1989.

Hewett, Ed. A., *Reforming the Soviet Economy*, Brookings, Washington DC 1988.

Inogo ne dano, Yu. Afanasyev, ed., Progress, Moscow 1988.

Kantorovich, L. V., *The Best Use of Economic Resources*, Harvard University Press, Cambridge Mass. 1965.

Karagedov, R. G., *Khozraschet, effektivnost i pribyl (ocherki teorii)*, Nauka, Novosibirsk 1979.

'Ob organizatsionnoi strukture upravleniya promyshlennostiu', *EKO*, 1983:8, 50–69.

Katsenelinboigen, A., *Soviet Economic Thought and Political Power in the USSR*, Pergamon, London 1980.

Katsenelinboigen, A., Lakhman, I. L. and Ovsienko, Yu, V., *Optimalnost i tovarno-denezhnye otnosheniya*, Nauka, Moscow 1969.

Katsenelinboigen, A., Ovsienko, Yu, V. and Faerman, E. Yu., *Metodologicheskie voprosy optimalnogo planirovaniya sotsialisticheskoi ekonomiki*, TsEMI AN SSSR, Moscow 1966.

Kornai, Janos, 'The Hungarian reform process: visions, hopes and reality', *Journal of Economic Literature*, 1986:4, 1687–737.

Kurashvili, B. P., 'Sudby otraslevogo upravleniya', *EKO*, 1983:10, 34–57.

'Kontury vozmozhnoi perestroiki', *EKO*, 1985:5, 59–70.

Lewin, Moshe, *Political Undercurrents in Soviet Economic Debates*, Pluto Press, London 1974.

Lisichkin, G. S., *Plan i Rynok*, Ekonomika, Moscow 1966.

Medvedev, V. A., *Zakon stoimosti i materialnye stimuly sotsialisticheskogo proizvodstva*, Ekonomika, Moscow 1966.

Upravlenie sotsialisticheskim proizvodstvom: problemy teorii i praktiki, Politizdat, Moscow 1983.

Nemchinov, V. S., *O Dalneyshem sovershenstvovanii planirovaniya i upravleniya narodnym khoziaistvom*, 2-e izd., Ekonomika, Moscow 1965.

'Novosibirsk Report', *Survey*, 1984:1, 88–108.

Novozhilov, V. V., *Voprosy razvitiya sotsialisticheskoi ekonomiki*, Nauka, Moscow 1970.

Problemy izmereniya zatrat i resultatov pri optimalnom planirovanii, Nauka, Moscow 1972.

Petrakov, N. Ya., *Khoziaistvennaya reforma: plan i ekonomicheskaya samostoyatelnost*, Mysl, Moscow 1971.

'Upravlenie ekonomiki i ekonomicheskie interesy', *Novyi Mir*, 1970:8, 167–86.

'Zolotoi chervonets vchera i zavtra', *Novyi Mir*, 1987:8, 205–21.

Popov, G. Kh., 'Polnyi khozraschet osnovnogo zvena ekonomiki', *EKO*, 1984:7, 20–36.

'S tochki zreniya ekonomista', *Nauka i Zhizn*, 1987:4, 54–65.

'O polze neravenstva', *Literaturnaya Gazeta* 4 Octover 1989, 10.

Problemy optimalnogo funktsionirovaniya sotsialisticheskoi ekonomiki, N. P. Fedorenko, ed., Nauka, Moscow 1972.

Reforma upravleniya ekonomikoi, problemy i poisk, Pod red. A. G. Aganbegyan, Ekonomika, Moscow 1987.

Saslawskaja, Tatjana, *Die Gorbatschow-Strategie*, Orac, Vienna 1989.

Seliunin, Vasili, 'Planovaya anarkhiya ili balans interesov', *Znamia*, 1989:11, 203–20.

Seliunin, V. and Khanin, G., 'Lukavaya Tsifra', *Novyi Mir*, 1987:2, 181–204.

Shatalin, S. S., *Funktsionirovanie ekonomiki razvitogo sotsializma*, Izdatelstvo MGU, Moscow 1982.

Shmelev, Nikolai, 'Avansy i dolgi', *Novyi Mir*, 1987:6, 142–58.

Sukhotin, Yu. V., Dementiev, V. E. and Ovsienko, Yu. V., 'O metodologii sovremennykh podkhodov k perestroike upravleniya ekonomikoi', *Ekonomika i matematicheskie metody*, 1987:3, 389–402.

Sutela, Pekka, *Socialism, Planning and Optimality*, Finnish Society for Sciences and Letters, Helsinki 1984.

Volkonskii, V. A., *Model optimalnogo planirovaniya i vzaimos-vyazi ekonomicheskikh pokazatelei*, Ekonomika, Moscow 1967.

Problemy sovershenstvovaniya khoziaistvennogo mekhanizma, Nauka, Moscow 1981.

Voznesenskii, N., *Voennaya ekonomika SSSR v period otechestvennoi voiny*, Gosudarstvennoe izdatelstvo politicheskoi literatury (no place indicated) 1948.

Yasin, E. G., 'Administrativnaya sistema tsen ili ekonomicheskii mekhanizm', *Ekonomika i matematicheskie metody*, 1988, 2:209–20.

Zaleski, Eugene, *Planning Reform in the Soviet Union, 1962–66*, The University of North Carolina Press, Chapel Hill 1967.

Index